# AN APPETITE FOR POETRY

As bad luck will have it, there are among these men with no great appetite for poetry—who don't understand the need for it and who would never have invented it—quite a number whose job or fate it is to judge it, discourse upon it, stimulate and cultivate the taste for it; in short, to distribute what they don't have. They apply to the task all their intelligence and all their zeal—with alarming consequences.

—*Paul Valéry*

# AN APPETITE FOR POETRY

## *Essays in Literary Interpretation*

FRANK KERMODE

COLLINS
8 Grafton Street, London W1
1989

William Collins Sons & Co. Ltd
London · Sydney · Glasgow · Auckland
Toronto · Johannesburg

BRITISH LIBRARY CATALOGUING IN PUBLICATION DATA

Kermode, Frank, *1919* –
An appetite for poetry: essays in literary
interpretation.
1. Poetry in English – Critical studies
I. Title
821'.009

ISBN 0-00-215388-2

First published in Great Britain in 1989


Printed and bound in Great Britain by
William Collins Sons and Co Ltd, Glasgow

*For John Hollander*

# *Contents*

# *Acknowledgments*

The chapters in this book originally appeared in the following publications:

1. *Daedalus,* The Journal of the American Academy of Arts and Sciences (Winter 1983), 1–11.
2. *The Southern Review* (Summer 1975), 513–529.
3. *Wallace Stevens: A Celebration,* ed. Frank Doggett and Robert Buttel (Princeton, N.J.: Princeton University Press, 1980).
4. *The Yale Review,* 78, no. 2 (August 1989).
5. *London Review of Books,* November 20, 1986 (originally entitled "On a Chinese Mountain").
6. *International Review of Psycho-Analysis,* vol. 12, part 1 (1985). Copyright © Institute of Psycho-Analysis. Presented as the 18th Ernest Jones Lecture, May 1984.
7. 'The Bennington Chapbooks in Literature', address delivered at Bennington College, and then published in *Bennington Review*, 8 (September 1980), 44–51.
8. *Midrash and Literature,* ed. Geoffrey H. Hartman and Sanford Budick (New Haven: Yale University Press, 1986), 179–194.
9. *The Bible and the Narrative Tradition,* ed. Frank McConnell (Oxford: Oxford University Press, 1986), 78–96. Copyright © 1986 by Oxford University Press. Reprinted by permission.
10. Presented as the Ethel M. Wood Lecture at King's College, London, December 4, 1984. Copyright © University of London, 1984.

Acknowledgment is also made to Alfred A. Knopf, Inc., for permission to reprint "The Plain Sense of Things" by Wallace Stevens (from *The Collected Poems of Wallace Stevens,* copyright 1952 by Wallace Stevens).

What am I to do, what shall I do, what should I do, in my situation, how proceed? By aporia pure and simple? Or by affirmations and negations invalidated as uttered, or sooner or later? Generally speaking. There must be other shifts. Otherwise it would be quite hopeless. I should mention before going any further, any further on, that I say aporia without knowing what it means. Can one be ephectic otherwise than unawares? I don't know.

—Samuel Beckett, *The Unnamable*

# *Prologue*

It might be thought that a collection of this kind should appear on its own, with at most a brief account of the provenance of its constituent pieces. I sympathize with that austere view of the matter, but once again feel obliged to do a little more than it would allow. An earlier collection, *The Art of Telling,*[1] seemed to require a longish apologetic prologue; it contained essays on the criticism of narrative, and on questions about canons and institutions, some of which depended on methods and assumptions that appeared to conflict with those endorsed by esteemed contemporaries. Hence the need for some preliminary argumentation. It is a need that has grown much more acute over the past few years.

In *The Art of Telling,* and also in an earlier book, *The Genesis of Secrecy,*[2] I was trying to do what William Empson held to be the right thing for critics, namely to follow my own nose, occasionally scenting value in certain modern techniques and theories, but never becoming their slave or their expositor. Possibly it was this measure of detachment that prevented my understanding the full extent of certain claims made on behalf of Theory, and notably that of the claim for its supremacy, which, in its simplest form, maintains that the primary use of literature, however defined, is to serve the needs of Theory—indeed, that the only reason for continuing the study of literature is that it can be pressed into this service.

I daresay it was my interest in such matters as the institutional control of interpretation that eventually led me to consider such claims with a proper measure of attention. For quite a long time I had been thinking about the literary canon, its intellectual and institutional status, finding the whole issue to be far more complicated than anybody seemed to have supposed. I presented a brief paper on the subject to the Modern Language Association meeting of 1974, and developed the theme in a lecture of 1978; both are included in *The Art of Telling*. But before that book appeared the topic of canon had quite spontaneously risen to somewhere near the top of the theoretical agenda. A whole issue of *Critical Inquiry,* later published in augmented form as a book,[3] was dedicated to the problem; W. J. T. Mitchell, the editor of the journal, told me he had not planned such an issue, that the contributions had simply arrived on his desk, as if the existence of the topic, and its contentiousness, had mysteriously and simultaneously declared itself everywhere and to everybody. In fact there is no real mystery, for the transfer of attention from works of literature to modes of signification, a transfer required by most modern critical theory, was bound to raise the question of literary value, and Mitchell must have been aware of this when he opened with Barbara Herrnstein Smith's essay "Contingencies of Value," which was later to form part of a book with the same title.[4] Smith observed that it has taken us a long time to perceive that value is the central issue in modern criticism. But it is so; and it cannot be separated from the issue of canon, now no longer ignored, but instead seriously misunderstood.

Believing this, I had myself published a little book called *Forms of Attention*[5] which argued, in part, that canon formation is not exclusively controlled by a professional clerisy, and that it was important to have a more accurate notion of what canons really are before demanding their abolition or dilution on admirable but oversimple social or political grounds. Later, in another book, *History and Value,*[6] I once again tried to attend to the interrelated topics of valuation and canon. Finally, during the years when these books came out, I had been writing quite a bit about biblical canons, including the chapter on that subject in *The Literary Guide to the Bible.*[7]

The purpose of these remarks is not advertisement or autobiography; I am only trying to suggest that some enduring preoccupations are reflected in parts of the present book, and also that since they differ so sharply from what is becoming the received wisdom I ought to deal more expressly with this conflict in these introductory remarks. Indeed, given the present critical climate, I almost feel it necessary to explain why other parts of the book show no interest in these fashionable problems, being about literature and not about theory. The fact is that I believe, against much influential opinion, that literary criticism should not be wholly or even principally a matter of rigorous investigation into what criticism is and does. Critics have a duty to interpret as well as to study the modes and fallacies of interpretative performance. They have equally a duty to evaluate, and to transmit interpretations of value (but not prescriptive valuations), as well as to make and study theory.

To continue a moment longer in this apologetic mode, I will add that over the period covered by these essays, roughly 1974 to the present, I have also written a great many reviews, some brief, as newspapers generally require, but some, appearing mostly in the generous pages of *The London Review of Books,* as long as many of these essays, and sometimes, as might be expected, displaying similar interests. Reviewing of this more ample and perhaps more serious sort is, in my view, as important as any other kind of literary criticism, and academics who think it an interference with graver matters need to give some thought to the whole question of the wider literary public on whose existence their own, with its mandarin privileges, must depend. However, there is only one essay in this book which appeared first as a review: it is the chapter on Empson, and I wanted to include it for the following reasons. First, at a time when there are so many models and techniques that can be got up and assiduously applied, there are individual and eccentric gifts which remain the prerequisite of the best criticism; and

Empson possessed them in the degree of genius. Second, there are at the moment attempts to enlist him posthumously in the ranks of a theoretical avant-garde; one sees why, but he does not belong there, and would have said so with his customary asperity and emphasis. It seems desirable to resist this kidnap attempt.

As Empson and many other more ordinary practitioners would have had no trouble in admitting, a normal critical career will contain many occasions for nontheoretical performances. There are festive or ceremonial occasions, such as the three hundredth anniversary of Milton's death, which the poet's college and university might well be expected to celebrate without deconstructive rigor; the current professor of English Literature in the university, called upon to do his part, would have caused much displeasure by devoting his hour to an examination of what that part was, and what must be the flaws in tricentennial rhetoric. He was very properly expected to say something about Milton. On the hundredth birthdays of Wallace Stevens or of T. S. Eliot it still seemed appropriate to discuss these poets as the authors of admired works, held to constitute a valuable *oeuvre*. And there might be other occasions to speak about literature without first asking at length what it is to speak about literature, or whether there is really such a thing to speak about. There are specialist audiences, audiences of specialists in fields other than literature, and audiences not properly specialist at all; and to speak sensibly to all such audiences remains, I think, the normal obligation of the professional critic. It should not be despised or neglected on the ground that one has more interesting things to do than talk about books and authors—for example, to demonstrate the uses of semiotic, narratological, psychoanalytical, or neohistorical models, though in themselves such demonstrations may be absorbing, life-enhancing, or at least career-enhancing. For it should be realized that the consequences of not doing this *normal* work are likely to be grave. Walking through the Life Sciences building at UCLA recently, I noticed affixed to a laboratory door the following words: "Les théories passent. Le grenouille reste.—Jean Rostand, *Carnets d'un biologiste.*" There is a risk that in the less severe discipline of criticism the result may turn out to be different; the theories will remain but the frog may disappear. Criticism seems to be in rapid decline, and is by many thought moribund, and all the better for that. But if we use the term in a different and now increasingly dominant sense, we can say that more literary criticism is now being written than ever before, and of a kind that is thought by many to be more valuable, more intelligent, and more exciting than any before it. I have a difficulty here. Although much of this new criticism is indeed intelligent and, to sympathetic readers, exciting, it is often the work of writers who seem largely to have lost interest in literature as such (the question of what that is I defer for a moment). It is not merely that they deplore earlier types of criticism and want to replace them with something that will do their work better; for the program contains instructions to annihilate them, and also to destroy the end they had in view, which, however ineptly they performed the task, was to deepen understanding of literature, and to transmit to others (including non-professors) interpretations and valuations which could and would be transformed or accommodated to new conditions as time went by. Anyway, it strikes me as worth observing that this great efflorescence of literary theory seems to entail an indifference to, and even a hostility toward, "literature."

What follows is not, however, intended as a jeremiad. Everybody in the business has too often heard superannuated or superannuable colleagues complaining that criticism, if that is what they happen to be talking about, has fallen into bad—almost though not quite synonymous with youthful—hands, and that only instant and severe reactionary measures will prevent things from falling apart. Such measures, even if anybody knew exactly what forms they might take, would be comprehensively self-defeating; those who wish to apply them no longer have the power to do so. It may be that old-style literary criticism, and even literature, in the once familiar sense of the word, are indeed on the point of extinction, that powerful obscure forces are extruding them from the culture. If that is their fate, it is one they share with a great many other things. The human race got along without literature and, *a fortiori,* without literary criticism, for very lengthy periods before, and no doubt it could do so again. All we could do in that case would be to take the advice of Shakespeare's Octavius, and let determined things to destiny hold unbewailed their way. But refusing to wail is not the same thing as surrendering, and it may still be possible, even if matters are desperate, to hold on for a while. It is at least worth considering what it is that we are apparently being asked or forced to give up in order to have the benefits of the present critical revolution.

In any case it may be too early to brace oneself in that way; experience suggests that this *nouvelle vague* may break like its predecessors; of course the next wave may be even rougher on those who are not riding it, but it too may pass. A further and better reason for declining to wail is the evident quality of much recent work. Nobody who considers the extent and subtlety of the thought of, say, Paul de Man and Jacques Derrida will want to join the chorus of uninformed complainants castigated by the former in his essay "The Resistance to Theory" and the latter in his *Mémoires*.[8] The "argument against theory" is by now a genre in its own right, and so is the counter-genre of defense; I have decided that in this prologue I should not try to comment on it directly, but, once more, to follow my own nose.[9] My sense of the matter is simply that it would be quite wrong to deplore theory as such, though quite right to contest some of its claims. That is to say, any complaint must be leveled not against new critical practices; it would be as intemperate to deny their propriety as it would be to decline questions about their cost, which arises not so much from the theoretical practices themselves as from the hegemonic claims they are often thought to justify.

Here it will be well to remind ourselves that in some form or other the dispute about the place of theory in literary criticism, and especially in its more pedagogical moments, has always been with us. Instruction in vernacular literature may originally have been meant to serve utilitarian purposes, or, in its loftier mood, ends that might be vaguely described as cultural or quasi-religious; but, once established in the universities, literary instruction needed to look more like a discipline comparable at least to the study of literature in the classical languages. "Appreciation" was almost crowded out by Old and Middle English, Gothic, Icelandic, philology generally. (Philology had the dignified status of a science; the first wave of periodicals dedicated to literary scholarship tended to call themselves by such titles as *The Journal of English and German Philology* or *Modern Philology,* and it was a long time before anything that would be described as criticism appeared in their pages.) At the new, science-oriented Johns Hopkins University, James Bright, a professor of philology, remarked that to call a philologist a professor of literature "would be as absurd as describing a biologist as a professor of vegetables." But these scientific pretensions did not impress the real scientists: "The practical man would hardly conceal his amusement at the assumption of a company of mere philologists that they were identified with the progress of the community, and were the custodians of our higher fortunes," wrote James T. Hatfield in 1901. And as philology lost its charm and authority the literary professors had to look elsewhere for support. In 1953 René Wellek argued that philology must be replaced with a new body of hard doctrine, "a new systematic theory, a technique and methodology, teachable and transmissible." He tried to provide these amenities, but before long new systematic theories and techniques replaced his replacements. There has not been a time within living memory when it did not appear to some that theory was swamping literature. Graduate students found that it was more interesting, and, in a way, easier, to study the philosophy and methods of criticism than to study literature; and they were happy to seize on new models provided by other disciplines such as semiotics, anthropology, and psychoanalysis. It became usual for old-fashioned professors to lament the growing divide between what was done in the study and what was done in the classroom.

The present hegemony of theory is therefore new only in its extended reach and power. It may be argued, as by the judicious

Gerald Graff (from whom I have borrowed the historical evidence in the preceding paragraph) that the complaints about "research" replacing teaching lead nowhere, and that we must expect the new theories and methods to be routinized, and defused not by opposition or repression but by assimilation.[10] There is something in this, though not enough to still one's apprehension that the frog may disappear in the meantime; at present it is tolerated as the humbly indispensable cadaver necessary to the grander purposes of theory. Of course the time is long past when the Common Reader could expect to follow the discourses of theoretical professors, and we have a rather remarkable situation in which literary theorists would actually be offended if it were suggested that they had any obvious relation to common readers. They claim to be specialists, with no more obligation to common readers than theoretical physicists have. And so there is an ever-increasing supply of books classified as literary criticism which few people interested in literature, and not even all professionals, can read.

Indeed that most persuasive spokesman of modern theory, Jonathan Culler, finds reasons for affirming that this is not only the way things are, but the way things ought to be. In a recent book he opens the subject very explicitly.[11] Over the past dozen years or so it has been Culler's somewhat paradoxical merit to say with exceptional clarity exactly what he means—paradoxical because we now find him very lucidly complaining that certain persons hostile to his cause are guilty of encouraging students to succumb to "an ideology of lucidity." According to Culler, who sounds positively and lucidly exultant about the virtues of obscurity, modern criticism of the kind worth bothering about (and, his own contributions excepted, it is presumably of a kind that is virtuously obscure) is a greatly expanded domain, in which attention is typically paid to "new sorts of objects, new kinds of texts." It has theoretical models that are new, or newly imported from other disciplines. And such is its present state of prosperity that literary "theory"—which he describes as the nickname of this new domain—is now exporting its products to other disciplines such as law, anthropology, and psychoanalysis, thus, as it were, balancing its terms of trade. (He could have added biblical studies and theology, but has let it be known that he disapproves of them.) If this modern array of theoretical machinery has any unity, Culler says, it is a unity of an unprecedented kind, deriving not from agreement about the value and authority of a canon, but from a common "attention to the mechanisms of signification," which of course can be studied almost anywhere. Another preoccupation common to almost all the new theorists is politics; that is to say, their new criticism regularly takes the form of a critique of the institutional context, of the ways in which the institution "frames the sign."

Culler justly observes that literary criticism can sometimes be "taken for granted"; it ceases to be so whenever it is seriously attended to, as, for example, when there exists a criticism that criticizes criticism—that examines critical assumptions and practices, including its own and those of the institutions (the universities) which "frame" it. He is at pains to show how the history of academic criticism bears him out in this opinion. He also suggests that the success of the old New Criticism in its battle against the established academic modes of history and philology was due at least in part to the chance that it came along at a time when there were, in the United States, new institutional demands for courses in General Education. What this means is that at some level, rather far below that of the most eminent practitioners, the New Criticism could be adapted to the requirements of classrooms full of students capable of attending exclusively to "the words on the page" because of the happy accident that most of them had brought very little with them to add to those words. However, the newer varieties of criticism, introduced by the revolution of the sixties, are different, not because they aren't at odds with their predecessors, for of course they are, and not because they don't, like the old New Criticism, attend to the words on the page, for they do so with unparalleled intensity, and not because the later students have more intellectual luggage when they arrive, for they haven't; but rather because the *new* new criticism does not have, or at any rate originally didn't have (success has entailed a certain amount of dealing), the same degree of complicity as the old with the institutions which, with whatever measure of reluctance or bewilderment, house it. For one thing, the new style of criticism is determinedly interdisciplinary, and administrators who like to keep everything in allotted compartments dislike this. For another, it is unlike the old familiar approaches in that it concerns itself not with "works" and the familiar arrangements whereby "works" are assembled in "courses," but with "the logic of signification." Despite their common devotion to the complexities of language, the newer criticism differs from the old New Criticism in that it challenges "the specificity of the aesthetic." It has no interest in well-wrought urns, and in fact denies the possibility of such things; the new analytic procedures cannot tolerate notions of aesthetic totality. What it offers instead of critical totalization is a many-sided rhetorical approach; its interest is in what is officially, or by institutional consent, concealed. The only reason why it continues to concern itself at all with what Culler still refers to as "literature" is that literary works can better than others be induced to tell us things that bear "crucially" on theoretical questions. Culler's opinion is that criticism really works best when texts of all sorts, literary and nonliterary, great and small, are used; but he cannot bring himself to deny precedence to the great.

There is a certain atavism here, a ghostly canonicity, for the assumption is that the literary and the nonliterary can be confidently distinguished; and, as we shall see in a moment, the old idea of literature and the great book still lingers in the best theoretical minds, even when the revived rhetoric, pioneered with such authority by Culler's hero Paul de Man, has done so much to dismantle the distinction between literature and other kinds of writing, and to call into question the old notion of the canonical. Such dismantlings are not unheard-of—it has been argued that it was the establishment of vernacular canons that displaced rhetoric when it had been for centuries the normal instrument of criticism,[12] and so we may be contemplating one of time's irresistible revenges. And no doubt it is in part the sense of having history on his side that allows Culler to deal so magisterially with the continuing disagreement between people who study literary works and people who study signs.

Such disagreements, he believes, reflect larger differences in the university's understanding of its purpose. These can be expressed roughly as follows. On one side are the people who think the function of the university is to transmit a cultural heritage—or, in more sharply political language, that its ideological function is to reproduce "culture and the social order." And on the other side there are those who, with Culler's advocacy, think of the universities as "sites for the production of knowledge." This division of opinion as to the purpose of universities, it is suggested, is intimately related to the disagreement about the function of criticism. Those who take the older view hold that this function is to interpret the canon, "elucidating the 'core' of knowledge to be conveyed." Their notions of a proper "humanist" education are represented polemically, and it must be said very inadequately, by E. D. Hirsch's *Cultural Literacy* as endorsed by William Bennett, the former U.S. Secretary of Education. Hirsch's book serves as an easy target, and it probably seemed convenient to identify canonical "humanism" and interpretation with Hirsch's variety of "recognitive" hermeneutics—a theory certainly inconsistent with his own, but, as Culler well knows, equally unacceptable to many who hold opinions on canon and interpretation quite different from his.

One thing Culler particularly deplores is his opponents' professed worry about the need to produce educated students. To confuse the argument by references to teaching, is, he thinks, a conservative, even a reactionary, gesture: "The suggestion that thinking and writing about literature ought to be controlled by the possibilities of classroom presentation is usually an attempt to dismiss new lines of investigation or abstruse critical writings without confronting them directly." In the context of Culler's cool prose this extraordinary (and de Manian) remark might pass without much notice; so it is necessary to observe that it cunningly elides the distinction between quite legitimate concerns (reading and writing must be taught, the matter is urgent;

institutionally the whole superstructure of abstruse theory rests on the infrastructure of classroom teaching; the expression "controlled by" insidiously stands for something more like "consistent with") and the base exploitation of these concerns by lazy or shifty enemies. Such persons are given the Gramscian label "experts in legitimation," a disgrace the theorists themselves of course avoid because, despite their occupancy of well-endowed chairs, and their occasional boasting about the successful infiltration of their disciples into university departments—despite, in short, their own manifest expertness in legitimation—they are engaged in a continual critique of legitimacy. Culler's most audacious claim is that in the presumed absence of a literary avant-garde to lead the struggle against reactionary authority, Theory itself is the avant-garde of our time: "The practice of reflecting on interpretation itself and pursuing the kind of contestatory, self-transcending movement associated with avant-garde literature has now," we are expressly told, "become an activity of literary criticism." It is clear that Theory (I follow Culler in using the term to describe the whole many-sided critical movement) thinks remarkably well of itself, and remarkably ill of its literary-critical predecessors, unless their reputation is such that, like Empson, they might, if presented in suitably legitimated versions, serve as honorable ancestors, household gods, or propaganda totems.

It is a tribute to Culler's rhetorical skill that his claims and prejudices rarely sound intemperate, but his essay titled "The Humanities Tomorrow" deserves, I think, to be called aggressive. He reduces the views of the opposition as follows: it operates with a "crisis-narrative," thus defined: "once upon a time there was a canon of great cultural monuments." It is the canon, so conceived, that is now thought by Culler's enemies to be under threat, and along with it culture as we know it. Culler is then able to argue firmly against this caricature of his opponent's views. Their procedures, he says, had nothing to do with "training in the habits of critical thinking." What they wanted was to perpetuate false universalist and foundationalist attitudes, such as the idea that studying masterpieces "will provide an understanding of 'man,' as we used to say." Theory, on the other hand, is especially critical of universalist and foundationalist claims, and uniquely adept at spotting covert ideology (mostly, it seems from the examples offered, in television programs, but also, by exhaustive de Manian analysis, in "literature"). The object of the new criticism being to "demystify"—a much-favored word—cultural norms, it rejects canons as repositories of "known truth and received values . . . given truths or lifeless texts." In canons what criticism infallibly discovers is some form of stupefying aesthetic ideology.

Manifestos, however calmly expressed, are generically disposed to prejudice: their attacks on ideology must themselves be ideological, and a certain amount of misrepresentation of opposed positions, whether willed or merely generic, is no more than one should expect. Consequently there is little need to seek to demystify Culler's general proposition, which is essentially defensive: for the wholesale condemnation of older pedagogy as failing to inculcate habits of critical thinking is little more than a means of countering the suspicion, right or wrong, that Theory fails in exactly that respect. But the best way to test the validity of these arguments is to examine Culler's concept of "canon."

It is equated, as we have seen, with "the 'core' of knowledge to be conveyed," and regarded as part of an attempt to transmit what its defenders regard as "certain moral values," or "known truths and received values" founded on "lifeless texts." To teach it is merely to transmit "a common heritage (familiarity with a series of cultural monuments)." But the canon, according to Culler, is not to be thought of simply as the product of the deluded belief that such a heritage and such known truths and values exist. It is far less innocent, and the charges against it are not merely that it is conceptually wrong, but that it is subversive of justice. In the first place, the canon is made up of works written by white males, and should therefore be odious to all who care about the privations hitherto imposed on women and ethnic minorities. Moreover, it embodies a concept of culture quite unlike that in which today's students grew up—a culture that includes films, television, and lots of monoglot *Trivialliteratur*[13] but not the canonical classics. To inflict the latter on these persons of alien culture is "cultural racism"—a disease not endemic, we are to suppose, in the culture in which the students were raised, and with which they are first infected in the classroom.

These are some of the arguments used to make the idea of a canon seem pernicious. The only reason why so dangerous a body of writings is not excluded from study altogether is that "the great works" can be shown by deconstruction to be "the most powerful demystifiers of the ideologies they have been said to promote." Two reforms are needed: a critique of canons and canon-formation, and an expansion of the canon to include "writings by women, blacks, and minorities and other sorts of discourse deemed sub-literary."

This, I think, is a fair summary of Culler's view of canon and what needs to be done about it. It is wrong; he has very little idea of what a canon is, merely identifying the term with a state of affairs which his own metanarrative or crisis-fiction (roughly, that of the revolutionary purge) requires him to deplore. This misunderstanding entails some obvious confusion in his argument. So let us consider some features of canon that are, to use two more favorite words of the theorists, "crucial" to any "radical" understanding of the concept.

First, canons are formed by exclusions as well as inclusions; of course they can be expanded as well as contracted, though if you include anything and everything you naturally lose the idea of canon completely. The logic of Culler's position is to do so, but he is still bothered by his intuitive acceptance of the distinction between the literary and the sub-literary; he still believes that there are "great" works, even if the reasons for their being great have only recently been revealed. It is not really surprising that people like Culler, who have undergone extensive training in the appraisal of literature, should stumble upon the idea that such distinctions exist, but in so far as they entertain it they are, however reluctantly, reintroducing the canon, though adding that noncanonical works will also serve to illustrate the modes of signification and so forth. The word *canon* still carries something of its early and humbly practical sense of "list," which merges easily into "recommended list," for choice is always involved, and choice means exclusions and preferences. This is understood by other opponents of the canon, who do not care as much as Culler does for great works, who indeed would be happy to get rid of them to make room for their own choices, though if they succeed they must look forward to a time when their own canon will have to be defended, the "greatness" of its inclusions and the rightness of its exclusions—for example, of works by white males—explained.

Second, canons are not, as Culler alleges, enclosures full of static monuments. The error of thinking them so may be explained and in part excused by the apparent rigidity of ecclesiastical canons. These may be in more than one sense fixed—they are, effectively, closed, and their texts are treated as virtually immutable, so they are tied linguistically and also in other respects to the time of their formation, which is likely to be remote. The criteria determining that formation may well be but dimly understood, and in any event of no clear relevance in later times. If texts were all, canons would quickly cease to be of much interest. But it is pointless to think about canons without also thinking about commentary; the two go together, there is never the first without the second; without commentary canons would, as such, simply disappear. Nor is commentary simply a process of mindless veneration, the blind preservation of ancient monuments. In principle the continuity of commentary gives the contents of the canon a perpetual modernity, which is to say that the contents are effectively not the same from one generation to another: it is as inapposite to say of somebody's canon that it is irrelevant because it was written and compiled by white males as to say that the Hebrew Bible is irrelevant because it was written by ancient Jews. The point is that the value and the sense of canonical documents are not fossilized, for new values and meanings (still historically related to older ones) are, if you prefer to put it so, continually conferred upon them; so that when Culler says a new way of reading has conferred new values and meanings on the "great works" of Romanticism he is saying nothing that would in principle sound absurd to orthodox canonists, and indeed it is absurd only on the presumption that theory works as well with sub-literary as with literary texts. However, his way of putting it is influenced by the identification of the new criticism as the avant-garde; the myth is that we are being led out of error into a new and strenuous polity, founded on a "radical" critique: henceforth a series of new times begin, and the transgenerational aspect of canon, part of a past triumphantly abandoned, can be ignored. No doubt it is thought to be humanist or sentimental to imagine a community, even if only a community of commentary, that includes the dead as well as the living; yet it is an empirical fact that such a community exists (much as Bakhtin, Foucault, de Man, and others now dead belong to the heterogeneous community of theory), and its existence helps to falsify any account of canons as necessarily inert.

Third, without canon there would be no tradition ensuring what can be thought of as the special forms of attention elicited by canonical texts; and so, incidentally, no room for such special forms of attention as deconstruction, which, as a mode of commentary, has indeed been likened to certain rabbinical forms of attention, themselves deriving in part from the forms of literary attention developed by the classical rhetoricians. For it is in the character of canonical works to be such that only intense scrutiny of their texts will serve. The point is made neatly by Alvin Kibel: there are, it is true, great works of which "the text can be otherwise formulated"—he gives as examples The Reform Act and Newton's *Optics*—but canonical texts are those to which textual reference is always necessary—and here he mentions Plato, St. Mark, Rousseau, Freud—because they are, as he puts it, a continual source of meaning. "A canonical text is one whose importance we recognize, although in some radical sense we are not able to understand it."[14] It follows that having established a continuity of meanings and an especially intense form of attention, we cannot hope for an end to the search, not even in that terminal aporia which is the deconstructive substitute for closure and "totality." It is further obvious that texts of this kind—whether their immunity from the charge is intrinsic or the gift of time—are not to be thought of as inert or monolithic. Scholarly care will, as far as possible, preserve the text from change, but its stillness merely hides the contortions, repetitions, typologies, consonances, and cruxes that are the proper business of the interpreter. The text is only part of the story; the canon is text plus commentary, and commentary is what gives the text its inexhaustibility of reference and self-reference. I have heard it described as a set of relationships seeking momentary forms, as a texture of relations between past and present, as a kind of state which, by virtue of interpretation, contains its own subversive other. And all such descriptions come closer to the facts than the representation of canon as an instrument of mindless cultural conservatism and political injustice.

Fourth, there is, indeed, no such necessary association between canons and political oppression as it now appears common to assume. The canonical form of the Hebrew Bible was established after the destruction of Jerusalem, when its makers and commentators were members of an oppressed culture and religion, outsiders in everything except Torah. As for the *academic* canon of literature, it has certainly been protected in the academy, but it was not formed there, and in fact made its academic appearance not in powerful institutions but in such establishments as the fledgling University of London, where it was a substitute for the classics unavailable at Oxford or Cambridge to women, Jews, and dissenters; in the United States it was developed in departments whose first objective was to give immigrants a better command of English. To express this more generally: it is by no means the case that canon-formation is invariably the project of a privileged class of priests or academics; the preferences and vogues of lay persons, the force of relatively uninstructed opinion, are often decisive, as I tried to show in *Forms of Attention.* And it should also be remembered that the introduction of *secular* canons can be seen as part of a more general process of secularization; their development implies that it is not only biblical and classical texts that merit special forms of attention—that the vernacular literatures deserve equally intense philological and rhetorical study, one variety of which happens to be modern deconstruction. Indeed it might have been expected that Culler, who approves of secularization and also of deconstruction, would approve of this adapted form of canonicity.

Finally, there is behind his dismissive remarks on canon a philosophical objection to them as partaking of the false notion of aesthetic totalities, an objection which is an important part of the critical program deriving from de Man and Derrida. I shall say more about this attitude later, but while canon is still the topic I ought to add that the hypothesis of unity in canons is one that has frequently been justified by the success of commentary which endorses it; of course it can get in the way if used ineptly, or prematurely, for instance by forestalling deeper local investigations into the operations of figurality in texts, which is what de Man accused the New Criticism of doing when it tried to reconcile minute textual examination with a belief in ultimate aesthetic totality. It is in fact true that such attempts fail—not sometimes but always—if the criterion of success is a total and definitive statement of the relation of any text to a totality of texts—a truth that was recognized, and indeed assumed to be the basis of their whole enterprise, by the rabbis. Partial and temporary successes are all that could ever be expected, which is why interpretation is endless—why it can make sense to speak of texts as inexhaustible, and of the "great" texts as calling for continued institutional inquiry.

It will be seen from all this that canons are not at all as Culler describes them when he wants to make them the tokens of his opponents' stiff-necked refusal to see the light. The rejection of canon is not, however, an end in itself. Despite some confusion about what literature is, as on those occasions when it is allowed a certain status and differentiated from non-literature, there is no mistaking the fact that the intention is to let the notion of canon stand for literature in a sense now deprecated, nor that the consequent subordination of literature, and thus of what used to be called literary criticism, to theory is strongly implied.

We must try to determine what this entails by considering the practical aspirations and presuppositions of "many-sided" theory. And here it will be as well to remark that although there are very subtle theorists, who regard the politics of theory as important but tortuous and abstract, there are others in the many-sided enterprise who are far from subtle, and whose political crudity the subtle expressly deplore. We shall encounter some of these less subtle persons a little later.

First, though, one needs to think in general terms about the claim that theory is a matter of "radical" political significance. And it is important at the outset to reflect that there are extremely large numbers of people in the world to whom such a claim would be unintelligible or absurd. That such doubts exist in the larger literary public needs no demonstration—literary periodicals meant for that audience are almost everywhere, and for obvious reasons, hostile. But in a different though related way, doubt must also afflict the practitioners themselves. In so far as criticism of this kind is developed by academics it is in institutional competition with science, and science, even in its purest forms, has links with matters of public interest outside it such as technology and industrial production; science, to put the matter crudely, has a legible bottom line. Listening to scientists talk together (and they seem to be much more cooperative, as well as more affable, than literary critics), one is struck by two things: first, they assume that their inquiries have a common aim, say a clear and unified explanation of the world, to be arrived at by methods which, despite certain disputed areas of the philosophy of science, are in practice shared by all the investigators; and second, that there is, as a matter of empirical observation, a continuous and fruitful two-way commerce between theory and technology.

One might use here a convenient example, the activities of the so-called Ratio Club.[15] The club was formed in the immediate postwar years by a number of exceptional young scientists, including Alan Turing and George Miller, all recently released from military projects. Their special skills and experiences were various, but they had all spent the war years thinking about gunsights, radar, ciphers, and so forth. Consequently they had long concerned themselves with the *practical* implications of, say, information theory; they knew that technological needs could initiate the development of "pure" theory, which in turn would make possible technological advances otherwise unthinkable. Henceforth theories of computation, cognitive psychology, neurology, immunology, linguistics, and other subjects were transformed—not just by autonomous meditation (and the readiness with which all concerned recognized the values it created) but by powerful and palpable technological incentives and interactions. The theoretical enterprises were very largely complementary and not divisive, and the common effort was controlled by empirical observations. The thinking of these young men, often abstract, always very speculative, but conditioned by and dependent upon their recent concrete wartime experience, has since the 1950s done much to transform the environment and the everyday life even of literary critics, who, for example (and for good or ill), can now work as I am now working, on a computer far more powerful than any writer needs for writing, yet so practical that in the ordinary way one uses it without bothering to reflect on its complexity, and certainly without the need to remind oneself that it is an "instantiation" of a purely conceptual Turing machine. Once that concept existed, the need for algorithms produced algorithms, and they found appropriate physical forms.

The point is not that it is a very superior thing to be a thinking scientist, but to indicate what it really means to engage in a form of knowledge production that impinges directly on the world, as the critical theorists think they must claim to do. Forms of abstract thinking exist in the academic environment which have visible effects on society and thus, in a way that must seem obvious to everybody (except governments who try to save money by destroying the conditions under which "pure" research is conducted), pay off. Now there seems to be no reason for saying anything of this sort about the latest criticism, which obviously has far more in common with the nice speculations of philosophy than with "hard" science, though if it is to have what it regards as its proper place beside those who think of universities as sites of knowledge production it must somehow suggest that although this philosophical affinity is one that must be acknowledged and even rejoiced in, there is also a strong claim to beneficial practical effects.

None of this means there is anything wrong in wanting to go on doing theory, unless you believe that all intellectual disciplines should be productive in the way science can be. What is wrong is the claim that theory can be appropriately measured by such sociopolitical standards. Culler's explanation of the practical use of theory seems to be that it offers a necessary critical opposition within the institution; what is opposed is of course not the party that endorses knowledge generation, but the rump that still talks about the preservation of cultural monuments and so forth, and in particular the bad faith of the old-fashioned critics, who by rattling on mechanically about canons and values support a false idea of the university and also of social justice. The claim is that in this way theory, a purer criticism, establishes itself as one of the branches of learning that make knowledge and also, by purging the sites of knowledge production, put it to civil use. However large the political claim, it can in practice only be expressed as opposition to a limited number of rival academic disciplines (none of them regarded as of vast importance by the regnant knowledge generators) and to an image of them that is in any case distorted. They are the disciplines which, in regarding themselves as somehow ancillary to literature, are held to represent a discredited concept of the university. That opposition to these disciplines by yet another discipline of very little interest to the bosses can be represented as having potentially a "crucial" influence on the academy, indeed on politics more generally, is a claim so fantastically inflated that it belongs not to the real world but to carnival.

One need not idealize the scientists, or disparage the achievements of these new critics, to apprehend the essential difference between this program for generating knowledge by criticism and the habit of scientific theory. It is simply that the mutually productive relationship between abstract reflection and technology mentioned earlier is not reflected in any similar relation between the new criticism and anything beyond it. For example, theory, as Culler acknowledges, has no discernible input from, or influence on, current literature—which is why it is necessary for him and others to claim that this kind of writing *is* the new literature.

Such professed confidence that the new style can have a beneficial though still presumably indirect effect on the world outside the institutions depends on the belief that certain forms of theory are specially adapted to the task of exposing covert ideologies, and can thus be politically purgative beyond the institution, the site of productive knowledge. Culler, for one, believes that theory will do good to suffering minorities. The days when the editors of *Tel Quel* supposed they could help with the revolution by turning up at the Renault factory and reading their pieces to the workers over lunch are presumably over, and anyway the exposure of the ideology of lucidity has made it even less probable that such audiences would understand what was going on. And it is hard to avoid the doubtless over-simple reflection that if one feels strongly enough about the matter there are probably more effective ways of drawing attention to political injustice than by deconstructing Hegel and Freud. Another crude reflection is that if this adversarial enterprise ever seemed likely to upset the cultural and political arrangements preferred by the patrons on whose benevolence it depends, they would soon find ways of putting a stop to it.

So far I have been speaking of theoretical ambitions given relatively modest expression, and concerned primarily with the use of critical techniques to adjust political attitudes at a certain level of abstraction, always of course in the hope that the effort would indirectly feed through to the world of power. But there are, in the many-sided movement, more belligerent elements, and they contend that their criticism, and the writings they choose to propagate, should work more directly toward political ends. They are not by any means the first critics to believe it possible and right to do so; for example, the early Soviet exponents of *proletcult* held the same belief in one form, and the advocates of Socialist Realism in another; and there have been more recent manifestations, parts of what René Wellek called, in an indignant essay of 1972, "The Attack on Literature."[16]

Wellek is the author (in six large volumes) of a history of the critical tradition now deemed largely obsolete; he also collaborated in a book called *Theory of Literature* (1949), which was for a generation a standard work; so it is easy to see why he was upset. In "The Attack on Literature" he cites pronouncements by various writers who, as it seems to him wrongly, associate literature itself with political injustice: among his examples are Roland Barthes ("literature is constitutionally reactionary"), Oswald Wiener ("the alphabet was imposed by higher-ups"), and Louis Kampf ("our aesthetics are rooted in surplus value"). Remarks of this sort were not unusual in the late sixties and early seventies, and should sometimes be taken at less than face value. Barthes was every inch a literary man, and some of his *obiter dicta,* for instance that syntax is fascist, can probably be treated as provocative flourishes rather than serious statements of opinion. Louis Kampf was a quasi-dadaist revolutionary of his moment and thenceforth, so far as I am aware, of no moment. I know nothing of Wiener, whose remark is of the sort that means to be *épatant* but on examination turns out to be trivial.

Yet the idea that literature (and *a fortiori* criticism which is complicitous with the old idea of it) is the invention of an oppressive class, and one that progressive critics have a duty to attack, cannot be regarded as just a passing fancy of the sixties. It might be possible to trace some of its present aspects to that epoch; as that intelligent but soured commentator Frederick Crews remarked, the demand in the sixties for an end to oppression turned into a demand for theories *about* oppression.[17] But the literary-political program seems in fact to have done rather better than many others that were formulated in those years; it has survived and become more influential, more varied, and more in touch with changes in public sentiment that have nothing to do with literary criticism. The political attack on literature considered as a belletristic canon imposed by unjust authority—often a theme, though an uneasy one, of Marxist criticism—has been greatly strengthened by our enhanced consciousness of sexist and racist injustice, and our wish to eliminate them: so that campaigns for women's canons, black canons, black women's canons, campaigns against male white dominance in literature as elsewhere, can be seen to reflect larger movements in public sentiment and public conscience. Political "attacks on literature" and on canon can thus be prosecuted in the knowledge that those who oppose them need to explain how they can do so and still be credited with a measure of political purity; and they themselves may suffer some disturbance to their social conscience, or just feel irked at being called reactionary, or even fascist. This partly explains one central aspect of the present situation—the lack of any resolute resistance to the decanonization of literature now in rapid progress in the United States, and probably elsewhere—a process often accompanied, strangely enough at first sight, since it is the project of people who think canons wicked, by the construction of rival canons *de novo* with, of course, no real pretense that their purpose is other than political and revolutionary. The canon having proved so successful a weapon in the hands of the enemy, it is proposed to use it against them in this new phase of the class war. I needn't add that not all criticism which takes account of politics deserves to be lumped together with that of these noisier and more provocative parties; but all seem to call for a change in the definition of literature, a change they prefer to think of in their various ways as the necessary deconstruction of a false and limiting aesthetic. It is maintained that the literary canon is a fiction invented to support the ideology of the modern capitalist state, and that literature cannot be treated as "a distinct, bounded object of knowledge,"[18] so it follows that to study literature is to study politics, and that any denial of this necessity is in bad faith.

And so the question, what is it that is studied when one studies literature?—or, what is the ostensible object of criticism?—is politicized and becomes very contentious. Even when what used, on the whole uncontentiously, to be thought of as literature is criticized, it is often not criticized as *literature:* and some criticism presupposes either that there is no such thing as literature or that there shouldn't be, or that, supposing there is, and that it has a right to exist, it is something the true nature of which we have come to understand that we do not understand.

Affirmative action programs, no doubt in some degree fortified by various brands of literary politics, have ensured that the balance and structure of university departments have of late been changing, which is a desirable thing, and there must be consequent changes in the way things are done. But such changes need not, and in fact will not, entail the conversion of literature departments into instruments of direct political action. A more probable reading of the future of the more extremist programs is that people will say of each of them—with appropriate variation—what Robert Scholes recently said of deconstruction: that "it allows a displacement of political activism into a textual world where anarchy can *become* the establishment without threatening the actual seats of political and economic power. Political radicalism may be thus drained off or sublimated into a textual radicalism that can happily theorize its own disconnection from unpleasant realities."[19] What the most radical political program for criticism is most likely to achieve is the kind of success represented by an appointment to a department that feels itself a bit short of help in the area of "radical" criticism, and thus at a disadvantage with others that are better balanced, and that attract more attention and support. The successful candidate will have about as much real political power as his or her colleagues in bibliography or Middle English.

The immediate issue is in any case not who gets promoted or who runs what, nor is it the possibility that a change of syllabus can be a prelude to political revolution. What we need to ask is whether the arguments against literature (and thus against the sort of criticism that was once thought to "serve" it and teach it) have validity, political or otherwise. And there are arguments not ostensibly political for the view that they have such validity. Some of these derive from Paris—Wellek cites Barthes's *écriture* and Blanchot's "disappearance of literature." Some are native to

America—the populist propaganda of Leslie Fiedler, extolling what the Germans call *Trivialliteratur,* and the less easily resistible arguments of Richard Poirier, who treats literature as a performance like other performances; not minding, and doubtless happy to be seen not to mind, that Wordsworth expressly condemned those who talked about a taste for poetry as one might about a taste for sherry or rope-dancing. But Poirier does not forget that unignorably good performance, in whatever field of activity—including writing and reading—calls for intelligent training and attentive preparatory effort; and this is a saving implication, for if Poirier is right we can continue to suppose that there is a learnable mode of performance called literature, and another called literary criticism, considered as the performed description of performances.[20] We may also infer that he thinks some performances more valuable than others. How can he tell? It is, as I remarked at the outset, the great question, and we may at present be paying a price for having put it aside, as Barbara Herrnstein Smith suggests.

Historically the concept of literature is inextricably involved with the presumption of quality in both text and reader. It is therefore not surprising that the dismissal of quality as irrelevant to the study of writing (or its exploitation for political purposes) should entail a denial of literature. This consequence is evident not only in the more extreme arguments, overtly supporting factional aspirations, but also in those uneasy equivocations of Culler on the subject of "great" literature and the dilution of the canon. Many-sided theory having dismissed the "classic" and banned the study of "great works" as such, it must go on to find new reasons for studying literature—or, to avoid arguments about that word, writing—at all. These reasons are ingenious and interesting, another reason why theorists find theory more exciting than literature, of which they have little further need, and of which, if necessary, they can claim to be the authors.

Theory is an absorbing preoccupation. Paul Valéry once remarked that among those whose responsibility or destiny it is to judge poetry, to talk about it, to cultivate a taste for it in others, there are many who lack any appetite for it, or any understanding of the need for it. These people, he goes on, are in the peculiar business of distributing something they do not possess. What makes the situation worse is that they do their work with intelligence and zeal; they think seriously and deeply about all manner of things that are not, however, what he calls "poetry."[21]

Anybody who accepts that there is a difference between poetry and other writing (and of course many avant-garde theorists, *sans grand appétit de Poésie* perhaps, do not) will feel that some modern criticism can be disposed of under Valéry's rubric, for there are certainly works which demonstrate nothing except the zealous acquisition of a new critical patter.[22] However, one can by no means dispose of all modern criticism by placing it in this category, to which, one need hardly add, a lot of earlier criticism, possibly most of it, also belongs. It must be remembered that deconstruction, say, or Heideggerian hermeneutics are not the easiest options for those who wish to avoid the ardors of poetry; as Dr. Johnson remarked in another context, to write thus it is at least necessary to read and think. The renunciation of literary criticism as a means toward the understanding and valuation of poetry betokens no diminution of zeal or intelligence, only a lack of interest in, or taste for, what Valéry calls "poetry," along with a desire—not new, for it has hovered over the academic study of literature from the beginning—to acquire scientific respectability; to have done with vague "appreciations" and inert cultural monuments, to be seen to participate in the modern business of knowledge generation by substituting for the philosophically flawed old models new ones borrowed from harder disciplines. Hayden White has recently given some reasons for thinking these ambitions as illusory now as they ever were. He describes humanistic studies as fragmented into separate disciplines "which must feign to aspire to the status of science without any hope of achieving the kind of procedures developed in the physical sciences . . . The result . . . is that in order to enable research in any field of humanistic studies, investigators must presuppose that at least one other field of study is effectively secured, that is to say, effectively free of the kind of epistemological and methodological disputes that agitate their own area of enquiry." For example, a dependence on historiography entails the belief that it offers a stable element over which critical pluralism can securely play: it takes no account of history's own insecurities and pluralisms.[23]

This observation suggests an explanation for, among other things, the rapid turnover of models—structuralism, for example, which took one kind of linguistics as a basis for a semiotic science of literature, was quickly superseded by many-sided poststructuralism. It left a legacy, the datum of nonreferentiality; and its devaluation of value "problematized" the concept of literature, necessitating a further and more ambitious flight from literary criticism.

The consequence is a degree of confusion such as opponents of the ideology of lucidity alone might welcome. In a late essay Paul de Man addressed the modern difficulties of those who are, according to Valéry, charged with stimulating in others a taste for poetry:

> The main theoretical difficulty in the teaching of literature is the delimitation of border lines that circumscribe the literary field by setting it apart from other modes of discourse. Hence the nervousness which any tampering with the canonical definition of a literary corpus is bound to provoke. In a manner that is more acute for theoreticians of literature than for theoreticians of the natural or the social world, it can be said that they do not quite know what they are talking about, not only in the metaphysical sense that the whatness, the ontology of literature is hard to fathom, but also in the more elusive sense that, whenever one is supposed to speak of literature, one speaks of anything under the sun (including, of course, oneself) except literature. The need for determination thus becomes all the stronger as a way to safeguard a discipline which constantly threatens to degenerate into gossip, trivia or self-obsession.[24]

De Man recommended an almost puritanical rigor in reading, and was certainly less likely than most to avoid discussion of literature by drifting off into anything under the sun, though here, as often elsewhere, he is more concerned with the difficulty of doing it than with doing it. In fact doing it is bound to be difficult when there is a problem about what it is, and what it means to talk about it. In the passage quoted above the word "literature" is used repeatedly; the existence of literature is clearly presupposed, but it is always thought of as a problematic area, with problematic borders. It is not only the old-fashioned who feel nervous about those borders. In fact de Man goes on to say that the fixing of borderlines within which literature may be thought to exist always implies a prior philosophical, religious, or ideological choice, a predetermination of what is literary. This stricture must presumably affect his own usage of such terms as "literature" and "literary," but he heads off this charge by claiming that literary *theory* is in a measure autonomous, that it is concerned with modalities of sense (usually, it is worth adding, the sense of literary works) and not with value; and that to define what the linguistics of semiology and literature have in common "has become the object of literary theory." Is this not, in a new and subtle form, the old longing for a "science of literature"? The form preferred by de Man is that of a modernized rhetoric. He is clear that criticism "involves the voiding, rather than the affirmation, of literary categories," and that it is "not *a priori* certain that literature is a reliable source of information about anything but its own language." Literature doubtless exists, but in some fashion that makes it excessively difficult to define or criticize.

De Man thrives on difficulties, especially when they seem insoluble, when attempts at solution are themselves doomed, by the very nature of discursive argument, to be self-defeating. A good example is the following kind of argument: there can be no frontiers between literature and other kinds of discourse. Since what is called literature is marked by the avowed figurality of its language, and since all discourse is marked by the figurality of its language, everything is literature. That nothing is, while everything is, literature is just the kind of opposition the de Manian mode of argument likes to set up. Similarly, it is maintained that the distinction between poetry and prose is an obsolete piece of mystification; yet de Man often talks about poetry as such, and, at any rate in some of his earlier work, seems to consider whether special claims may be made for it; they are admittedly different from those of the old New Criticism from which he is always strenuously, though also with a certain nostalgia, distancing himself, and doubtless avoid the more obvious kind of aesthetic totalization, but claims they nevertheless are, and they would not be made on behalf of anything that might as well be called literature simply because the borderlines don't exist.

For de Man theory means "reading"—an activity of which he holds an extremely rarefied notion. It is possible only for an élite of theorists, prepared for a rigorous engagement with the resistance inevitably encountered in the application of language to language. All the same it *is* called "reading," and presumably has a relation of some sort to the activity that normally goes by that name. One thing the two ideas of reading have in common is that they work best, or most interestingly, on texts which have long been held in esteem, and are usually classified as literature: Proust, Hölderlin, Rousseau, Wordsworth, Shelley. Apart from a remarkably celebrated allusion to Archie Bunker, de Man rarely performed his readings on anything to which the *ancien régime* would have denied the epithet "literary," though to the old ones the term was simply honorific, while to de Man it is hopelessly problematic.

A critic of de Man's age (exactly my own) must of course have dragged into his later life a burden of notions about intuitions of value that are now questioned or discredited. And being well aware of what has to be given up, he tried in another late essay called "Return to Philology" to say what that was. This short piece makes the polemically exaggerated assertion that it is the secret aim of more conventional literary teaching (abandoning specificity in its quest for themes and totalities) to conceal what close reading reveals. But it also raises what seems to have become the fundamental question, whether "aesthetic" values are compatible or incompatible with linguistic structures, bearing in mind that it is from supposed entities consisting of linguistic structures that any such values must be derived. De Man calls this an open question: it will be answered, if at all, he says, by the teaching of literature as rhetoric or poetics prior to its being taught as hermeneutics and history. The work would have to be done in small specialized departments, where the usual justification for large ones, namely that literature has to do with aesthetic values or "standards of cultural excellence," would presumably be deconstructed at the outset. As I say, he knew a lot about standards of cultural excellence, but maintained that such standards are "in the last analysis always based on some form of religious faith." For this suspect foundation he wished to substitute "a principle of disbelief." It is not difficult to see that such a principle can mean little to a subject lacking the experience of belief, and de Man's formation was such that he had indeed experienced belief in a form that led him to believe he needed to cultivate disbelief. This is certainly not the place to enter into the controversy about his wartime juvenilia; it is nevertheless worth pointing out that the mature de Man was in many respects inconceivable except as the product of an education not to be had outside continental Europe, and he is often applying the principle of disbelief to beliefs it might never have occurred to the rest of us to hold, or possibly even to consider very seriously. For example, when Heidegger says that the German language alone "speaks Being" while all the others merely "speak of Being," a person of my formation is likely to feel, if not say, that on this occasion at least Heidegger is being silly. But to arrive at a position of disbelief in respect to such views was for de Man an arduous and fruitful task, involving a deconstruction of a powerful philosophical tradition that sponsored certain beliefs he came to regard as abhorrent, whether they were related to German political and cultural hegemony or to the false idea of aesthetic totality. Thus it was for him a matter of moment that *no* poetry, not even Hölderlin's, can be said to "speak Being," whereas to most people the claim that this is what poetry does would hardly seem worth arguing about, since it could only be done in a philosophical mode which we don't in any way believe capable of making our kind of sense. But none of this means that the principle of disbelief is not a valuable principle, or that de Man's often melancholy and sometimes desperate application of it is irrelevant to our present crisis. He is very much between two worlds, and immobilized by his belief in disbelief. Disbelief entails uncertainties, and nobody was ever so hot for uncertainties as de Man. He believed that his skeptical critique could detect covert or blind ideologies, unfounded theological assumptions about totalities, in the work of others; but he would not have denied that "in the last analysis" a comparable scrutiny would detect similar deep flaws in his own. His desire to remain always aware of this consequence is one reason why he sometimes seems bewilderingly autocritical; yet he needed to show some confidence in the power of his own writing to perform just the feat it denied to be a possibility for others' writing, namely to say what it meant. And he is always aware of the pressure upon him of the traditional assumptions he is constantly obliged to put to the question.

De Man, who was, among other things, a historian, a philologist, and at least at one time a conventional critic of the arts, seems not to have been able to embrace fully his own total aesthetic abolitionism. The uncertainties that, as he remarks, characterize the history of "the discourse about literature" are *his* uncertainties. The difficulty about the question "what is literature?" (from which necessarily springs the question "what is literary criticism?") is *his* difficulty. And it is very much his problem that the "resistance to theory" remains when the naive and facile objections have been scornfully swept away. It remains, he says, because it is an internal resistance. It was in de Man's nature to detect resistances; the telos of his theorizing is not closure but aporia, which becomes for all deconstructionists a perpetually hesitant substitute for closure. The more complex the argument, the more certain is that destination of conclusive uncertainty. And this would be true of any answer to the question, "What is literature?" or, as de Man puts it, "literature as such." There is much to admire in this subtle self-resistance which can be stilled only by aporia, which becomes a source not of dismay or philosophical despair but of a sober exultation. At least once de Man discussed the problem of getting stuck in an aporia with unusually good humor, questioning whether it was possible, as Gérard Genette recommended, "to remain *within* this whirligig *(tourniquet)*." Is it possible, asks de Man, to remain "*within* an undecidable situation? As anyone who has ever been caught in a revolving door or on a revolving wheel can testify, it is certainly most uncomfortable."[25] But the tone seems to tell you he doesn't really mind. And, in itself, the predicament must seem quite a desirable end to arguments of all kinds that are conducted according to the principle of disbelief. De Man provides a model, not only for a pedagogy he was sadly sure could never be institutionally established, but also for a certain poise, a certain stillness, induced by considerations of the aporetic difficulty of the case. This hesitant poise could be a useful example to critics whose thought has led them into antithetical positions, yet who have not renounced—perhaps cannot renounce—value or history. Aporia, undecidability: these now ubiquitous expressions are often covert ways of achieving critical closures which the favored line of argument ostensibly forbids and avoids. But they can also reflect, in the best practitioners, a degree of prudence and sanity. For the great question of value and history may, at any rate for the moment, be described as undecided, if not undecidable.

Nobody could read de Man—even in the old sense of the word—without being aware that his was a very remarkable mind, essentially a dark mind as well as an abnormally acute one; what he writes is, in a perfectly recognizable sense of the word, literature. We value a texture and a personality. So with Derrida, the other writer who gives a genuine prestige to theory. What becomes of literature in the thought of Derrida? We find him saying, with that hesitant irony he so often employs, that "there is no—or hardly any, ever so little—literature,"[26] which must mean that there is *some*, and that it can be identified. If you read him on, say, Mallarmé or Jabès you can see how he delights in the little there is. Of course, he also says that "there is no essence of literature, no truth of literature," and that the concept is habitually used or misused in a way that depends on an assumed reference to a transcendental truth, on an oppression of the signifier by the signified: he has many ways of saying it, and they mean that the very little literature there is obeys the rule that modern writing, a return to the most original form of writing, must be an activity that subverts logocentrism: it must, in fact, be the sort of Derrida himself chooses, with such virtuosity, to discuss.

The "hymeneal" puns he finds in Mallarmé remind one a little of Empson, though expressed in a very different dialect; this is worth saying because it is here that "reading" (and de Man once said that Derrida was the first Frenchman ever to *read*) rejoins literary criticism. The point is that even on this view literature (and consequently a need for commentary identifiable as literary criticism) still exists, if you know where to look for it (if your nose leads you to it), as writing that has in some elusive sense more *value* than non-literature, the merely *lisible*—literature in the false idea of it, considered as something that effectively expired in the nineteenth century. Derrida once remarked in an interview that he was first drawn not "toward philosophy but rather toward literature," though he immediately qualified the statement, adding: "no, toward something which literature accommodates more easily than philosophy." Lacking essence, lacking literariness, literature nevertheless remains, if only in order to accommodate something else. Perhaps its value is a function of its resistance to critical analysis; in any case, as Derrida's excellent commentator Rodolphe Gasché justly remarks in discussing it, this attitude clearly cannot be regarded as a dismissal of literary criticism.[27]

Yet where there is very little literature, there need presumably be very little literary criticism. The old version—castigated as commentary, covert theology, a leaping over the signifier, a false assumption of some transcendental signified—is tolerated only as a marginally useful "doubling" of the text. And here, I think, the demarcation of the borderline between old and new is sharper than de Man usually felt able to make it. The position seems to be that the old habits of thematization and totalization are rejected; they form horizons that restrict textual polysemy; they are false as well as naive. Yet they cannot be wholly dispensed with, if only because there must be something to subvert.

Again, as usual with the finest practitioners, whatever their programs, we find Derrida—more cautious than might be expected of one who has acquired the reputation of the Great Anarch—considering his position in relation to what must be wholly or partly superseded, recognizing in his idiosyncratic way a certain measure of dependence or interdependence. Now even "thematic" critics of the old school are aware of the loss of textual specificity entailed by the very nature of their methods, just as they are aware of at least some of the problems of closure. They may well think that Derrida has given this awareness a clearer definition, and allow themselves to hope that the older styles of criticism needn't after all be abolished, only made more rigorous and more self-critical.

That reform is close to what de Man was after when he advocated the revival of rhetoric and poetics as the foundations of a pedagogy to be refined in the classrooms of a tropological élite. But these theoreticians seem not always to have been read in quite the intended sense; the radical now seems more interesting on its own than in a dialogue with the stuffy old, and the "principle of disbelief" is here in abeyance. Yet as Gasché and others have remarked, Derrida's unthematizable units—supplement, remark, and so on—have been used by his followers, involuntary resurrectionists of the older criticism, in a shamefully *thematic* way. Perhaps the only writer who can truly sustain Derridean flight is Derrida; others make forced landings on terrain that is likely to be treacherous in the manner explained by Hayden White.

Praise for exquisite hesitations at the expense of bold postmodern offensives and, equally, of unquestioning commitments to an older aesthetics, is unlikely to be regarded by the embattled on either side as of any relevance to their lives. It isn't easy to squat on the fence. On the other hand, traditionalists (who may think it in principle a good place to be) need to acquire some understanding of the new, which is often more than they want to do; while the innovators, on the other hand, are too happily aggressive to sit still, and are continually reinforced. If one leader fails others spring up to take his place—potent advocates of the new, who deplore thematization and closure, and less equivocally than Derrida. Barthes, for instance, was vehement on the subject. Lyotard makes slogans against the totalizers. Another sect, the Heideggerians, though they disagree with others of the many-sided party, hate closure just as much, detesting anything that obstructs the continuous participation of the reader in the discourse. Any disposition to totalize meets with flamboyant opposition. Who, then, needs fences? Certainly not the proponents of the revolutionary purge, the champions of text against works.

It is nevertheless possible to maintain that what some Derrideans are inadvertently doing is to bring about the exact opposite of their wishes by "sealing up" the text, putting it back behind the prison bars of the New Criticism. Such is the opinion of Robert Scholes, who wishes, as a semiotician, to break "the hermetic seal around the literary text," to "open up the way between the literary text and social text in which we live."[28] He wants no elite classroom, but a place in which by being taught to criticize some texts students can be made capable of criticizing all texts, social as well as written—all the tissue, one might say, of the human world. Scholes condemns the opponents of closure for covertly imposing their own closure, and so joining the old-style opposition, who need closure to enable them to talk about aesthetic wholes. He makes some points against Derrida's own self-contradictions—for instance, his defense of his own *intentions,* his complaints that his meaning has been misunderstood—and against the errors of some of his American disciples. Yet in treating literature mostly as just another semiotic system, and by espousing putatively value-free methods, is not he himself leading his troops out of criticism as such into the supposedly more secure ground of semiotics? Elsewhere he refers to himself as "a teacher of language and literature—or, better, of textuality,"[29] which tells us what literature has become for *him*—a semiotic sample, convenient because more portable than the entire social environment. On this view the redemption of the literary text seems to require its relegation to the position of one among an inexhaustible and indiscriminate array of other texts: in short, to save it is to destroy it. Such are the contradictions in which we find ourselves when we lose confidence in the existence and value of "literature as such."

I have been discussing the subtle, and must now make good my promise to consider also the less subtle—those who are not given to backward glances; who care little for the exact nature of the risks to be taken or the size of the stake; who would think exquisite learned hesitations pusillanimous, not maturely cautious, find not poise but paralysis. They do not share de Man's diffidence about getting their programs accepted by their institutions, and they are not bothered by the extreme intricacy of the relation between academic criticism and politics. We have recently been told in some detail about one institution where programs are unhesitantly intended to have a direct impact on the larger society. In order to achieve this they need to propose iconoclastic ideas about literature.

On February 2, 1988, the *Wall Street Journal* decided for some reason to investigate the English faculty at Duke University. David Brooks, literary editor of the *Journal,* visited the star-studded department and came up with quotes that must have startled the stockholders, among whom, it is reasonably safe to conjecture, were at least some of the trustees of the university. "Students are not taught that there is such a thing as literary excellence . . . [We] are throwing out the notion of good and bad, or ignoring it," said one young teacher. Another claimed that "we" were de-emphasizing the "phalluscentric [*sic*] canon" by attending more to nineteenth-century black women writers than to Shakespeare. There are courses with such titles as "Paranoia, Politics and other Pleasures," doubtless intended primarily for the delight of the instructors, and courses on movie Westerns and Zane Grey and comic books, more for the delectation of the students. They are said to be popular; job vacancies, we are told, attract hundreds of applications from young scholars who keenly approve of the abolition of quality, canon, and so forth. A woman professor was reported as saying that the canon which includes Shakespeare, Twain, and Tolstoy was the invention of "white, male Northeasterners" as part of a plot to oppress minorities and women. She confessed to teaching Shakespeare, but only in order to "use" him as an illustration of the way seventeenth-century society mistreated women. And so on. The English department at Duke, one might add, is said to have attracted big critical names by offering six-figure salaries, and by this means, we are assured, it has "made itself one of the two or three most respected departments in the nation."[30]

Now we know better than to believe all we read in the papers; moreover, it seems likely that some of his interlocutors were teasing Brooks. But the trustees of the university may have felt some dismay at the article, and Barbara Herrnstein Smith of Duke, then the president of the Modern Language Association of America, whose study of value I mentioned earlier, thought it necessary on February 26 to appease them with a more qualified account of what was afoot. She explained to them that literary study has a history of change, and that institutions make and can therefore break canons, which is certainly true. She added that her colleagues were not "trashing" the classics; nobody was saying that Shakespeare and Milton—and presumably Mark Twain and Tolstoy—could be "replaced" by anything else. They were, she went on with some apparent inconsistency, teaching people to read literature—some literature, any literature? and what, by the way, *is* literature?—thus enabling them to grow familiar with American culture and Western thought, and even, she went so far as to add, with "eternal truths" and "higher values." It seems to be implied, though Smith goes out of her way to deny this, that a "new" canon, or perhaps any canon or no canon at all but simply the first books or films or videos that come to hand or mind that are likely to please students largely unfamiliar with anything very different from these chosen works, will for these purposes do as well or better than any old literary canon.

Smith is conciliatory, apologetic, and no doubt, in the circumstances, prudent to suggest that there had been no real change in purpose, only in means; the virtues of literature as a civilizing force are not being questioned. She is a distinguished scholar, and for all I know she might, in other circumstances, talking to specialists rather than nonspecialist trustees, be as radical, as subtle, as melancholy as de Man: but on this occasion the message was simple, the speaker defensive. She was telling the trustees that in her department—one of the two or three best in the land—it was believed that the teaching of literature as a means to eternal truth and so forth could be done with books and methods quite different from those used by earlier and presumably misguided teachers who had had the same end in view. But the expert on value is a least aware that she may be entering a minefield. On the other hand Annabel Patterson, if she was correctly reported, maintains that the proper use of Shakespeare is to convey information, eternal truths perhaps, about the oppression of women in the seventeenth century. Her intentions are not of the sort that used to be called literary—they are political, quite expressly so—and one does not need a subtle de Manian reading to detect *this* ideology. The reform of the canon to include representatives of minorities neglected by white northeastern males is frankly described not as having anything to do with literature but as a stage in a revolutionary political program aimed at the discomfiture of white northeastern males. Here are no delicately excogitated aporiai or liminal hesitations; here are no wrestlings with the problem of reference; in fact, there is very little of anything that could be described, on any definition of the word, as *reading*. If the old escape route from reading always led, as de Man believed, to mere chat and self-indulgent aesthetics, then the new one must be said to have its own ways of escaping from the rigors of reading, whether into ready-made political positions or into easier intellectual exercises such as the mechanical use of formulas not originally mechanical at all, like those of Paul de Man himself, and those of Jacques Derrida.

It is as true of the best of the new, as it is of the best of the old criticism—let us risk saying, of criticism in general when it is the work of sense and intelligence—that it does not always lead us into the morass of triviality described by de Man. It remains a mark of the best that they rarely find matters to be simple, or suppose that all who came before them were absurdly wrong; thus they will not easily assume that the attribution of value to something known as literature is nothing but an obsolete piece of theology, left over from the days before they discovered "reading." They will remember, too, that value is the product of intergenerational transactions. So are institutions, and the canons with which they have a reciprocal relation. They can certainly change—canons, institutions, and values—but such changes are perforce a matter of intricate negotiations (conducted by acts of reading, talking, and writing) and rarely of abolitionist propaganda.

I have come this far without saying much about the general condition of literary criticism today, and will try briefly to remedy this omission by referring to a new history of American criticism, covering the years 1930 to 1980, by Vincent B. Leitch. It is a solid survey, packed with names and theories; I had not thought criticism had undone so many. The longest entry in the index is, not surprisingly, for Derrida. But one of the first things to notice is that certain names one would expect to find mentioned, if not honored, in any account of modern American criticism are absent: John Hollander, for example, an important poet but also a critic of wide learning and exceptional gifts, who happens to be hostile to much modern critical theory. The book is arranged according to schools or types of criticism; Hollander, since he belongs to none of them, has no place in it. Another independent critical performer whom I have already mentioned, namely Richard Poirier, is, by a taxonomy as weird as Borges' famous Chinese dog system, affiliated to "The New York Intellectuals" because he has lived in New York and was once an editor of *Partisan Review,* standards by which I too am a New York intellectual. Poirier is simply bundled into the handiest category; no reader will take away the slightest notion of the character of his work, of the penetration of his reading, or of his importance in the present crisis of the subject. He has to be put into a school, whether he likes it or not. Leitch's readers will easily add further instances of exclusion or of relative neglect; Hugh Kenner, for instance, cannot be accommodated. Leitch, aware of the danger of his method, alludes to the exclusions in his Preface ("Displaced from this history are the individual careers of such critics as [eleven famous names follow]"),[31] and one understands that certain distortions and omissions of this sort are hard to avoid; historians need to give their books some sort of organization. Moreover, the organizing principle he has chosen does seem to reflect the mood or morale of the profession of academic criticism at this moment. Critics are most admired and noticed when associated with a particular creed or method; a superior, well-balanced department will have representatives of Marxism, feminism, deconstruction, psychoanalytic criticism, neo-historicism, reader-response criticism, and so forth. The pronouncements by members of the Duke faculty, whether or not the report was wholly accurate and allowing for an element of caricature, do represent the present current of feeling. So does Leitch's conscientious account of the way we live now. Critics of idiosyncratic talent—often, on a sustainable view of the matter, the best critics—are left out, while large numbers of practitioners, by adherence to this or that doctrine forming part of many-sided theory, achieve a place in the story. Although their books and articles, patiently listed by Leitch, are overpoweringly numerous, they are for the most part compliant with his categorizations: Myth Criticism, Phenomenological and Existential[ist] Criticism, Reader-Response Criticism, Structuralism and Semiotics, Deconstruction, Feminism, Black Aesthetics, Leftist Criticism, and so on. Many of these types of criticism profess to engage in a critique of power structures, yet it is obvious that their authors are replicating those structures within the world of academic criticism, struggling for visibility, keeping an eye open for passing bandwagons, looking for the valuable mutation, the new set of tricks that will ensure success or at any rate survival. They are encouraged to do so by the nature of the academy, which promotes the generation of knowledge, or at least a mimesis of it, by insisting on publication as a condition of tenure.

Few people can take much pleasure in modern academic literary criticism except its practitioners, who do not mind that an intelligent outsider would surely find it both arcane and depressing. One of the questions such an observer might reasonably but naively ask is whether there is a connection between such work and teaching. Isn't teaching the primary reason why these people have their jobs? Of course there are, or used to be, critics who worked outside the academy and had no classroom responsibilities—Edmund Wilson was a notable instance—but few of these mavericks survive, and even such writers as Alfred Kazin, normally thought of as extra-academic, have long had bases in universities. Nearly all critics are contractually obliged to teach for a living, though their tenure in practice depends more on published "research" than on teaching. Not many can claim a close relationship between what they do in their studies and what they offer their students, and some would not wish to. Leitch dutifully takes up the question of pedagogy; and, to be fair, we should remember that he sees himself more as a dispassionate reporter than as a critic. Here and there he notes in some practitioner an unusual, even a perverse, interest in the classroom and records a few opinions as to what should be done in it. Some schools of criticism, for instance the reader-response theorists and the psychoanalytic critics, have a vested interest in students, who are for them a convenient source of data. But they, like the others, must publish books and articles which as a rule can be read only by colleagues, or those who aspire to be colleagues; certainly not by the mass of undergraduates who take "English" courses, and only rarely by interested "common readers." And, according to Leitch, the classroom connection "seemed neither inevitable nor desirable to . . . groups of critics ranging from the early Marxists and New York Intellectuals to the later existentialists and deconstructors."[32] Curiously enough, some critics—Leitch names Geoffrey Hartman—have actually protested against "the reduction of criticism to pedagogy."

And here Leitch quotes Lionel Trilling's observation that

"pedagogy is a depressing subject to all persons of sensibility," apparently without recognizing the rather obvious irony of the statement. It occurred originally in a memorable essay, the subject of which is precisely what the teaching of *literature* to undergraduates is meant in the modern world (or was meant, in Trilling's modern world) to achieve. (The answer, when it comes, is certainly not that the students should be brainwashed into reverence for boring cultural monuments.) Trilling modestly asks whether it might not be better for students to *know* something, "almost anything that has nothing to do with the talkative and attitudinizing present."[33] He even suggests, in his polite, rather formal way, that it is possible in the university to confront "the power of a work of art fully and courageously," and even to "discover and disclose power where it has not been felt before," especially if that power has been concealed by the very fact of the work's having become "a classic," and by the other fact that its relation to immediate modern problems, as formulated by philosophy, sociology, and politics, is *not* immediate, *not* "relevant."[34] No wonder Trilling is nowadays rarely referred to; in the modern world of academic criticism there is no leisure for discovering the answers to his questions, which are concerned with teaching in its relation to a much wider area of culture.

In another place this same unfortunately obsolete critic spoke of the need "to keep the road open," by which he meant that one should do something about the way in which the literary culture has been cut off from the imaginative lives of educated people in general—in short, about "the great gulf between our educated classes and the best of our literature."[35] He saw that intellectuals had long ago given up thinking that what they had to say should be made intelligible to all educated persons; he believed that this direction had fostered the growth of an alienated intellectual class, and that it was a responsibility of the intelligentsia to try to reverse this trend.

Most would agree that in some respects the situation is more difficult now than it was in Trilling's time; to put it at its simplest and in a formula hardly anybody would contest, people arrive at universities less well prepared for the study of almost anything than they used to be. For most of them it is surely a considerable misfortune to encounter teachers who are not interested in teaching but only in their own theoretical speculations, which even well-educated nonspecialists would describe as recondite.

What I am saying should not be regarded as praise of things past, mere nostalgia for the time when the acquisition of knowledge was not, as it is for example by Lyotard, thought of as a quaint and obsolescent practice. I should prefer to call it a matter for urgent consideration and action. It is obvious that the character and purpose of literary criticism can be changed, has been changed. The changes may be, and sometimes evidently are, the result of intense and fruitful work; there is much to admire. Yet a possible consequence is the destruction of reading—to use the word in an old, but still permissible, sense. The desire to read is in modern times acquired for the most part in universities. Almost all the potential readership passes through the college classroom, and is numbered in millions. Since the whole business of reading is today acknowledged to be very difficult, so difficult that until recently nobody ever really managed to accomplish it, it will be allowed that the university must be the proper place to try to teach it. But how? To a few, in very rigorous classrooms, on a narrow range of Mallarméan texts? Or to the many who could not hope to get around such an assault course? Or perhaps one should instead take the opportunity to explain to students what they are doing when they watch Western movies? Should one try to impart to people who have only the slightest acquaintance with literature an expert knowledge of the modes of its production? These are real questions, to which a great many people would give positive answers.

The fact that they would do so means that the problem has an ethical dimension. Can one be asked to teach in a manner that might incur the self-criticism of bad faith? One ought not to pretend that Milton should be taught in preference to Zane Grey if one has reason to think there is no evidence for believing this, and some for not believing it. But a more urgent issue is whether, suffering from such doubts, one has any genuine place in the academy.

It is not really possible for me (and for the remnant to which I suppose I belong) to think that the values we give to (or, more boldly, that we *recognize* in) *Hamlet* or *Coriolanus* or the "Horatian Ode" (considered, of course, as works, totalities, not simply stretches of text) are the product simply of our own brainwashed responses. They are instances of literary value. It is true that the capacity to recognize such value is sometimes hard to distinguish from its shadow, the trained but vacuous response, the stock cultural OK. But that is far from being a reason for giving up faith in the real thing. To do so might entail the destruction of literature, be its quantity ever so little, and the substitution of the kind of theory that may exhibit zeal and intelligence but abandons what Valéry calls poetry.

That zeal, intelligence, and poetry can after all live together can be demonstrated by the practice of very good literary critics. I think of a sentence of William Empson, who did his own sort of theory, but believed its object was only to prevent inadequate theories from getting in the way of literary criticism. For "a critic ought to trust his own nose, like the hunting dog, and if he lets any kind of theory or principle distract him from that, he is not doing his work . . . There is the same position about a moral or ethical theory; however firm your belief in it, and however definite its ruling on a particular case, you still have to see whether your feelings can be brought to accept the results in that case. If they can't, well, you may be wrong, but if it gets too bad, you have to give up the theory. All the same, there is clearly a need for such theories; for one thing, without a tolerable supply of handy generalisation you can't stretch your mind to see all around a particular case. And the theory alters the feelings no less than the feelings alter the theory."[36] Of course Empson is admittedly talking about "fit" readers, the kind likely to find themselves in this predicament, hesitating on a borderline between poetry and theory—the kind likely to see this tension between theory and poetry as serious (hence the analogy with moral choices). It is another representation of the limit across which the flight from literature and literary criticism is occurring. It would be very good if all those in flight were to pause at the limit, look back, and reflect not only on the undoubted brilliance of some recent theory, but on what remains of literature and literary criticism; to meditate not only their choices but the cost of their choices; to consider seriously whether zeal and intelligence may conceal a lack that they might, even in present circumstances, be unwilling to admit, a lack, namely, of the appetite for poetry: "de quoi les conséquences sont à craindre."

In the essays that follow I have trusted my own nose but tried to keep in mind the need for theories, which ought on occasion to be declared, on occasion kept out of view, and on occasion, as Empson suggests, given up. Admittedly this arrangement doesn't suit Theory, which tends to be ostentatious: "brave Theory puffing by / in silks that whistle . . ." But the answer to any complaints will have to come from literature, not from me. It is not yet quite dead, and now and again it is possible, I hope, to write about particular cases of it without dispensing with a tolerable supply of handy generalizations, and without refusing to let the feelings alter the theory, or the theory the feelings. And when I come to think of it, the writers who best maintain this balance are not critics but poets; and some of them discussed in this book—Milton, Stevens, Eliot, and Empson himself—provide excellent demonstrations of how it is done.

CHAPTER I

# *The Common Reader*

Over the past few years, we have heard a good deal about a possible and desirable "science of literature" that would have linguistics as its principal model; and it would be reasonable to maintain that we have seen marked advances in descriptive and taxonomic techniques, especially in the analysis of narrative. Unprecedentedly large numbers of people now seek, or are compelled to undergo, formal instruction in literature, and part of the motivation of this new science is undoubtedly a desire to develop a systematic body of information that can be taught and learned. Another part is the wish to establish a decent claim to exactness; for in the modern university, whatever is spent on the "humanities" must be obtained at the expense of the natural sciences, with their insatiable appetite for money.

There is nothing very new about such desires and claims; in some form or other, they have existed ever since the vernacular literatures were admitted as subjects for study in the universities. In former times, the model for imitation might have been classical philology or comparative philology; more recently, it has been post-Saussurean linguistics. Yet there has always existed, along with these scientific aspirations, a strong current of "antipositivism," a conviction that the study of literature could only be frustrated by attempts to ape either the exactness or the utility of the hard sciences. And this opinion has survived along with all the latest things in "theory." Over the past few years, we have seen the successful publication of new kinds of literary criticism that are frankly incomprehensible—and of course totally without interest—to nonprofessional readers, and it ought not to seem surprising that they have produced a backlash. The protesters argue that the business of literary criticism, however they may define it (as the common pursuit of true judgment, the elucidation of works of literature, and so forth), is certainly not the arcane and pretentious affair it is represented as being by the latest "theorists." And as often as not, they will at this point refer to Samuel Johnson as a great critic seraphically free from the taint of theory, and remind us that Johnson said that he rejoiced to concur with the Common Reader, implying that all good critics must do likewise.

Johnson concurred, specifically, with the opinion of the Common Reader on Gray's "Elegy in a Country Churchyard," and added this: "By the common sense of readers uncorrupted with literary prejudices, after all the refinements of subtilty and the dogmatism of learning, must be finally decided all claim to poetical honours." And it is to this Common Reader, endowed with common sense but innocent of subtlety and learning, that many refined, subtle, dogmatic, and learned literary critics now profess to cede all judgment.

It is as well to be clear about what Johnson meant. In rejoicing to concur with the Common Reader, he was of course making it evident that he himself was a different animal altogether, though capable of understanding judgments that were unprejudiced and incorrupt. That he could speak so of the consensus of unspecialized opinion is an indication that he was talking about a state of affairs historically very different from our own. Johnson was not a teacher of literature in the modern manner, and critics who nowadays say that they yield to the authority of the uninstructed are in a very different position from his. Why, what, and whom are they teaching? Helen Gardner, a devout supporter of the Common Reader view, has spent her life teaching literature to the expensively educated. In a recent book[1] she compares her students to camels, who pause at the Oxford oasis to fill their humps with reading before striking out across the desert of modern life. But she also believes that some people are better readers than others, and I suppose she would number her Oxford students among them; they are already *un*common readers, and unless the teacher secretly believes that reading cannot be taught, will presumably be even more uncommon by the time they leave the university. To believe otherwise would surely destroy the spirit of all but the most cynical and self-serving of teachers. Yet Dame Helen warmly applauds Dr. Johnson and Virginia Woolf, who took *The Common Reader* as a title for her collected literary essays, for appealing from the judgment of professionals to the common sense of "those who read widely for enjoyment."

The Common Reader is of course not a person but a constituency, and everybody not seeking to grind an ax must know that by now it is a pretty rotten borough. Whether or not there is a causal connection, the dissolution of the Common Reader has proceeded *pari passu* with the establishment and growth of the profession of which Dame Helen is such an ornament. A large-scale history of the Common Reader is certainly a professional desideratum (though it might find but few common readers). Erich Auerbach sketched a part of that history when he investigated the expression *la cour et la ville:* "The absence of function, common to the aristocracy that had been stripped of its feudal character and to the wealthy bourgeoisie which had begun to turn away from gainful occupations toward *otium cum dignitate,* fused these two groups into a single class, namely *la cour et la ville.*" But as this class expanded, it recruited on a large scale from *la ville,* and in the course of the eighteenth century, "the 'public' came . . . to be dominated by *la ville,* the bourgeoisie." This public came into existence as a direct consequence of the development of the vernaculars and of printing. Auerbach says that it "determined the character of literature and the literary language throughout Europe."[2] It was an "elite minority," clearly differentiated from the uneducated on the one hand and the specialists on the other. In fact, it was Johnson's Common Reader.

Johnson took an interest in this phenomenon, and of course understood that it had undergone a historical development. He remarked, for instance, that in Milton's time reading was not a general amusement: "Neither traders nor often gentlemen thought themselves disgraced by ignorance. The women had not then aspired to literature, nor was every house supplied with a closet of knowledge." Of his own time, however, he says that "general literature . . . pervades the nation through all its ranks." There is here a touch of hyperbole, but it is clear enough that Johnson characterizes the Common Reader sociologically; he speaks of him (or it) as a class. Reading was one of the things that was done, in his time, by people of some income and some leisure. Occasionally he even suggested that they read because they could think of nothing else to do: "People in general do not willingly read, if they can have anything else to amuse them."[3]

That last sentence might adorn the wall of any modern publisher's office, but the point is that leisure and income are now for the most part otherwise employed than in reading. We still speak of "the general reader," but not very hopefully, and it is acknowledged that the kinds of people who constituted the class of the Common Reader have now thought of other things to do; the class is as nearly obsolete as "polite literature," which is what it once chose to read. Its rapid decline dates from the last quarter of the nineteenth century; one symptom of it was the sudden demise of the three-decker novel that had helped to fill the leisure time of large numbers of bourgeois families. The effect on literary production is very noticeable in the same period. Crudely speaking, there was a new public to satisfy, but its requirements were not always consistent with the aspirations of authors who thought of themselves as artists. Hence the new importance of such editors as Edward Garnett, middlemen between artist and public. Garnett wielded extraordinary power over a host of writers, including Conrad, Galsworthy, and Lawrence, and they submitted to it because the gap between art and the public had to be closed if they were to survive.[4] The literary agent was another new trade, another sign that the concurrence of specialist and Common Reader now called for professional intervention. The ample provision of ephemeral writing for the masses made it more and more obvious that serious writing must be content with its own small audience; the avant-garde took pride in the fact, but eventually its products were to be saved by the creation of an artificial class of readers who taught, or were taught, in colleges. The division widened as cinema, radio, and television took over the task of filling people's leisure time; and all the duties of the old Common Reader have now virtually devolved upon professional students of literature. The competition for mass markets (for common readers in a looser sense) is something that does not concern these professionals, who generally have nothing whatever to do with the promotion or censure of the most widely read books. Pale descendants of the Common Reader, they have none but the most transient contacts with common readers.

The nature and extent of such contacts are worth more study than they get. We must expect a good deal of variation from one country to another; the only study I know of confines itself almost exclusively to West Germany, where the position is different from those in the United States or in the United Kingdom. Yet there are resemblances also, and we have something to learn from the work of Peter Uwe Hohendahl,[5] who assumes a split between "elite" and "mass" culture and sees that it must affect criticism. Broadly speaking, the elite is still under the influence of notions of aesthetic autonomy that had their origins in the thought of the late eighteenth century; the masses assume that naive realism is the proper aim of writing. This division indicates the end of what Hohendahl refers to as "the public sphere," a Frankfurt term that in this connection means something very close to Johnson's Common Reader. Hohendahl happens to believe that the remedy for this split is the socialization of private property; but we need not follow him in that direction to benefit from his empirical observations.

In Germany there is still a clear difference between the reviewing of books, *Tageskritik,* and the study of literature in the universities, *Literaturwissenschaft,* such that it is unusual to find the same persons doing both. The effect of *Tageskritik* on readers seems to be very limited; at a date in the late 1960s, it appeared that of the one hundred seventy thousand people who read reviews in the journals or class newspapers (a number estimated to be about a quarter of the total professing some interest in literature), very few took any serious notice of book reviews. The aesthetic assumptions of the reviewers do not coincide with those of the readers; indeed, "the literature that is actually read is not the literature that is discussed" by reviewers.[6] Best sellers are rarely reviewed at all, except in provincial newspapers. Rather, the publishers work directly on the public, arranging "media events" and general support from newspapers whose owners find the promoted book ideologically congenial. Such books are, in their way, instruments for the capitalist oppression of consumers; and by paying no attention to them and concentrating on work that meets their own irrelevant standards of merit, the reviewers are abetting the exploitation. All they do is serve as cultural extras to the papers they write in; and they use a narcissistic jargon mostly incomprehensible to their readers.

It was for these reasons that the New Left eventually turned its fire on the practitioners of *Tageskritik*. They served the ruling system; aesthetic autonomy has no real meaning in an age of mechanical reproduction. What the critics ought to have concerned themselves with was political praxis; they ought to stop reviewing randomly chosen books and concentrate upon the mechanisms by which books are produced and sold. As it turned out, both *Tageskritik* and *Literaturwissenschaft* survived these assaults. There is, to be sure, more consideration of "trivial literature"; the authority of professors is somewhat reduced; but the end of bourgeois criticism still seems a long way off. In a famous essay[7] Walter Benjamin spoke of an art appropriate to an era of mass production, an art lacking *aura*—that uniqueness, authenticity, historicity, which mass reproduction necessarily destroys. But *aura* is what most of us literary critics are interested in. To the New Left, and indeed to Benjamin (who had marvelous antennae for *aura*), our interest makes us more or less unconscious kin to fascism.

As I remarked, Hohendahl's material is not quite the same as ours, and any critique we ventured would also differ from his.

We rarely think of criticism as an "institution"—rarely consider it as part of the entire social nexus. But it is hardly to our credit that we fail to do this, and the absence of any effective critique of criticism goes some way to explaining why our criticism is in such a peculiar state. One significant difference from the German situation might be mentioned at once. In the United States and perhaps even more in the United Kingdom, *Tageskritik* is very often, perhaps one could say normally, the work of the same hands that produce *Literaturwissenschaft*. The writers use a different tone, but are essentially academics; either they are talking to an audience that consists, approximately, of their former students (the new Common Reader), or they indulge themselves as wits or punsters. The dyer's hand is visible, though there may be attempts to conceal it; and it can hardly be denied that their aesthetic expectations, the general set of their interests, are very different from those of their audience, even in the posh Sunday papers, which have a circulation of a million or more. That circulation is maintained by means quite other than those employed by the academic reviewers, and it is easy enough to see that, to the New Left, the reviewers must seem to be passive instruments of a vicious system, contributors to "systematically distorted communication."

The historian of the Common Reader would need also to be the historian of reviewing. He would find in the great nineteenth-century quarterlies, and in *The Atlantic Monthly* of Brownell's day, long and lucid reviews of important books. The Common Reader still existed; such reviews were bourgeois family reading. To find anything comparable now he would have to look to such journals as *The New York Review of Books* and *The London Review of Books,* but even there he will find dons writing for dons and their pupils—a very different audience, very differently recruited. The reasons for the change I have already adumbrated: first, the relatively uneducated have found amusements they prefer to reading; second, the universities have taken over both the production and the criticism of literature, except—and it is of course a large exception—for the books that are read by millions.

A few freaks aside (the latest being *The White Hotel*), how do English-speaking critics respond to best sellers? On the whole, when they look at them at all, they do so with a holiday air, as if they were doing something that wasn't really their business. Edmund Wilson was, among many other things, the greatest *Tageskritik* of his time. In a piece called "'You Can't Do This To Me!' Shrilled Celia," he took a look at Lloyd C. Douglas's wartime best seller, *The Robe*. ("I lately decided that it was time for me to take cognizance of it," he says, meaning by "lately" not, I think, "recently" so much as "belatedly," for he explains that the book has sold about a million and a half copies in hard cover in rather less than two years.) Having provided samples of the prose, he goes on to say how very old-fashioned the book is, just like *Ben Hur* and *Quo Vadis*. The puzzle for Wilson is that this "almost unrivalled fabric of old clichés" should hold the attention of seven million Americans, when it is "difficult to imagine that any literate person could ever get through more than two pages of it for pleasure." Yet the work has "a certain purity"; and the fact that all those readers should prefer this long and tedious novel to "livelier and easier productions which have been specially flavored to please them" testifies to the longing of the ordinary reader for "moral light." Wilson concludes that "the ordinary reader, even in our ghastly time," is in decent moral shape; but that anybody who supposes Mencken had improved American taste had better think again.[8]

I doubt if the attitude of reviewers to popular books has altered much since that article was written, almost fifty years ago; Wilson cannot conceive of himself concurring with ordinary readers. When they read, they do different things, and for different reasons. Like shepherds in a pastoral, the Common Reader is granted a certain moral purity, but no refinement. Or, like the shepherds' flocks, they look up, and Douglas feeds them. Nowadays we might rather say that his successors exploit them. The latest notice I have seen of a current best seller in a highbrow journal—*The London Review of Books*[9]—is by John Sutherland (author of a good book on the publishing of best sellers). His subject is Jeffrey Archer's *The Prodigal Daughter,* topping the list as I write. Sutherland tells the story, which is about Florentyna, a prodigious child who grew up to be vice-president and then president of the United States. He then criticizes the style, just as Wilson did: "The result is the kind of novel one imagines a *Time* Magazine team turning out." Why, then, do people like it so much? Well, there is "an insatiable appetite for fables of success"; and such fables do best in America, which is why Archer, an Englishman "with a shrewd eye to the market," made his book a "tatty rewrite of the American dream." Like Wilson, Sutherland censures the derivative nature of the best seller's prose, and associates the success of the book with what he takes to be well-understood characteristics of the American way of life. The space between the reviewer and the novel, and the people who like the novel, is accepted as unbridgeable; and there is no attempt to explain why this should be so, or what the consequences are of its being so. Sutherland has, exceptionally, made a point of studying the best seller; that is, when he is wearing his *Literaturwissenschaft* (subsection, sociology of literature) hat. As a reviewer, in the *London Review,* he assumes that he is talking to the new Common Reader, who shares his assumptions and wouldn't be seen dead with a copy of *The Prodigal Daughter,* but might be amused to read a bit about it, simply as a curiosity having nothing to do with literature but only (as Leavis said unfairly but brilliantly of the Sitwells) with the history of publicity.

Meanwhile the academics go on producing their editions of the classics, or, more usually nowadays, developing theories of everything; of both classes of work, it may safely be said that the ordinary reader cannot afford to buy them, and could not read them if he did. Even in Germany, the most successful new critical school—that which deals in "reader response"—has very little to say about that reader as a social being, a person who opens a book and reads it. In England and America, a few Marxists—and they pretty rarefied—apart, the matter of the relation between professional critic and audience is hardly ever referred to, except in the sort of vacuous observation about the Common Reader I have mentioned. As to why ordinary readers should be so different from us—why they used to be moral and dull, and are now possessed of an insatiable appetite for success and are still dull—nobody ventures an opinion.

Yet such power as there may be to influence our literary culture must be in the hands of these critics, who teach in the colleges and moonlight in the reviews. How do they, and how ought they, use that power? I have assumed that the modern Common Reader passes through a university. The number of people now teaching literature is probably greater than the total of critics who formerly existed throughout history, and they must have some effect on the millions of readers who frequent their classes. Does good come of this? Richard Poirier says he sees "no reason in the world" why common readers should care to read the classics or serious contemporary fiction and poetry; "I don't think it makes them better people, better citizens, better anything." By some criteria, he must be right. Indeed, it is immodest to propose that by making people read these things we are improving them, ethically or civically. All we dare claim is that we are making them better readers. We might or might not go on to claim that bad reading (of the Bible, for example) has often had disastrous consequences; or that a society containing subtle readers is at least a more interesting, perhaps a richer, society than one that does not; or that good readers are likely to be more resistant to the exploitative forces of "the ruling system." But we should not say we are improving them, except as readers.

And that is surely enough for anybody to attempt: the reconstruction of the Common Reader on a new, historically appropriate plan. We need to remember Johnson's remark, that reading is not willingly undertaken if there is something else to do; that the acquisition of the knowledge and technique to do it well is arduous. People will sweat for them only if assured of the authenticity of the authority that asks them to do so. Such authenticity is largely institutional, but we have to manage without any central authority ourselves. If there were one, with power to bind and loose, to make and uphold canons, even to issue an *index librorum prohibitorum,* the job would be easier. It would be easier, too, if we did not devote quite so much of our energy to showing how clever we are, either in the manipulation of texts or in the rarefied exercise of theory and methodology. If, in short, we had a full and daunting sense of our responsibilities toward the Common Reader, conceived not as some fictive outsider whose word, it pleases us to say, is our law, but as the students in our class, who, as we are now continually lamenting, know nothing and have never acquired our own need to be on speaking terms with the past. As Philip Rieff likes to point out, the world of rock and pop pretends to have no past, and they live partly in that world. Some make the mistake—understandably, but it *is* a mistake—of treating the past as synonymous with authoritarian oppression. I am sure Rieff is right in speaking of them as "disinherited."[10] He believes that the only remedy is the restitution of authority, the promulgation of "interdicts" and the inculcation of "the knowledge that is in repetition." It is true that "unified cultures" tend to be authoritarian, so the culture of the new Common Reader, however subtle and various, would need authority. There is something to be learned, perhaps, from the success of F. R. Leavis as a teacher: these books prescribed, those proscribed; a bold doctrine of minority culture, and the creation of an image of it that made the young want to join it. As Donald Davie, who underwent that influence, has recently remarked,[11] it was at least as encouraging to be told what you should not read as what you should. There was a canon; and where there is a canon there is authority.

Philip Rieff believes that by authoritarian prescription we can make our students "sovereign selves."[12] I imagine he would allow in that remark a certain ethical component. There, I hesitantly disagree; hesitantly, because I don't know what Rieff could bring off, but know the sensible limit of my own ambitions. I agree with Poirier; I daresay he would accept my view that reading, as we ought to teach it, can make not a good person, but a subtle, questioning one, always with the possibility of corruption yet richer and more enriching. How did we ever come to suppose that we were equipped to make people good? To be realistic, we cannot do that, any more than we can fill the humps of the young with supplies of reading for later use. There are soft drinks available everywhere; nobody needs that warm stale water. To be realistic again, we have little to do with the oppressed, with the hapless victims of television and advertising, insofar as they constitute an inaccessible mass. We have to do with the new Common Reader, who has to be our creation, who will want to join us, as people who speak with the past and know something of reading as an art to be mastered. We are carrying something on, but have the responsibility of making the generation that will agree that carrying it on in its turn is worth the effort. In the end, that is the only feasible task of reviewers as well as academics. And every narcissistic, venal, or impudent review, every clever academic stunt, is a dereliction of this duty of continuance and creation. That, I think, is where we may speak of the morality of the business: in terms of our duty to the only real Common Reader, and the strong temptations to neglect it.

CHAPTER 2

# *Milton in Old Age*

Milton died on the eighth or ninth of November, 1674, a little before his sixty-sixth birthday. At the time of the Restoration he was in his fifty-second year. Had he died then—or even if he had suffered those penalties short of death proposed by Parliament for men not technically regicides but criminally associated with the regicide cause—we should have been deprived of all but a fragment of *Paradise Lost;* and of *Paradise Regained* and *Samson Agonistes*—two works concerned in their very different ways with the patterns of heroism to which Milton desired his own life to conform—nothing would have been written.

It is the author of these works—an old man, blind and quiet—rather than the ardent scholar of Christ's, or the exalted chiliast of the forties, that I discuss here. Always, according to his lights, a hero and "separate to God," he now understood better than before what was required of a man honored by such an election.

AN IMPARTIAL HISTORIAN'S ACCOUNT of the political crisis of 1658–1660 would be unlikely to devote much space to Milton; the relevant volume of the *Oxford History of England,* though it is the work of a writer exceptionally well acquainted with Milton's biography, mentions him in this context but once. Yet to the poet himself it must have seemed otherwise, and he would have been surprised to learn that his part in the story had come to seem so inconsiderable. He could not have denied that he had failed to save the Republic; but he would surely have defended himself against the charge that his efforts were trivial. Nor would he have thought himself to blame for their failure: "That fault I take not on me, but transfer / On Israel's governors and heads of tribes." While his fickle countrymen betrayed their historical mission and, as he put it, crept back into servitude, Milton continued to see himself—older though he was, and partly incapacitated—as the same elected champion he had more manifestly been in the days when he was the very voice of England's newly won Christian liberty, the agonist who lost his eyes when they were

> overplied
> In liberty's defence, my noble task
> Of which all Europe talks from side to side.

That great task had not fallen to him by chance. "It is a singular favour of the Divinity towards me that I, above others, was chosen to defend the cause of liberty. . . . This favour I have acknowledged, nor can the time ever come when it will cease to be my duty to acknowledge it." Thus the *Defensio Pro Se* of 1655, in which the poet, not for the first time, represents himself as elected, as "separate to God," and confident that no historical circumstance could ever induce him to deny either his duty or his privilege.

As General Monck's army moved southward to London, Milton spoke out once more, in the *Ready and Easy Way to Establish a Free Commonwealth,* for liberty as he understood it. There was still some hope that Monck would decide in favor of the Rump, and had he done so Milton's pamphlet would not have mattered much. But since there was at least a clear chance, and probably a good deal more than that, of Monck's deciding otherwise, Milton's act must be called very bold. Johnson found in it occasion for another gibe at egotistical whiggery: "he was fantastic enough to think that the nation, agitated as it was, might be settled by a pamphlet." And it is true that Milton was always prone to this kind of exaggerated estimate of his influence. Perhaps he was incapable of imagining that God might produce for his Englishmen a scenario of national crisis in which there was no major role for Milton. At any rate, he would not have thought himself free to abstain, though he must have known perfectly well that on this occasion obedience to divine prompting, to that intimate impulse which moves the elect as agents of the divine plot, was more hazardous than it had been in the past.

He showed no precautionary politeness to the Stuarts. "If we return to kingship, and soon repent, as undoubtedly we shall when we begin to find the old encroachments coming on little by little upon our consciences, which must necessarily proceed from king and bishop united inseparably in one interest, we may be forced to fight over again all that we have fought, and spend over again all that we have spent, but are never like to attain thus far as we are now advanced to the recovery of our freedom." Even before these words appeared in print the ejected members were reseated in the Commons, and the Restoration became virtually certain. Milton knew this perfectly well; but he retracted nothing, rather added, at the beginning of his book, this almost cavalier defiance: "If their absolute determination be to enthral us, before so long a Lent of servitude they may permit us a little shroving-time first, wherein to speak freely, and take our leaves of liberty."

For he would, he says, have spoken out in the language of "the good old Cause" even if there had been no hearers save "trees and stones." But he was determined to bring his words to the notice of more dangerous auditors. He wrote Monck a letter, more or less summarizing the pamphlet and advocating a republican government "without single person." And then, when he despaired of Monck, he produced a further edition of the *Ready and Easy Way* in which he positively invited attention to his past record as the defender of the lost heroic cause, and as the voice of the English people against tyranny.

Though he did them such dangerous service, the English people have in general found it hard to love Milton. Yet surely one can withhold admiration for such unconsidering courage, only condemning it as excessive. Milton must have known, or must have thought he knew, what would follow if the newly restored king should take note of him, as he seemed to require. The son of the supposed author of *Eikon Basilike* could hardly be expected to feel clement toward the undisputed and unrepentant author of *Eikonoklastes,* or to forget that Milton had published *The Tenure of Kings and Magistrates* only two weeks after the judicial murder of his father the king. Royalists who had professed to believe Milton's blindness a divine punishment for such earlier presumptuousness might now be expected to hold that these renewed outbreaks of heretical impudence called for more immediate discipline, humanly administered.

Even before the king reached London the newly enlarged Commons was considering how to deal with his enemies. There was to be an Act of Oblivion pardoning all treasons committed between 1638 and 1660, with certain specified exceptions. The regicides—defined by Charles himself as "the immediate murderers of my father"—were excepted; they would suffer death. A second class of offenders, to be nominated to the number of twenty, were to suffer penalties short of death. A few great men not technically regicides were separately named, Lambert and Vane among them. Not to be named was, of course, to escape retribution altogether.

Milton might well have expected to be named in the second group of twenty, but he was not. Edward Phillips, his nephew, says he had friends in both Council and Parliament who "made a considerable party for him." This must be true, but the story is more complicated than Phillips suggests.[1]

Early in the summer of 1660 Milton rather uncharacteristically went into hiding. About the same time the Commons requested the king to call in the *Defensio Populi Anglicani* and the *Eikonoklastes,* and ordered the attorney general to arrest the author. Meanwhile they went on with the grisly business of choosing twenty names for the list of second-class culprits. Milton was proposed for the twentieth vacancy, but the proposal was not seconded, and so not debated; the place went to Ralph Corbet, a colonel who had disagreed with Monck. Milton's friends were serving him well, for some of the names on the list were of persons who had, on the face of it, been much less injurious to the royal cause than he.

The order for his arrest was mysteriously held up; it was issued only on August 13, seven weeks late. Godfrey Davis conjectures that the poet's friends contrived this, supposing that the order would be ineffective if delayed until after the Lords had accepted the Bill of Indemnity. This they eventually did on August 9, having made some more exceptions not including Milton. A proclamation of the Council now let it be known that Milton, and another offender named Goodwin (nineteenth on the Commons' list, though a much less important figure than the poet), had "fled, or so obscured themselves, that no endeavour used for their apprehension can take effect, whereby they might be brought to legal trial and deservedly receive condign punishment for their treasons and offences." This curious announcement, apparently designed to discourage the officers responsible for the pursuit, was probably another device of Milton's friends. They had done their work well, and he was as good as saved.

Or so it must have seemed; but now something went wrong, and Milton was arrested by the Sergeant of the House of Commons, a man insensitive, we must suppose, to the tone of the proclamation. So Milton went to prison after all, and remained there long enough to run up a large debt for keeper's fees. Eventually, as we are told by the reliable Anonymous Biographer, he "sued out his Pardon," and was released on December 15.

Probably, as Godfrey Davis suggests, the friends of Milton had arranged a deal: he would not be named in the Act, but he must suffer the disgrace of having two of his books burned by the common hangman. And that would be the end of it; but the machinery proved too complicated, the proclamation trick went wrong, and the order for Milton's arrest, never seriously intended, was carried out. Had all gone well he would hardly have suffered at all, but in the event this unlucky accident not only sent him to prison but compelled him to sue for pardon. That he hesitated before doing so is perhaps suggested by the length of his imprisonment. But there was no other way to safety; he had to sue, and thus acknowledged the authority of the king.

There is little direct testimony to Milton's mood in these days. Richardson says "he was so dejected he would lie awake whole nights"; but though he claimed to be reporting the words of a contemporary of Milton, Richardson was writing seventy years after the event, and perhaps remembering the opening of *Paradise Lost,* book 7:

> though fallen on evil days,
> On evil days though fallen, and evil tongues;
> In darkness, and with dangers compassed round,
> And solitude . . .

According to Marvell, one of his boldest champions, Milton now "expiated himself in a retired silence"; but Marvell had good reason at this stage to be politic. Still, it is reasonable to guess that the poet was not exactly delighted at the course of events. All about him his enemies were systematically destroying everything he had worked for, and he could say nothing about it. He was blind and also poor, for he had lost his savings in the failure of a Commonwealth bank. And worst of all, perhaps, he had been compelled to sue for the royal pardon and add to his other afflictions the sense of a vocation or an allegiance betrayed.

In the past he had been calm, even in a measure exultant, in adversity. His blindness, he tells us in the *Second Defence,* brought him no sense of divine displeasure; on the contrary, he had enjoyed, in the most critical moments of his life, a full consciousness of God's favor and protection. In the fifties he would write in autograph albums the motto "My strength is made perfect in weakness," alluding to 2 Corinthians 12:9–10: "And he said unto me, My grace is sufficient for thee, for my strength is made perfect in weakness. Most gladly therefore will I rather glory in my infirmities, that the power of Christ may rest upon me. Therefore I take pleasure in infirmities, in reproaches, in necessities, in persecutions, in distresses for Christ's sake: for when I am weak, then I am strong." *In contumeliis, in necessitatibus, in angustiis pro Christo* . . . In 1654 Milton, in the *Second*

*Defence,* paraphrased the apostle and brought him into conformity with his own case; for at that time his infirmity lay not in persecution or poverty but in blindness: "Let me be one of the weakest, provided only that in my darkness the light of the Divine Countenance more brightly shines. For then I shall be at once the weakest and the mightiest—at once blind and of the most piercing sight. Thus through my infirmity I may be consummated." *Cum enim infirmor, tunc potens sum.*

Since the troubles of these earlier years could not shake his confidence in his election, in his power to respond to the intimate impulse, he had no occasion to qualify what he had written in *Eikonoklastes* concerning his political responsibilities: "They who with a good conscience and upright heart did their civil duties in the sight of God and in several places to resist tyranny and the violence of superstition banded both against them we may well be sure will never seek to be forgiven that which may be justly attributed to their immortal praise, nor will assent ever to the guilty blotting out of those actions before men, by which their faith assures them they chiefly stand approved." These words have unexpected ironical force when we think of Milton in the last days of 1660, for they occur in the course of a discussion of a possible Restoration and a possible Act of Oblivion. To the Milton of 1649 these expedients were as undesirable as they were unlikely to occur. But they were included in God's plot; and when they came to pass Milton was forced, apparently by a mere accident, to seek forgiveness for what, in justice, ought to have been attributed to his immortal praise, and to assent not only to the Restoration (for he acknowledged the authority of the king to pardon him), but also to the guilty blotting out (what else was the Act of Oblivion?) of actions by which his faith assured him he chiefly stood approved.

One can scarcely exaggerate the significance of that plea for pardon. Such a man, one may think, could easily have borne all the disgraces and dangers of 1660 except this one. He who had called it a singular favor of God to defend regicide now humbled himself before inherited and unjust royal authority. Such was the position into which God had compelled him. He might now have used the words he later gave to the injured Adam: "Inexplicable / Thy justice seems" (*Paradise Lost* x.754–755), or those of the Chorus in *Samson Agonistes,* commenting upon God's apparently "contrarious" treatment of his elect:

> Not only dost degrade them, or remit
> To life obscur'd, which were a fair dismission,
> But throw'st them lower than thou didst exalt them high,
> Unseemly fall in human eye
> Too grievous for the trespass or omission . . . (687–691)

But we must note that Milton nowhere encourages us to believe that he held himself guilty of any trespass or omission, or thought his miseries in any sense the consequences of his own acts. It might now be more difficult to understand the *purpose* of his sufferings, but it is not suggested that their cause lay in his own acts. We note that when Samson offers that explanation he is proved wrong.

IN WHAT FOLLOWS, as in what I have already said, I assume that *Samson Agonistes* is a late work of Milton. It has lately been the fashion to treat it as early, usually as belonging to the last years of the forties. W. R. Parker, the author of the most recent full-scale biography, was the chief proponent of this view, and it has the support of John Carey, the most recent editor of the tragedy. Nevertheless I feel as sure as it is possible to be, in the absence of positive evidence either way, that these scholars are wrong. This is not the occasion to argue about it, but I ought to say, I suppose, that if Parker and Carey are right the argument of this essay is, like Eve in the ninth book of *Paradise Lost,* separated from its best prop.

I shall discuss the tragedy in relation to Milton's own life and hope in doing so to avoid the errors with which others are perhaps justly charged. I shall not be saying that *Samson Agonistes* makes detectable allusions to events in post-Restoration England that displeased Milton, though I will admit that I should not be very surprised if it sometimes did. What I believe, without reservation, is that Milton was extremely interested in the problems created by the peculiar conduct of God toward his elected heroes, including Milton; and that in writing a tragedy about Samson he was exploring these problems and giving privileged expression to complaints about, though of course also vindicating, that inexplicable justice.

It is important not to be melodramatic about this. We are under no necessity to think of the poet as living in perpetual despair, eyeless in Gaza, bleakly preoccupied with the suffering elect. Aubrey testifies to the contrary, reporting his subject as "cheerful even in his gout-fits" and "extreme pleasant in his conversation . . . but satirical." Others represent the old man as handsome and musical, of a deportment "sweet and affable," and a gait "erect and manly, bespeaking courage and undauntedness." He was, we learn, studious and industrious; a little hard on his daughters, perhaps, but patient under many provocations. He proved capable of "demeaning himself peaceable," as the Anonymous Biographer puts it, adding that he "was so far from being reckoned disaffected, that he was visited at his house on Bunhill by a chief officer of state, and desired to employ his pen on their behalf." (I suppose we must not presume to remember this interview when reading of Samson's encounter with the Public Officer of the Philistines.) We have no cause to think the old poet desperate of demeanor, and all we can hope to say is that we have a faint conception of the process by which he achieved his heroic calm of mind.

*Paradise Regained* meditates the heroism of the saint who suffers rather than acts. Jesus undergoes all the temptations exactly as a man might who sees and knows and yet abstains. Even at the climax of Satan's assault, when all the temptations of sense, pride, and curiosity have failed and we see the hero *agonistes,* in combat with the adversary, he *does* nothing, strikes no blow, merely rejects: "Tempt not the Lord thy God, he said and stood" (iv.561). All the action, all the energy, is demonic, and to obey Satan, Jesus would have to break the law; to leap from the pinnacle would be to subject God to an impious test.

But not every hero is called upon to reject and stand. Some must *act,* in order to alter the world and history. And the ways of God to them are more difficult to understand. They are subject to promptings and impulses which impel them to break the laws of man, perhaps the laws of God. If in consequence they find themselves suffering as if they were common criminals or sinners—suffering even beyond the measure usually meted out to such offenders, with pangs "too grievous for the trespass"; the temperate afflicted by the diseases of intemperance, the noble sharing the fate of the felon—they may be tempted to complain that the impulse was untrustworthy, or that God has deceived them. For example: an impulse, thought to be of God, impels a man, against the law, to marry a Philistine woman; and time proves that the prompting was indeed divine. A second impulse urges him into marriage with a second Philistine woman, there being no palpable difference between the two cases; but this time the outcome is by all appearances disastrous. To the first wife the hero reveals a secret; and the consequence is not shame and condemnation but the glorious slaughter of many enemies of God. To the second he reveals a secret, and the consequences are mutilation, degradation, and separation from God. Was the second prompting false, and if so, how was this to be known? It almost appears that God neither cares for nor understands his human agents.

Let me, for a moment, consider another *electus*. This man was educated in an atmosphere of purity fanatical beyond the fantasies of Nazarites. He learned that only in performing unconditionally the will of another could he hope to enjoy true liberty; that freedom was obedience, that obedience was continually tested by irrational prohibitions; that all offenses, and especially sexual "pollutions," were certain to attract extremely severe punishments. This man lived a chaste and useful life until, in his forties, he suffered a breakdown characterized by the formation of a delusional system of which the main element was the patient's special relationship with God. He maintained that it was God's way to enter into such relations with exceptionally gifted men. He himself had been chosen as the instrument of a millennial change; he would give birth to a new race of men. In order to do so he must suffer emasculation and become a woman.

At first he thought this command "contrary to the order of things," but later he came to see it as consonant with that order. It was God's method to manifest his power in miracles that might well seem to men, with their limited information and understanding, futile, absurd, or cruel.

The case is that of Schreber, as described by himself, by Freud in his classic study of paranoia, and by Schatzman in his book *Soul Murder.* Schreber's delusional system was extremely complex—he invented, for example, a whole heavenly hierarchy. He never doubted his election, always denying that he was insane, and in general behaving with intelligence and affability. There were, however, many occasions when he complained with apparent justice of God's inexplicable and arbitrary dealings. God, he once remarked, "has more or less absurd ideas, which are all contrary to human nature." God "did not know how to treat a living human being"; for some reason he felt that his authority was precarious, and therefore formed conspiracies against the innocent and degraded without compunction his most temperate and obedient servants.

After such complaints Schreber invariably rallied to the defense of his God, annulling blasphemy with reverence. God may behave as if he wants to be rid of his human agent. God never seems to learn from his experience of human beings. Nevertheless he is supremely just, and the torments of the elect are devised by Love.

I mention the Schreber case not because I am concerned with its etiology, as disputed between Schatzman and the Freudians; and certainly not to suggest that Milton was paranoid; but simply because it offers another famous instance of the human imagination at work on the questions of election and suffering and the divine plot. There does seem to be a measure of similarity between the delusional systems of paranoia and tragic plots. Oedipus at Colonus is certain of the innocence of his life, certain that the gods contrived his misery and then abandoned him to a punishment unrelated to any criminal intention on his part; yet he swears by them still, and they return to him at the end. "We share in his blessing," says Theseus, telling the daughters of Oedipus not to weep. The mutilation of the elect in his "apprehensive tenderest parts" (*Samson Agonistes* 624) follows divine election and somehow leads—for Schreber, for Oedipus, for Samson—to the renewing of the intolerable world.

*Samson Agonistes* IS SO UNDENIABLY a tragedy in the Greek manner that we forget the rest of the truth; it is a tragedy in the manner of an imagined Hebrew archetype, of which the Athenian plays are but deviant descendants. That is why Milton's irregular strophes shun the Greek model and look back to Old Testament poetry; and that is why his hero, antecedent to the Greek tragic heroes, is drawn from the list of the Old Testament elect, as certified by the eleventh chapter of the Epistle to the Hebrews. Such a saint has obvious advantages—in a Christian world which knows the truth about such matters—over his Greek derivatives, Oedipus or Heracles; though there is a wide and troublesome space between the Paul Bunyan-like figure of the folktale in Judges and the God-abandoned hero of Milton.

Scholarship has attempted to fill some of his space by telling us what centuries of exegetes made of Samson. He was an argument for chastity, or at any rate for marriage within one's tribe. He was, according to Gregory the Great, an exemplum of the authentic *hubris* and the authentic *hamartia;* or of the possibility, as some said, of godly suicide; or simply of the turning of Fortune's wheel and the inevitable falls of illustrious men. But when such conjectures occur in the tragedy they are credited to the Chorus or to Manoa, or to Samson himself at his lowest point. They are all erroneous conjectures, made by characters who erroneously suppose that they are commenting upon a completed action and therefore can hardly avoid the inference that Samson is responsible for his own plight and is therefore being punished. Milton, you might think, had said enough in his time about moldy exegetes to discourage us from thinking they could explain his tragedy. In making sense of the bully-boy of Judges he imposes his own interpretations and uses those of the exegetes merely as instances of erroneous opinion.

What happens in *Samson Agonistes?* Samson breaks the law

three times, twice by marrying and once by going to perform for the Philistines. He married the woman of Timna, "the daughter of the infidels," against the wishes of his parents:

> they knew not
> That what I motioned was of God; I knew
> From intimate impulse . . . (221–223)

Samson does not doubt—nor, incidentally, does the author of Judges—that this marriage, in which he gave away the secret of the riddle about sweetness and strength, was the occasion of his beginning "Israel's deliverance." The Chorus, however, does doubt it. Why should a Nazarite be prompted by God

> Against his vow of strictest purity
> To seek in marriage that fallacious bride,
> Unclean, unchaste? (319–321)

However, it goes on to reflect that the woman of Timna was not unchaste till later, so that Samson contracted from her no moral stain but only, one is left to suppose, some merely ceremonial pollution. This curious distinction has some importance. Milton later alters the account in Judges by marrying Samson to Dalila, probably to make a similar point: the law he broke was not moral but ceremonial. And we remember that he omits any reference to Samson's famous misdemeanor with the harlot of Gaza. He will not, it seems, allow Samson to be like Hosea, whom God commanded to take a wife of whoredoms; the laws he breaks are all of the kind subsequently abrogated by reason and by revelation. So that whether or not the Chorus is right in asserting that God breaks his own laws when he chooses (314), he does not, it seems, force Milton's Samson to break the moral law.

Nevertheless, by inducing Samson to marry the woman of Timna, God does, in the furtherance of his own designs, cause Samson to break his vows as a Nazarite. Samson understandably supposed, when he conceived a desire for Dalila, that the same process was beginning again: "I thought it lawful from my former act, And the same end . . ." (231–232). So he married

Dalila, though Judges neither calls it a marriage nor suggests that the union was in this instance the consequence of divine prompting. And something went wrong; instead of slaughtering Philistines Samson found himself eyeless in Gaza. As Manoa remarks, it seems hard that a hero twice before his birth described by angels as having a special relationship with God should end by suffering such "foul indignities" (371). Samson, however, says he himself must take all the blame; he should have known by the experience of his first marriage that a Philistine wife would betray him. That was the only correct inference; he had been wrong to think that lusting after their women would always place him in the position of slaying Philistines, as if God were bound not only to devise absurd bits of plot but also to repeat them.

It is at this point that we first hear from Manoa about the Philistine intention to display Samson at the feast, that is to say, to compel him into uncleanliness. A thousand lines later the invitation is delivered, and Samson, stimulated by his successes against Dalila and Harapha, rejects it; his reason for doing so is precisely that he will not break the law and present himself as "a Nazarite in place abominable" (1359). However, he now experiences an intimate impulse, feels "some rousing motions" (1382); and this familiar sensation causes him to change his mind and commit the uncleanness after all. God, he observes, will no doubt provide dispensation:

> that he may dispense with me or thee
> Present in temples at idolatrous rites
> For some important cause, thou need'st not doubt. (1377–79)

This is the peripeteia, brought on by Samson's deciding to obey his impulse and break the law, just as he had done to good effect in his first marriage and, as will now appear, in his second as well; for this genuinely Aristotelian complexity (metabasis, peripeteia, and anagnorisis all at once) requires us, among other things, to reevaluate the consequences of the Dalila marriage and the authenticity of the impulse that led to it.

When God overrides Samson's scruples about appearing in the unclean place—and we know from the outcome that it was his doing—we have no choice but to believe that all of Samson's intimate impulses, however wanton, however contrary to his vows of purity, are authentically of God. There is accordingly no doubt that, like his uncleanness, his misery, mutilation, and humiliation, cruel as they are, form part of the divine plot—especially since his wretchedness arises from a remorse he has no real cause to feel, since he had simply obeyed God's orders. God had never stopped using him, and so, despite appearances, had never abandoned him:

> all this
> With God not parted from him, as was feared,
> But favouring and assisting to the end (1718–20)

says Manoa, relieved to find his son's election authenticated, and now ready to speak of torture as evidence of love.

We now see the structure of God's peculiar plot; it takes this form:

> intimate impulse
> lawbreaking
> condemnation
> vindication.

He has scruples, it seems, about breaches of the moral law. It is clear from the divorce tracts and the *De Doctrina* that Milton would regard Old Testament limitations on exogamy as mere "national obstrictions" and the rules about ceremonial purity as completely abrogated; so it must be said that God shows a respect for the moral law (his own) and causes Samson only to violate unimportant taboos. We note that when Dalila argues that Baal can dispense with his own laws, Samson at once condemns the position as illogical:

> gods unable
> To acquit themselves and prosecute their foes
> But by ungodly deeds, the contradiction
> Of their own deity, Gods cannot be. (896–898)

So the Chorus is presumably wrong, as usual, in arguing that the Hebrew God can do it. But there are certain ironies in this situation, which seem not to have attracted the attention of expositors. For instance, Dalila also claims the authenticity of her impulse, which she thinks is proved by the outcome—she has saved her country from Samson. And she boasts that she will be posthumously celebrated and have flowers brought to her tomb. But of course she is wrong, and Samson gets the flowers (983–997, 1741–43). These passages are eight hundred lines apart, but we are presumably expected to put them together; and perhaps there is a certain openness in the whole treatment of the question whether Jehovah and Baal can dispense with their own laws.

What is clear, however, is that Samson's sufferings are not his fault, though he allowed himself to be polluted, and revealed what ought to have been kept secret. Under another dispensation these would be the crimes of Oedipus, unintended yet requiring punishment. Samson's sufferings *feel* like a punishment, but are not. They are none the less intense, of course; when we read his lament, "O that torment should not be confined / To the body's wounds and sores" (606ff.), we remember that Milton seems to have had a special horror of physical mutilation, which he here applies to the agony of remorse. For although Samson has been physically mangled in his "apprehensive tenderest parts" he is here applying the expression of his spiritual torment to the guilt he supposes himself to have incurred by mistaking the nature of a sexual impulse.

The question why God should encourage such an error, and then punish it savagely, naturally gives rise to some stifled complaints. But in the end both Samson and God are explicitly exonerated. Samson was never what he seemed, nor what people said about him: not a suicide—"self-killed / Not willingly" (1664–65)—not false to his vocation, since he has "fulfilled / The work for which he was foretold / To Israel" (1661–63), and not even truly blind—"with inward eye illuminated" (1687)—for which last point there is a parallel in the *Alcestis,* but also in the *Second Defence*. As for God, his self-vindication is so complete that in the end the Chorus can utter words of which its descendant in *Oedipus at Colonus* dares offer only a watered-down, relatively noncommittal version. Not only is there nothing here for tears, but

All is best, though we oft doubt
What the unsearchable dispose
Of highest wisdom brings about,
And ever best found in the close. (1745–48)

It is occasionally remarked by commentators that very little in fact came of Samson's act, and that Israel went on serving just the same, notwithstanding Samson's annihilation of many important Philistines; the suggestion is that since Milton was of course familiar with this fact we must suppose he wanted us to bear it in mind when considering the triumphant end of the tragedy; the millennial opportunity afforded by Samson's feat was missed. It is true that Samson complains of Israelite backslidings in the past, and Manoa observes that the tribes must "find courage to lay hold on this occasion" (1716). But I cannot attach much importance to this. It is a bit like the suicide problem: Milton knew that Samson's last prayer was "let my soul die with the Philistines," so takes steps to prevent suicide from becoming an issue in his tragedy; he knew that Israel went on serving after Samson, and so touched on the point without making a central issue of it. Instead he makes the slaughter as complete as possible: "The vulgar only scaped who stood without" (1659). Whatever happened next, an epoch had been completed by the successful exertions of the elect. His separation from God—however perverse God may sometimes appear, with his trivial miracles of fox's tail and ass's jawbone, his irrational prohibitions, his willingness to dismiss his heroes into uncleanness and servitude, mangled in their apprehensive tenderest parts, suffering under a "sense of heaven's desertion" (632)—was quite illusory. He suffered in innocence, and his ceremonial lapses were of no significance except as elements of God's peculiar plot.

I BEGAN by speaking of Milton and went on to talk about Schreber and Samson. I must now explain this peculiar plot. Milton tended always to see his life according to patterns of various kinds, doubtless divine in origin; in this he somewhat resembles Luther. The long choosing and beginning late, the emergence from contemplation to action (parallel to that of

Christ in *Paradise Regained*)—the return from Italy under the compulsion, as he tells us in *The Reason of Church Government,* of an "inward prompting"—the coming to maturity of his heroic career in the Defences—all are part of a pattern. He was an agent of God: "When God commands to take the trumpet and blow a dolorous and jarring blast, it lies not in his will what he shall say or what he shall conceal," as Milton remarks in the same work. We know how he came to write against episcopacy, then against the divorce laws, and then against licensing; but in his own account of these matters in the *Second Defence* he omits all tribute to chance and the tide of his personal affairs, representing this part of his career as a systematic effort toward "the promotion of real and substantial liberty," duly divided into subordinate topics. And, as we have already seen, his taking his election so seriously sometimes involved exaggeration of his heroic achievement.

After the Restoration he had the time, and the store of memories—some painful—to devote himself to an old and very characteristic project. As early as *The Reason of Church Government* he had announced a desire to discover "what king or knight before the Conquest might be chosen in whom to lay the pattern of a Christian hero." He now knew that the pattern must be sought not in romance but closer to the source. The passive hero was, indeed, Jesus himself. What of the suffering elect who must act, possibly against the law, or what passed as the law, in the furtherance of God's purposes?

Tillyard once remarked that if Milton had found himself in Adam's position he would at once have eaten the fruit and sat down to write a pamphlet justifying his act. Probably he would have attributed his disregard of an arbitrary prohibition to an intimate impulse. Certainly he is on record as believing that laws might on proper occasion be broken: "No ordinance, human or from heaven," he wrote in *Eikonoklastes,* "can bind against the good of man"; and, in the same book, "Great worthies heretofore, by disobeying law, oftentimes have saved the commonwealth." The law in question here was that by which the king commands obedience; Milton had already, in

*The Tenure of Kings and Magistrates,* explained the circumstances in which he did not.

The deposition and killing of the king, Milton always represented as rational and indeed virtuous acts. It is by no means part of my purpose to inquire whether, in the dark of his mind, he may have experienced some trace of atavistic guilt, some sense of pollution or parricide. W. R. Parker has noticed how some of Milton's insults upon the dead king in *Eikonoklastes* return to plague their inventor: "Whom God hardens, he also blinds." And, of course, Milton's enemies liked to think of his blindness as a punishment. But for all we know he was quite untroubled by such superstitions. He lost his eyes as part of God's plan, suffering, like the Apostle, persecution, hardship, contempt, and poverty that he might be the stronger instrument of the one true arbitrary and autocratic master. He was right to break the law of kings, which he thought human and not from heaven. Confident of his election, he could explain all his actions and all his sufferings; except, perhaps, his submission to the authority of Charles II.

This was a violation of his own purity, and could well have seemed likely to be the worst of his pains. Yet to accept those pains as a punishment would be to destroy the structures of belief that had made sense of his life. It might seem necessary to redesign those structures so that they incorporated the violation as a necessary part of the divine plot. A man, one of the elect, who had, with justified confidence in the authenticity of his impulse, repeatedly broken what others took to be the law, now finds himself, on obeying the same impulse, apparently condemned to misery and impurity. It must turn out that this is an illusion. The submission to Charles II—a purely ceremonial submission—is part of a plot, the end of which will prove that after all every impulse was authentic. The justice of God, expressed in his arbitrary designs (Milton's friends were thwarted in their attempts by what seemed the merest accident), must not be expected to make immediate human sense.

For God often seems indifferent to human beings; he seems not to understand them. His plots cause them excruciating pain and are unrelated to the human sense of justice. He is contemptuous of equity, even of sanity; think again of those trivial miracles, set between the great miracle of the annunciatory fires at the beginning, and the great miracle of the hero-phoenix at the end, dying into a new *saeculum*. Schreber's god, with his absurd angels and petty miracles, his enforced pollutions, his disregard for human pain in the apprehensive tenderest parts, and his absolute rightness and justice, is, of course, a god of madness. But Milton's is his distant ancestor, the God of the archetypal Hebrew tragedy, perceived behind its Greek shadows, and defined by Milton's experience as his Christian agent. Human kings he could set below the law, but there was another monarch, who called fear love and bondage freedom; in the end, however, he would reveal the purpose for which he required his elect to suffer and to commit uncleanness.

Milton's old age was a little too like the one Manoa planned for Samson—domestic comfort under the license, dearly bought, of the Philistine lords. I do not say he waited for some last prompting, some last occasion to offer freedom to his fickle tribe, some explanation of that interlude of misery. Indeed it is unnecessary to do so. The divine plot naturally contains its peripeteia; the last intimate impulse was to write *Samson Agonistes,* a heroic examination of all such intimate impulses, and a vindication of the peculiar justice of a God whose arbitrary decisions and devices alone make sense of the hero's world, and are that of which he must make sense.

# CHAPTER 3

## *Wallace Stevens*

### DWELLING POETICALLY IN CONNECTICUT

The last poetry of Wallace Stevens, which may be his greatest, seems not to have found the critic who can speak for it. The present essay will not do so, for my purpose is the marginal one of reflecting on various interests that we know Stevens to have had in his last years, in the hope that they may have some relevance to those venerable poems. They are mostly poems of death, or of the achievement of a posture in which to meet it correctly. Stevens was a correct man. There was also a proper mise en scène for poetry; he cared for the physical presentation of his and other people's poems, as if their disclosures, even the most exalted, the closest to a final truth, required the art of the typographer and the gold, leather, and linen of the binder as accompaniments to revelation. Propriety is not always satisfied by grays and blacks; ideas, poems, and persons may need or deserve some decorous slash of vivid color from the remoter parts of the lexicon, some gaiety. Or, if they do not deserve it, they should get it: "Merit in poets is as boring as merit in people" (*Adagia, Opus Posthumous,* p. 157).[1]

In these years Stevens was also interested in Friedrich Hölderlin, who also knew that merit was not enough: "Full of merit, yet poetically / Man dwells on the earth." And because of Hölderlin he looked toward the poet's great explainer, the philosopher Martin Heidegger. Whether he ever found Heidegger is an interesting question. Between them, Hölderlin and Heidegger form a kind of model of that composite poet, virile youth and old tramp, who seized on Stevens' imagination. But Stevens himself was not very like them. For him the poetical, the supererogatory grace might be a gaiety, "light or color, images," or a gilt top edge. Like Hölderlin, he thought of the poet as "the priest of the invisible"; but unlike him, he would choose a wild word with sane care and give his poems wry titles to make them self-ironical. Like Heidegger, he thought of poetry as a renovation of experience; unlike him, he thought that the truth in the end did not matter. And even as he grew old, Stevens was never the tramp, as he had never been the virile youth. The encounter of being with death was not far off, but there was time for these interests, the well-made typeface or rich binding, the Germans, mad and obscure.

AS FOR THE FINE BINDINGS and limited editions, Stevens came to like them more and more, and not only for his own poems. He wrote letters to printers and binders about the way books should be produced. He told his editor, Katharine Frazier, that he would rather rewrite lines in *Notes toward a Supreme Fiction* than have ugly turnovers in the printed copy (*Letters,* p. 407).[2] Later he had a bibliopegic correspondence with Victor Hammer, a Viennese who operated first the Anvil Press in Lexington, Kentucky, and then the Aurora Press at Wells College. In 1946 he bought Janet Lewis' *The Earth-Bound,* beautifully published by Mr. Hammer, and negotiated for a bookplate. On January 22, 1948, he wrote to Hammer ordering a copy of his limited edition (fifty-one copies only) of Hölderlin's *Poems 1796–1804*—"I read German well enough," he remarked—and he later thanked Hammer for the book in terms that bore entirely upon the beauty of the printing (*L,* pp. 576, 681). He spoke not of Hölderlin's art but of Mr. Hammer's.

It was not unimportant to Stevens that Hammer was living in Kentucky. Reality changes, he observed, and "in every place and at every time the imagination makes its way by reason of it." He thought of this Viennese printer in Kentucky and reflected that "a man is not bothered by the reality to which he is accustomed, that is to say, in the midst of which he has been born. He may be very much disturbed by reality elsewhere, but even as to that it would be only a question of time" (*L*, p. 577). He wondered whether Hammer could procure him a drawing of a necessary angel by Fritz Kredel. Mr. Kredel was "to state in the form of a drawing his idea of the surroundings in which poor people would be at rest and happy." A few weeks later he explained why this was desirable, referring to his "Angel Surrounded by Paysans": "There must be in the world about us things that solace us quite as fully as any heavenly visitation could." The plan was given up; perhaps Kredel could not see that particular angel (*L*, pp. 656, 661, 662–663).

Although he said nothing about the contents of Hammer's *Hölderlin*, Stevens was presumably interested in them. He had recently acquired a German edition of the *Gedichte*, published in 1949. This book is described in the catalogue of the Parke-Bernet sale of Stevens' books (March 1959) as a small folio, full niger morocco, gilt fillets on sides, gilt edges. "In a morocco-edged linen slipcase . . . A SUMPTUOUS BOOK PRINTED WITH A SPECIALLY CUT TYPE-FACE AND PRINTED ON HAND-MADE PAPER." Angels visiting the poor were, for Stevens, none the worse for top-edge gilt, even though they might themselves claim to have no "wear of ore" and to "live without a tepid aureole." Still, he must have looked inside this splendid package. He was certainly reading *about* Hölderlin, for example, an essay by Bernard Groethuysen, which he read in May 1948. Four years later he discovered that "Heidegger, the Swiss philosopher," had written a little work on Hölderlin, and he asked his Paris bookseller, Paule Vidal, to find him a copy. He would prefer, he said, a French translation, "But I should rather have it even in German than not have it at all" (*L*, p. 758).

As it happens, his local bookseller could have provided him with the essay in English, for a translation of the *Erläuterung zu Hölderlins Dichtung* was included in a collection of essays by Heidegger, *Existence and Being*, in 1949. Perhaps its workaday appearance would not have suited Stevens in any case. He asked Mme Vidal for a copy from "some bookseller at Fribourg." Probably she did not find one, for when Stevens' Korean friend

Peter H. Lee was in Freiburg in June 1954, Stevens wrote asking him about Heidegger in terms that do not suggest close acquaintance with his work: "If you attend any of his lectures, or even see him, tell me about him because it will help to make him real. At the moment he is a myth, like so many things in philosophy." At the end of September, still unsatisfied and still apparently under the impression that Heidegger was Swiss, he asked Lee whether the philosopher lectured in French or German (*L,* pp. 839, 846). That letter was written two days before the publication of *Collected Poems,* three before Stevens' seventy-fifth birthday, and less than a year before his death. At that late date his knowledge of Heidegger seems scanty enough, more myth than reality. The only certain fact is that Stevens was mixing up the Swiss and German Freiburgs, which is why he used the French form of the name of the city and referred to Heidegger as Swiss. He can therefore have known nothing of the philosopher's brief tenure as the Nazi-appointed rector of Freiburg University. It is an odd mistake, if one reflects that Heidegger spent about as much time outside of Germany as Stevens did out of the United States.

Still, he must have heard talk of Heidegger and the Hölderlin essays (though he mentions only one). His belated career as a lecturer and reader at colleges and universities had made him acquainted with philosophers—people who did their probing deliberately, he said, and not fortuitously, like poets. But we can be sure that he did not know Heidegger, even in French, as he knew, for example, Emerson, Santayana, and William James. Heidegger's was a book he did not, as a reader, "become." Years before, a philosophy professor had asked him why he did not take on a "full-sized" philosopher, and, when asked by Stevens to name some, included C. S. Peirce on the list. In his relation of this episode to Theodore Weiss, Stevens added, "I have always been curious about Pierce [*sic*], but have been obliged to save my eyesight for THE QUARTERLY REVIEW, etc" (*L,* p. 476). Since his correspondent was the editor of *The Quarterly Review,* we must take this as banter, but all the same, he probably meant that he preferred being curious about Peirce to reading him.

Perhaps for his purposes a smattering of knowledge was more useful than an understanding. Some image of Heidegger in his peasant clothes, darkly speculating upon his hero and supreme poet, precursor of the angel most necessary when, after the failure of the gods, our poverty is most complete, suited Stevens better than a whole philosophy, however vatic in expression. Perhaps the notion of this venerable man as having thought exhaustively about death and poetry and about the moment of their final encounter was enough. Stevens would try by his accustomed channels to acquire the sage's book, but if it did not come, it would still be interesting to know how he looked and what language he spoke in his Freiburg lecture room, in the midst of his accustomed reality.

It is sometimes argued that Stevens' poems are suffused with the philosophy of others, indeed, that they are sometimes virtually paraphrases of such philosophies, so that the sense of, say, "The Bird with the Coppery, Keen Claws" must be sought in William James's *The Pluralistic Universe*.[3] However that may be, the focus here is on something else. Heidegger thinking about Hölderlin—his great poet of the Time Between the failure of God and the birth of a new age, and of the sense in which man dwells poetically on earth—was meditating on the essence of poetry, its disclosures of being and its relation with death, which completes and annihilates being. He was probing these matters as deliberately as his extraordinary pre-Socratic manner allowed, and the text he meditated was the text of a schizophrenic seer who also loved those philosophic origins and sought to subvert the civil languages that had supervened upon them. Perhaps, borrowing Housman's joke, one could say that Stevens was a better poet than Heidegger and a better philosopher than Hölderlin, and so found himself, in a manner, betwixt and between. But there he was in the accustomed reality of Connecticut, meditating these very problems, probing fortuitously, and commenting on his own text. The projects were related. It was a leaden time; when reality is death, the imagination can no longer press back against it. When you live in "*a world that does not move for the weight of its own heaviness*" (*The Necessary Angel*,

p. 63),[4] you may imagine how differently it might appear to a young virile poet, but in the end you must find out for your aging self how that weight is to be lifted, what fiction will transform death.

IN "THE POET'S VOCATION," Hölderlin calls upon the angel of the day *(des Tages Engel)* to awaken the people, stupefied by their world, and enable them to help the poet by interpreting him. But even if he is denied that help, he goes on all the same

> And needs no weapon and no wile till
> God's being missed in the end will help him.[5]

Stevens was capable of a fair degree of rapture at the poetic possibilities opened up by the death of God; indeed, on this point he is less gnomic than his precursor. But like Hölderlin, he also felt the cold: "wozu Dichter in dürftiger Zeit?"[6] What are poets for in the time of poverty? is a question he often asked in his own way. In his own way he also maintained, though his obscurities are not Hölderlin's, that "Voll Verdienst, doch dichterisch, wohnet der Mensch auf dieser Erde [full of merit (what would be a better translation?), yet poetically, man dwells on this earth]."[7] Does the approach of death make this a little difficult to see?

In his essay "Effects of Analogy" (1948), Stevens proposes: "Take the case of a man for whom reality is enough, as, at the end of his life, he returns to it like a man returning from Nowhere to his village and to everything there that is tangible and visible, which he has come to cherish and wants to be near. He sees without images. But is he not seeing a clarified reality of his own? Does he not dwell in an analogy?" (*NA*, p. 129). He thinks that the being-toward-death, as Heidegger would call it, finds its form in the roofs, woods, and fields of a particular accustomed reality. It is a theme not altogether remote from that of Hölderlin's "Homecoming" ("Heimkunft"). And it is central to Stevens. The place where the poet dwells, especially if it is his place of origin, will be his *mundo,* a clarified analogy of the earth he has lived in, the more so as death approaches. In the same essay he explains that a poet's sense of the world, his sense of place, will color his dealings with death. James Thomson has a melancholy sense of the world; his place was a city of dreadful night, and he writes "We yearn for speedy death in full fruition, / Dateless oblivion and divine repose." Whitman, on the other hand, speaks of a "free flight into the wordless, / Away from books, away from art, the day erased, the lesson done . . ."[8] Stevens does not enlarge upon these disclosures. They are effects of analogy; death is understood analogously, the last reality has the color and the shapes of a clarified reality of one's own. In "Imagination as Value," delivered as he approached his seventieth birthday, Stevens spoke of Pascal as one who, for all his hatred of the imagination ("this superb power, the enemy of reason"), clung "in the very act of dying" to the faculty that, however "delusive," might still create "beauty, justice and happiness" (*NA,* pp. 135–136). As Pascal needed it to comprehend his death, so the poet needs it, especially in a time when "the great poems of heaven and hell have been written and the great poem of the earth remains to be written" (*NA,* p. 142).

The point is Heideggerian; Stevens does not quote Heidegger here, one feels, only because he had not read him. Instead, he thinks of Santayana, whom he had known well at Harvard fifty years before. He thinks of him as one who gave the imagination a part in life similar to that which it plays in art. For the art of dying depends on our having dwelt poetically on earth. And so Santayana in old age "dwells in the head of the world, in the company of devoted women, in their convent, and in the company of familiar saints, whose presence does so much to make any convent an appropriate refuge for a generous and human philosopher. . . . there can be lives in which the value of the imagination is the same as its value in arts and letters and I exclude from consideration as part of that statement any thought of poverty or wealth, being a *bauer* or being a king, and so on, as irrelevant" (*NA,* p. 148). Reflecting on Santayana's death in a letter to Barbara Church (September 29, 1952), he thinks again of one who abandoned poetry for thought but made this imaginative gesture, the choice, for a long old age, of a Roman convent, of a kind of poverty (he "probably gave them all he had and asked them to keep him, body and soul" [*L*, p. 762]), of an image of oncoming death founded in the accustomed reality of prayer, liturgy, and the earthly city, which, being the heart of one world, may be the figure of another, the more so if, in dwelling poetically, we dwell in analogy. So the poem he might have written for Heidegger became a poem for Santayana.

"To an Old Philosopher in Rome" is about such dwelling, and about the moment when accustomed reality provides a language for death, invents it, as it invents its own angels, by analogy. The poem straddles the threshold, "the figures in the street / Become the figures of heaven. . . . The threshold, Rome, and that more merciful Rome / Beyond, the two alike in the make of the mind" (*Collected Poems*, p. 508).[9] It is, one may say, a great poem, though perhaps not wholly characteristic of Stevens in the persistence with which it fills out its scenario of antitheses: "The extreme of the known in the presence of the extreme / Of the unknown"; the candle and the celestial possible of which it is the symbol, life as a flame tearing at a wick; grandeur found in "the afflatus of ruin," in the "Profound poetry of the poor and of the dead"; splendor in poverty, death in life. It is language accommodating itself to that which ends and fulfills being, an image of that "total grandeur." This is a grandeur made of nothing but the bed, the chair, the moving nuns, the bells, and newsboys of the *civitas terrena;* but it is total, and the only image of a grandeur still unknown.

Note also that it is *easy:* "How easily the blown banners change to wings." Somehow it has become easy to find heaven in poverty's speech. The ease is the "ease of mind" mentioned at the beginning of "Prologues to What Is Possible," where the rowers are sure of their way, and "The boat was built of stones that had lost their weight and being no longer heavy / Had left in them only a brilliance, of unaccustomed origin" (*CP*, p. 515). The voyager easily passes into the unfamiliar—into death—as if it were the known. I do not mean that for Stevens this step is always easy, only that there is a kind of comfortable grace in some of his accounts of the threshold, an absence of what might be called, after Heidegger, *care* (to say nothing of dread), a grace that arises from acquiescence in the casual boons of the world of poverty, even at the moment when suffering caused by the absence of the gods might be most acute.

Heidegger called Hölderlin the poet of the Time Between—between the departure and the return of the gods—the midnight of the world's night. Stevens is consciously a poet of the same time. His answer to Hölderlin's question, "wozu Dichter?" (which Heidegger took as the title of his astonishing lecture on the twentieth anniversary of the death of Rainer Maria Rilke), would not be, in essence, different from either the poet's or the philosopher's. He had long been trying to make poetry out of commonplaces, for instance, in *Owl's Clover* in the thirties, and in 1949 he said that in "An Ordinary Evening in New Haven" his interest was "to try to get as close to the ordinary, the commonplace and the ugly as it is possible for a poet to get. It is not a question of grim reality but of plain reality. The object is of course to purge oneself of anything false" (*L,* p. 636). At the end of that poem reality, plain reality, is given some of the imagery of death: "It may be a shade that traverses / A dust, a force that traverses a shade" (*CP,* p. 489). Those "edgings and inchings of final form," those statements tentatively closing in on the real, are in their way a figure for the imagination's edging and inching toward the comprehension of death. Hence, too, the idea of self-purgation; the moral and the poetic functions of imagination grow toward identity and in virtually the same way labor to include death in being. Death is a threshold, the commonplace on one side of it, its transcendent analogue on the other, as the Santayana poem at once asserts. And that notion is much prefigured, for Stevens is a poet of thresholds: even summer is a threshold and, in "Credences of Summer," an image of death. At the end of "The Auroras of Autumn" the "scholar of one candle" opens his door and sees across the threshold "An Arctic effulgence flaring on the frame / Of everything he is. And he feels afraid" (*CP,* p. 417). Finally, the supreme poet understands, out of the partial fact that we are "An unhappy people in a happy world":

> In these unhappy he meditates a whole,
> The full of fortune and the full of fate,
> As if he lived all lives, that he might know,
>
> In hall harridan, not hushful paradise,
> To a haggling of wind and weather, by these lights
> Like a blaze of summer straw, in winter's nick. (*CP*, pp. 420–421)

Here all the accustomed realities are known and accommodated to a summerlike brilliance in an icy world. Hölderlin would have called this poet a servant of the wine god, bearing all such care, seeing that blaze on behalf of all, imagining everything for them, including death. Knowing poverty ("His poverty becomes his heart's strong core" [*CP*, p. 427]) is the means to find a way through the world, which "Is more difficult to find than the way beyond it" (*CP*, p. 446). This is what Stevens calls the will to holiness. It is a favorite word of Hölderlin's. *Wozu Dichter?* They must dwell in their huts, their accustomed reality, framed by their commonplace thresholds, and do all that angels can—intimate, by use of a perhaps delusive faculty, what lies beyond, the fullness of the encounter when Being has inched and edged its way to death. Santayana's choice of Rome as a place to die is a poet's choice; he seeks out this central city as affording the structures, the rituals, even the ritual compassions, that, out of accustomedness, the imagination confers on death. "These are poems," wrote Randall Jarrell of *The Rock,* "from the other side of existence, the poems of someone who sees things in steady accustomedness, as we do not, and who sees their accustomedness, and them, as about to perish."[10] Or, as Stevens himself puts it, "The thing seen becomes the thing unseen" (*Adagia, OP,* p. 167). Nevertheless, as he states elsewhere in the *Adagia,* "The poet is the intermediary between people and the world in which they live . . . but not between people and some other world" (*OP,* p. 162). Thus, in concerning himself with death, the poet must concern himself with the poverty of the accustomed, with the mystery of dwelling poetically in its midst. And perhaps, as Hölderlin remarked, "God's being missed in the end will help him." Perhaps it will also help him to see the poet's words comfortingly coated in the adventitious splendors of decorative bindings, rendered easy by sharp, clear type, the blessings of richness in poverty, of ease in the world of care.

STEVENS WAS QUITE RIGHT to be curious about Heidegger and to want to know what the philosopher said about Hölderlin. The intense meditation on poetry that Heidegger produced in the series of works inaugurated by the 1936 essay on Hölderlin represents, in a way, the fulfillment of an ambition evident in Stevens' prose. Stevens could not achieve it fully for various reasons. The desire for ease could have been one. Then again, his philosophy, as he himself admitted, was a philosophy of collects, an amateur's philosophy. Heidegger was professional as well as incantatory; he thought as the pre-Socratics (or some of them) thought, poetically. But he thought accurately. Albert Hofstadter says that as a thinker Heidegger did what a poet does: *dichtet.*[11] Like the poet, he was concerned with "the saying of world and earth," with their conflict—not unlike the conflict of world and *mundo* in Stevens—and so with the place of all nearness and remoteness of the gods. "Poetry is the saying of the unconcealedness of what is. Actual language at any given moment is the happening of this saying." This is the *truth,* for Heidegger looked to the etymological meaning of *alētheia,* which is "unconcealedness." Thus, although it sets up a world, the work of art also *lets the earth be an earth.* "As a world opens itself the earth comes to rise up." And so it happens that "art is the becoming and happening of truth." All art is in essence poetry, a disclosure of the earth, a "setting-into-work of truth." The appearance of this truth is beauty.[12]

There are times when Stevens would have recognized this voice as that of a remote kinsman in poetry, for example, in the "thinking poem," "Aus der Erfahrung des Denkens" ("The Thinker as Poet"):

> When the early morning light quietly
> grows above the mountains. . . .
>
> The world's darkening never reaches
> to the light of Being.
>
> We are too late for the gods and too
> early for Being. Being's poem,
> just begun, is man. . . .[13]

Or, one can just imagine these aphorisms occurring in the *Adagia:*

> Poetry looks like a game and yet it is not.
>
> Poetry rouses the appearance of the unreal and of dream in the face of the palpable and clamorous reality, in which we believe ourselves at home. And yet . . . what the poet says and undertakes to be, is the real.[14]

Yet the affinity, I think, goes beyond these resemblances. It is of course mitigated by differences of a kind at which I have already hinted; Stevens was less bold, less willing to be oracular than Heidegger. And then there is the matter of those new typefaces and fine bindings: wear of ore for the angel of accustomedness, precursors of a transfigured commonplace, patches of Florida in the world of books. Likewise, there are the *trouvailles* and the collects and the fortuities of dizzle-dazzle that interrupt disclosures of pure poverty. But for all that, there is an affinity.[15]

If we think of the idea of dwelling and death we may come to understand this affinity. "Poetically man dwells on this earth," said Hölderlin. In the poverty of the Time Between, one establishes this dwelling by finding the poetry of the commonplace, in the joy of Danes in Denmark, in the cackle of toucans in the place of toucans, in Elizabeth Park and Ryan's Lunch. Stevens did it over and over again, observing the greater brilliancies of earth from his own doorstep. He dwelt in Connecticut as Santayana dwelt in the head of the world, as if it were origin as well as threshold. He wanted to establish Hölderlin's proposition, and every reader of Stevens will think of many more instances of his desire to do so. Freiburg, Fribourg, were elsewhere. The foyer, the dwelling place, might be Hartford or New Haven, Farmington or Haddam. The Captain and Bawda "married well because the marriage-place / Was what they loved. It was neither heaven nor hell" (*CP,* p. 401). It was earth, and the poetry of the earth was what Hölderlin sought and Heidegger demanded. Stevens was always writing it and naming the spot to which it adhered. This is what poets are for in a time of need. They provide a cure of that ground; they give it health by disclosing it, in its true poverty, in the nothing that is. The hero of this world, redeemer of being, namer of the holy, is the poet. Stevens has many modest images of him, yet he is the center. In that same central place Heidegger sets Hölderlin and adorns him with words that have special senses: *truth, angel, care, dwell.*

Heidegger gave the word *dwell* a special charge of meaning. Drawing on an old sense of the German word, he can say that "Mortals dwell in that they can save the earth," that is, "set it free in its own presencing," free, as Stevens would say, of its man-locked set. There is much more to dwelling,[16] but I will mention only that to dwell is to initiate one's own nature, one's being capable of death as death, "into the use and practice of this capacity, so that there may be a good death." Furthermore, "as soon as man *gives thought* to his dwelling it is a misery no longer"; so out of its insecurity and poverty ("man dwells in huts and wraps himself in the bashful garment," says Hölderlin;[17] "a single shawl / Wrapped tightly round us, since we are poor . . . ," says Stevens [*CP,* p. 524]) he can build, can make poetry.[18] For Heidegger is here meditating on Hölderlin's enigma, that we dwell poetically on this earth, even in a time of destitution, and that our doing so is somehow gratuitous, independent of our merits, a kind of grace.

Where one dwells is one's homeland, and to return to it is to see it in its candid kind. Heidegger's first essay on Hölderlin is about the elegy "Homecoming," a poem of serenity and angels but also of the poet who names the town and makes it "shine forth." The angels are best summoned in one's homeland because the "original essence of joy is the process of becoming at home in proximity to the source."[19] The gods have failed; the poet "without fear of the appearance of godlessness . . . must remain near the failure of the god until out of that proximity the word is granted which names the High One." For he is the giant of the time that follows the default of the god. He is the first among men; others must help him by interpreting his word (which is the life of the world) so that each man may have his own homecoming.

In a second essay on Hölderlin, Heidegger deepens these apprehensions and speaks of the godlike power of his poet. Man has been given arbitrariness, and he has been given language, with which he creates and destroys and affirms what he is. What he affirms is that he "belongs to the earth and gives it being: Only where there is language is there world." (The "words of the world," says Stevens, "are the life of the world" [*CP,* p. 474].) The naming of the gods ("This happy creature—It is he that invented the Gods" [*OP,* p. 167]) was only the first act by which language—poetry—established Being. To dwell poetically is to stand in the proximity of being; when the essence of things receives a name, as the gods once received a name in the first poetic act, things shine out.[20] These things are commonplace and accustomed till thus named: only then is it the case that "The steeple at Farmington / Stands glistening and Haddam shines and sways" (*CP,* p. 533).

The completion and delimitation of Being come with death, with *my* death, for we cannot think authentically about the deaths of others. Heidegger had written much about this in *Being and Time,* and he thought about it in relation to poetry in essays written between 1947 and 1952, when Stevens' not dissimilar meditations were in progress and when he was saying he would like to read Heidegger. Only on the subject of care, on the necessity of speaking heavily and with radical plainness of being and ending, might he have found in the German a weight as of stones he chose not to lift.

But perhaps, after all, Stevens did know something about *Being and Time.* Perhaps it was knowing about it that sent him looking, in his seventies, for news of what that Swiss philosopher might have to say about his supreme poet. Heidegger wrestled with ideas we all wrestle with: the potentiality of no more being able to be there, he remarks, is the inmost, one might say the own-most, potentiality. We have many ways of estranging death; for example, we say, "Everybody dies," or "one dies." So we conceal our own "being-toward-death"; yet death is the "end" of Being, of *Dasein*—and the means by which it becomes a whole. To estrange it, to make it a mere fact of experience, is to make it inauthentic. Being understands its own death authentically not by avoiding that dread out of which courage must come but by accepting it as essential to Being's everydayness, which otherwise conceals the fact that the end is imminent at every moment. There must be a "running forward in thought" to the potentiality of death.

Only where there is language is there world, says Heidegger; and only where there is language is there this running in thought, this authentication of death. It is the homecoming that calls for the great elegy; it is "learning at home to become at home," as Heidegger says of the Hölderlin elegy.[21] "All full poets are poets of homecoming," he says. And he insists that Hölderlin's elegy is not *about* homecoming; it *is* homecoming. Stevens knew this, whether he learned it from Heidegger or not. He knew the truth of many of Heidegger's assertions, for example, about the nature of change in art. "The works are no longer the same as they once were. It is they themselves, to be sure, that we encounter . . . but they themselves are gone by."[22] The work of art "opens up a world and at the same time sets his world back again on earth."[23] The perpetuation of such truth is the task of an impossible philosopher's man or hero. Stevens' poet works in the fading light; the "he" of the late poems has to make his homecoming, has to depend on his interpreters to make it for themselves and understand that it is impermanent. The advent of the Supreme Poet, who would stop all this, is like the return of the god. Heidegger's most impressive meditation on this coming event is in the lecture on Rilke, "Wozu Dichter?" (1946). The time is completely destitute; the gods will return only when the time is free. Poets in such a destitute time must "sense the trace of the fugitive gods" and, in dark night, utter the holy. Of this night Hölderlin is the poet. Is Rilke such a poet? Certainly he came to understand the destitution of the time, a time when even the trace of the holy has become unrecognizable, and there is lacking "the unconcealedness of the nature of pain, death and love."[24] Certainly he understood the need for "unshieldedness" and the need to "read the word 'death' without negation." But it is not certain that he attained the full poetic vocation or spoke for the coming world era, as Hölderlin did.

The long, dark essay on Rilke is finally beyond the scope of Stevens. But Stevens knew that language makes a world of the earth and includes death in that world; he knew that it effects the unconcealment of the earth, that this is the poet's task in a time of destitution and seclusion. He could imagine a vocation for a supreme poet. Sometimes he could speak or chant of these things majestically enough, but in the last poems he would not dress the poet in singing robes. The poet is, mostly, at home and old, shambling, shabby, and human. He does not say "'I am the greatness of the new-found night'" (*OP,* p. 93). But he accepts that what one knows "of a single spot / Is what one knows of the universe" (*OP,* p. 99). His Ulysses strives to come home; he seeks a new youth "in the substance of his region" (*OP,* p. 118), in its commonness, like that of the great river in Connecticut, which one comes to "before one comes to the first black cataracts" (*CP,* p. 533) of the other, Stygian river.

It should be added that the "he," the poet, of some of the last poems, can be a "spirit without a foyer" and search among the fortuities he perceives for "that serene he had always been approaching / As toward an absolute foyer . . ." (*OP,* p. 112). It is a different version of the running-toward-death, and Heidegger would have approved of that "serene," for Hölderlin used the word and his glossator turned it over many times in his mind. Is this ordered serenity too easy? When we climb a mountain "Vermont throws itself together" (*OP,* p. 115); Vermont does the work, provided, of course, that we climb the mountain. It is not quite easy, but it is of the essence that it is also not quite difficult. The greatest image of the being at the threshold of death is, I suppose, "Of Mere Being," a poem that is also, one may be sure, very late. It contains a foreign song and a foreign bird. There is dread in it. Heidegger, I dare say, would have admired it, but there is no reason to suppose that he would have been less severe on Stevens than on Rilke.

SO ONE FORCES THEM TOGETHER, Hölderlin-Heidegger in Freiburg or Fribourg, and Stevens in Hartford. But Stevens always draws back, as if to examine a binding or to keep some distance between himself and a mad poet or a very difficult philosopher. "Philosophical validity," he assured a correspondent in 1952, was no concern of his; "recently," he added, "I have been fitted into too many philosophic frames" (*L*, p. 753). Perhaps the Heidegger frame would have pleased him better than most; for one thing, Heidegger's thought is very different from any that Stevens was accustomed to think of as philosophical. But Stevens would have drawn back. Not to find a copy of *Existence and Being* was, in a way, to draw back, to seek Heidegger instead in Paris, where his bookseller knew the kind of book he liked, and it would arrive like something exotic. Then again, there was a crucial difference of origin: Stevens was an American in America, Heidegger a German in Germany (not Switzerland), all life long. Part of this difference is reflected in varying styles of solemnity, in the fact that Heidegger is wholly without irony, while Stevens always has it within call.

There was an affinity between the ways in which they felt the world and understood poetry; between the truths they disclosed in the night of destitution by dwelling poetically in—that is, by saving—their worlds. Stevens had something of the quality that made Heidegger describe Hölderlin as himself having that third eye he attributed to Oedipus; he was virtually talking about it in the last lines of "The Auroras":

he meditates a whole,
The full of fortune and the full of fate,
As if he lived all lives, that he might know. . . . (*CP*, p. 420)

But few could have refused more obstinately the fate of Hölderlin. For Stevens the world was by no means always a haggling of wind and weather or even of an *unheimlich* "serene." It was often, perhaps daily, a place of ease, of "Berlioz and roses" if that happened to be "the current combination at home" (*L*, p. 505), of postcards from Cuba, tea from Ceylon—fortuities of earth that solace us and make a world, or, like the Tal Coat painting that hung in his house in these years, an angel of reality. Such, too, though more elegant and more ornate, were the finely printed books of Mr. Hammer, a Viennese "without a foyer" but now growing accustomed to the reality of Kentucky, whence he might send surrogate angels to Connecticut. There dwelt the poet, watching the shining of the commonplace (occasionally, a distant palm, an unclassifiable, fire-fangled bird) and, for the most part, easy among his splendid books, though soon to die.

CHAPTER 4

# *T. S. Eliot*

## THE LAST CLASSIC

Early in 1988 I received from Washington University a letter outlining the program of its Eliot centennial celebration; the 22-cent stamps on the envelope bore an image of the head of the poet. Evidently it was not only Washington University, and the city of St. Louis, birthplace of the poet, who wished to celebrate the occasion of his hundredth birthday; the United States took official cognizance of it; by implication the country of his birth had forgiven him for his change of citizenship and for what can be represented as his Euro-centered views on practically everything.

Yet there are voices, and powerful voices, which would speak against the propriety of such celebrations. Eliot has often been accused of betraying his American origins, of having, in his practice as poet and critic, blocked or distorted the authentic native tradition in poetry. This opinion has, over the years, been variously but persistently expressed. William Carlos Williams, Eliot's contemporary, called *The Waste Land* "the great catastrophe to our letters . . . There was heat in us, a core and a drive that was gathering headway upon the theme of a rediscovery of a primary impetus, the elementary principle of all art, in the local conditions. Our work staggered to a halt for a moment under the blast of Eliot's genius which gave the poem back to the academics. We did not know how to answer him." And again: "It wiped out our world as if an atom bomb had been dropped upon it . . . Eliot had turned his back on the possibility of reviving my world. And being an accomplished craftsman, better skilled in some ways than I could ever hope to be, I had to watch him carry off my world with him, the fool, to the enemy. If with his skill he could have been kept here to be employed by our slowly shaping drive, what strides might we not have taken! . . . I have never quite got over it."[1]

Williams' allegation of defection or betrayal may smack of a more general isolationism, though at the front of his mind it was certainly a question of technique—a question ultimately bound up with those of American origins and independence. Williams advocated and practiced a new metrical freedom controlled by an indigenous American discipline. He wanted a distinctive American poetry, responsive to the patterns and idiosyncracies not of just English but of American English. This hope he thought Eliot had frustrated by his voluntary assimilation of British English, and by his choice of a relevant past that was European, and more and more, as time went by, specifically English.

The complaint is not groundless, and its recurrence in New World societies probably inevitable; the conflict between inherited allegiances and the changed conditions of life in a new world has been reenacted, for example, in Australia, though in a different mode. An older language has to be changed—indeed it changes of itself—to suit different and more recent cultures and polities; but it cannot, in the nature of the case, quite cut itself off from its roots, or quite disown membership in a larger language community, which is why the attempt of some Australians to find a new language for poetry by admixing aboriginal words proved unsuccessful. And after a time during which there may linger a sense of deracination, of cultural inferiority, there may develop a mood of defiant self-sufficiency. At that point there can be a revolt, a determination to go it alone, sometimes accompanied by an exaggerated gesture of rejection.

The terms in which quarrels of this nature are conducted inevitably derive from the discourse of the moment when they happen to arise. On a long historical view Williams and Eliot had a good deal in common. They were both, though in different ways, associated with and affected by Ezra Pound, who was himself *echt* American, though also a very European American, at that time and subsequently not a rare type, though Pound was a rare enough specimen of it. They were both influenced by Imagism, a doctrine ultimately of European origin but raised, as it were, by American hands. At our distance from the events we might suppose the difference of opinion need hardly have been represented on an international scale at all. But that would be to ignore the deeper issue, the natural impatience felt by nations as well as individuals with the burden of an unwanted or inappropriate resented past. Later complainants found other ways of signaling what was essentially the same rejection of or revulsion from Europe—for example, Charles Olson and the Black Mountain school, with its cult of indigenous origins, of the immediacy of American speech and its independence of British-English rhythms.

For a time, it would seem, this American revolt against Eliot attracted no support from the literary academics. Williams must have expected this to be the case when he spoke of Eliot's "giving the poem back to the academics," a group perhaps too brainwashed by Europeanism, too inveterately committed to "paleface" cultural values, to produce the American "redskin" response he wanted. But as time went on, the academics themselves found ways of strengthening the cause of the republican American homeland against the authority of the classical, royalist émigré. For father and sponsor they chose Ralph Waldo Emerson, perhaps a somewhat palefaced redskin surrogate, but a thinker denied his due both by those who reduced him to a homespun pokerwork popular philosopher and by those loftier persons who preferred to pay homage to European sages certain to be more important simply because they were European.

Let me cite some authorities for this account of the contemporary opposition, some representative modern academic-Emersonians, persons of power and influence. Richard Poirier is perhaps the most measured, but he still blames Eliot for his part in the repression of native American literature. As Poirier puts the case (and I quote but one of a number of variously stated indictments), the relation between Emersonianism and "the modernist episode in Anglo-American literary culture" is reflected in the "predominance, over the past sixty years or so, of Eliot as against, say, a combination of Frost or Stevens with William James." In the 1920s, says Poirier, "American literature was up for grabs." So, in a sense, it was. D. H. Lawrence, a renegade Englishman, himself in revolt against the paleface, had almost singlehandedly begun the revaluation of "classic" American literature in the remarkable essays he wrote during World War I and just after it. (By calling anything American "classic" you at once dissociate yourself from Eliot's idea of the classic as something involving Virgil, Dante, Catholicism, and Empire. You are talking about a new civilization, or even of an empire that has decisively taken its westward course, and is not just a new shoot growing out of an old one.) So the 1920s saw the beginning of the rediscovery of Melville, the revaluation of Cooper and the rest; "but the hegemony of Eliot at that time and later delayed if it did not prevent the recognition that America had a literature."[2]

Thus Richard Poirier. To the charismatic Harold Bloom, "the American Sublime" and "the Emersonian Sublime" are interchangeable terms, each standing for an ideal in which Eliot had very little discernible interest. Bloom has throughout his career cheerfully disparaged Eliot, which, for an admirer of the Divinity School address and "The American Scholar," is after all a very logical thing to do. "The malign influence of T. S. Eliot still lingers on," he says, "in most contemporary accounts of literary tradition," though he now admits that Eliot sometimes unofficially recognized the truth of the Bloomian version of influence, and calls *Ash Wednesday,* which he once thought somewhat vacuous, a "crucial crisis ode." However, this partial reprieve for Eliot seems conditional on his accepting Whitman as his unacknowledged precursor.[3] One could complete this sketch of the modern American case against Eliot by observing that Helen Vendler, often described as the most sensitive and authoritative reader of modern American poetry, has never had much time for him, and I am not sure she has ever discussed him in print.

We may be sure that these influential voices speak for many others, less articulate yet still calling for vengeance on the suppressors of the native Emersonian tradition. All three, by the way, are warm in their praises of Wallace Stevens, another great modern poet who professed, perhaps not quite candidly, to have little time for Eliot. Far from emigrating, Stevens carefully avoided physical contact with Europe, and evidently harbored a certain dislike and suspicion of the British, and even of their language, for he maintained that despite appearances the roots of American poetry were actually French. Eliot, on the other hand, did not content himself with merely becoming British, which might have been achieved with the quiet discretion we associate with his habitual manner; rather he felt it necessary to make an announcement about it, and evidently regarded his naturalization, and his conversion to Anglicanism, as a matter of intellectual and public interest. Indeed he showed some of the enthusiasm of the convert, even, on occasion, presenting himself as a presumably slightly ironic caricature of the royalist; he liked to wear a white rose on the anniversary of the battle of Bosworth, and a red tie on the feast of St. Charles—the Church of England's sole martyr, and appropriately a royal one—much in the manner of the dandy Decadent Jacobites of the nineties. On another occasion one might indeed argue that his debt to the English nineties has not been fully counted. It amounted to much more than a reading of Arthur Symons' *The Symbolist Movement in Poetry* and a taste for the London music halls. It might be fair to add that he probably acquired this taste for the music hall in Boston; but the man who gave such cultural importance to Marie Lloyd was behaving like the English literati—like Ford Madox Ford, for instance, who is said to have edited the *New English Review* in a music-hall box. And anyway my present concern is with the poet's apparent preference for England and Europe over his native land.

As one would expect, this transfer of allegiance did not happen suddenly, as his early letters show. When Eliot arrived in London, hurrying out of Germany at the start of the 1914 war, he could make very little of the English. "It's ever so much easier to know what a Frenchman or an American is thinking about than an Englishman."[4] In the same fall he says he doesn't think he can ever be at home in England. He detested the English middle classes, with their hideous family life and contempt for education. But he was already moving in more exalted circles, introduced to them by Bertrand Russell, whom he had known at Harvard; and before the end of the war he is saying he gets on better with the English than with Americans, who "now impress me, almost invariably, as very immature." He urges his brother to join him in London; life there was a struggle, but that would be better than living among Americans who had "no consciousness at all."[5] For years he had debated whether he should go home and take up a philosophical career, probably at Harvard; his English wife, and the self-exiled Ezra Pound, had a lot to do with his decision to stay, or anyway not to go. But by the time he wrote that letter to Henry Ware Eliot he had pretty clearly made up his mind.

The English, or perhaps one should say the London, way of life suited him very well. He was a serious clubman, and notoriously wished to be recognized as a connoisseur of British cheese. He believed in empire and the established church (though the one was, to him, not vulgarly terrestrial, more the allegorical representation of an empire laid up in heaven, while the other was the form of Catholicism which he had, after much deliberation and possibly with some reluctance, declared the most appropriate). He had an unaffected but upper-class English accent, with no trace of American. I need say no more by way of establishing that it would be easy to represent him as, from the American point of view, quite exceptionally alienated, cut off from the language and culture of his native land.

Why, then, those centennial stamps? Why do his grandfather's university, and the citizens of his home town, put themselves to the trouble and expense of celebrating his foreign song and alien fame? Possibly they have considered and rejected the hostile versions of Eliot's career; or perhaps they are only obeying an instinct to commemorate a distinguished native son, however he may have been thought by others to have lost his way in the world. Or have they rather taken note that there has of late been a good deal of scholarship devoted to establishing or reestablishing Eliot as, after all, a genuinely American poet?

For there has been a change in fashion, and Eliot is nowadays looked at from a new angle. Over the past twenty years or so many commentators have found it necessary or expedient to give up the idea that his poetry was as impersonal as on his own theories it ought to have been; and having become familiar with biographical detail that was inaccessible during the poet's reticent lifetime, they have warmed to the notion that his poetry was after all written by a real person, indeed that it is in a rather curious way profoundly autobiographical. And if this really is so, St. Louis will presumably have its place in the story, and has accordingly a perfect right to take some proprietary interest in that story.

Eliot himself, lecturing there in 1953, spoke of his grandfather William Greenleaf Eliot, a man of whom it was said that the Day of Judgment seemed to attend him wherever he went. This very remarkable man, who went to St. Louis from Massachusetts as a young Unitarian preacher, was one of the heroes and makers of the city. On his monument it is written that "the whole city was his parish." After the cholera epidemic of 1849 he took twenty-six orphaned children into his family, adding them to his own five (it is reasonable to assume that Mrs. Eliot was equally remarkable). He entirely reformed the educational arrangements of the city, and his grateful colleagues wanted to name the present Washington University for him; characteristically, he would not allow it. His whole career, as recounted by Herbert Howarth, was as extraordinary as it was noble.[6]

William Greenleaf Eliot died the year before the poet was born, but, as Eliot remarked in his lecture, his Law of Public Service—to Church, City, and University—still governed the conduct of the household. The poet carefully specified the physical location of these three institutions: Locust Street, Washington Avenue, and the city of St. Louis itself.[7] He also remarked that behind the many cities in his poetry there was always the shade of what for him must be the essential city, St. Louis—apprehended by him as the beginning of the Wild West, yet also a displaced piece of New England, dominated by the disciplines of his grandfather.[8]

When we think about the idiosyncratic and predominantly Anglo-Saxon attitudes of the mature Eliot, it is worth keeping in mind his early and protracted experience of living on the margin. He was born into a place that for all its familiarity and excitements, and for all its essentiality, was not quite his own place; possibly we could say that the essential place must, for him, always be a place to which he could not quite belong. It was manifestly important to him that this city stood on the border between two worlds, at the very limit of the East and facing the relatively unknown and cityless West, where not only the landscape but the people and their rules of conduct must presumably be very different. Dividing these worlds was a strong brown river, "sullen, untamed and intractable, / Patient to some degree, at first recognised as a frontier." Later, on the Massachusetts shore, the young man had another experience of margins—the margin of land and sea, which was also a margin of past and present, offering to our eyes "its hints of earlier and other creation"—of a history, a territory of time, a west, inconceivably precedent to human history, surveyed from a narrow stockade, the ill-marked frontier of humanity.

In the frontier house in St. Louis there lived another poet, a poet very much of the paleface East, namely Eliot's mother. It seems usual to speak with some condescension of her poems, and even in her time she had trouble getting them into print. But Herbert Howarth justly commends her "preoccupation with form and with the extension of her technical range"; and it would seem that the first poet Eliot himself ever encountered set an example of precision, and a respect for the transatlantic English as opposed to the Emersonian manner.

> Nay, while the soul was in the body pent,
> Thy face so shone we knew not what it meant—

this couplet, which occurs in a poem called *A Musical Reverie,*[9] is interesting for several reasons. It is a clear reminiscence of Donne:

> her pure and eloquent blood
> Spoke in her cheeks, and so distinctly wrought,
> That one might almost say, her body thought—

lines which were remembered even in a century which had not yet accorded canonical status to Donne. They express an idea which Mrs. Eliot gives in attenuated form: the soul of the dead person could be perceived during life as animating her physical beauty. Donne's couplet is of course more powerful: according to his physiology the blood carries the soul so that when it "speaks" its eloquence—its illumination of the flesh—is a statement about its own nature; and as it speaks through flesh it is as if the body itself, perhaps *this* body uniquely, were capable of making apprehensible such spiritual pronouncements. It was this depth of sense that made Donne's lines available as an allegorical program for poetry: this is how poems should be, expressing spirit through sense, being indivisible as to what was said and the means of saying it. Here was an emblem of that undissociated sensibility which the Eliot of the early 1920s attributed to Donne and some other poets before the catastrophe of the English Civil War—a sensibility that the modern poet was required somehow to restore, with a new poetry that could not avoid being difficult.

Throughout his life Eliot's head was full of poetic associations, scraps remembered with or without their original context, and it is easy to imagine that these lines of Donne were made familiar to him in very early life by a mother who admired and imitated them. But, as he was later to remark, immature poets imitate, mature poets steal. Eliot himself was often to steal and often, in doing so, to misquote, but his mother's imitative lines are an illustration of what must absolutely be avoided: they are not stolen and put to new use, but copied, either consciously or—much worse, he believed—unconsciously. And yet it may be that the mother's unsatisfactory borrowing became the son's worthy theft.

The different uses to which mother and son put Donne's lines illustrate the son's sense of what it is to be at once new and traditional, whether in the reading or the writing of poetry. Mrs.

Eliot must have read them as the apt expression of the truth about the mysterious spirituality of a privileged physical beauty; she could hardly have thought of them as the emblem of a lost tradition to be restored, in an unpropitious age, by immense and lonely effort.

In reading them thus, Eliot was indeed following a tradition partly invented by himself, partly inherited or stolen from his predecessors. Just as the Jacobite red rose for Charles I was the kind of thing the Lionel Johnson era loved, so the thinking body takes one back to Arthur Symons, the propagandist of Decadence, and through him to the offbeat Laforgue, and to Mallarmé, and the serious French doctrine of Symbolism.

Inventing his version of the modern from such an unusual array of sources—Cavalcanti, Dante, Donne, Baudelaire, Laforgue, Symons, John Davidson, and so forth—Eliot certainly seemed to be invoking a tradition quite different from that of his American contemporaries (Pound, that other renegade, always excepted); but it is equally obvious that his tradition was not that of his English contemporaries, either. It is true that he was writing in London, but it was in America that he was, at the insistence of Pound, first published. It was, admittedly, in London that he was soon to establish himself as a writer, but he did so in the first instance rather as a critic than as a poet—original, certainly, holding many unusual opinions and expressing them with remarkable assurance, but doing so in a manner not too outrageous for publication in the *TLS* (he was many years later to thank Bruce Richmond, the editor of the *Supplement,* for teaching him "to write in a temperate and impartial way").[10]

The *TLS* was an "establishment" journal; Eliot was proud of being asked to write for it, but to do so was not to write for a minority culture, much less for an alienated avant-garde. Only when he had obtained from Lady Rothermere the funds that enabled him to publish his own quarterly, *The Criterion,* was he able, without fear of editorial rejection, to lay *The Waste Land,* a poem whose principal reader and critic to date had been Pound, before the English intelligentsia. And although the reception of the poem was far from entirely frigid, one of the things people tended to say about it was that it attacked the native tradition—"a gash at the root of our poetry," said G. M. Young,[11] and others offered like judgments with even more distress and sometimes with contempt. F. L. Lucas, in a notorious review, quoted Santayana on those who "never . . . dig deep or build for time," and who "Forsake the path the seeing Muses trod."

Perhaps Eliot's "rhythmical grumbling" succeeded as well as it did because it expressed the disillusionment of a generation, as some claimed; perhaps the recent war had induced the young to wonder whether some traditions were worth having anyway. Or possibly, as Eliot himself remarked, it expressed only their illusion of being disillusioned. In any case the old generally disapprove of disillusion, or the illusion of it, in the young, and if they disliked the poem they would only dislike it more for fostering defeatism or lowering morale. Certainly the complaints of traditional Englishmen continued long after the twenties, and they do seem to form a sort of counterpoint to the American lamentations and accusations of desertion. On both sides of the ocean there were those who felt that Eliot was somehow deviant from, and even destructive of, a native tradition—to the Americans a deserter, to the English a stranger in their midst, *metoikos,* as he sometimes called himself. The indigenous English view, that he had somehow beglamoured us, induced us to forget our true heritage, was given forceful expression in 1960 by Graham Hough in his book *Image and Experience,* which treats the "modernist" movement as an instance of "wilful Alexandrianism"—thus repeating and strengthening one of Lucas's charges. It was an American-influenced departure from the native mainstream, to which English poets should now return. Later still the powerful example of Philip Larkin (a poet of extraordinary powers, yet so *echt* English that Americans tend to find him dull and insular) encouraged some to affirm that the true line ran through Hardy, not the Americans; and Donald Davie also spoke up for Hardy. Davie is another good poet, and less insular than Larkin—witness his remarkable translations of Mickiewicz and Pasternak—and unlike Larkin he had also wrestled strenuously with Pound and Eliot. Yet he speaks in his turn for counterrevolution.

The point is obvious: a certain resentment, or anxiety about Eliot's relation to a national tradition, was felt and expressed both in America and England. It was the more potent when, as with most of the writers I have mentioned, it was informed by a real knowledge of poetry and a willingness to admit Eliot's remarkable gifts.

Looking at the Eliot of the 1920s, we see a youngish poet, who had been exiled from Boston in St. Louis, from St. Louis in Boston, from America in London, and from Europe in England. He has assumed the tone and the manners of an English literary establishment. However, he edits for the English a journal expressly dedicated to propagating the thought of Europe. Soon, on a platform in Charlottesville, Virginia, he is expressing (though he had hardly ever visited the South) his sympathy with Southern Agrarianism, a doctrine to which one supposes New England as well as old England to have been indifferent or unsympathetic. In the same series of lectures he also accused some of his most illustrious contemporaries, including writers who were friends of his and even shared many of his convictions, of what he described as "heresy"—deviation or exile from a central tradition. For he was by now a Catholic, though an Anglo-Catholic, one foot in the universal, one in the regional—a member of the established church and subscriber to a state religion, but dedicated to a universal church; in religion as in politics a European—wearing a red tie for Charles, the single saint of the Anglo-Catholics, and warmly approving of the Roman Catholicism of the atheist Charles Maurras, *classique, catholique, monarchiste,* disowned by the Vatican but not by Eliot, who managed thus to be an Anglican yet *plus catholique que le pape*. Bernard Bergonzi even suggests that the papal condemnation of *Action française* may have been responsible for Eliot's decision not to enter the Roman Catholic church.[12] He not only borrowed Maurras' credal formula but dedicated his book on Dante to this French anti-Semite, sponsor of the fascistic Camelots du Roi; the dedication gets what propriety it has from his having, years before, called Maurras the "Virgil who leads [some disciples] to the temple gate." He found in Maurrasian doctrine, sometimes admittedly fascistic, the antidote to both Communism and Fascism. Yet the evidence suggests that even the few Englishmen who knew anything about Maurras and the even fewer who read *Action française* regarded his ideas as "too alien to British tradition and too foreign to Britain's twentieth-century interests to be regarded as more than curiosities."[13]

I have been trying to establish that Eliot is not really to be thought of as an exile from this place or that, but rather as one who lived in a condition of permanent exile. We can add, if we wish, that in the years between the wars, as editor of a journal of exiguous circulation, held in an unusual posture by its dual loyalties, he was, despite his growing celebrity, in a condition of increasing literary and political exile. And without straining the argument we can say further that in his personal life he was an exile from marriage. It is evident, too, that in many of his personal relationships he was constrained to avoid the degree of intimacy that might require him to confide in, or simply to feel easy with and approachable by, another person. Lyndall Gordon tells us repeatedly of the rhythm by which he would seem to come close to friends or possible lovers and then back off, without explanation and perhaps inexplicably rejecting them, as if isolation or aloneness were something he was compelled to choose.

But we need not dwell on anecdote or gossip, for the real need is to explain that taste for or choice of exile, and perhaps to ask why, for all its apparent eccentricity, Eliot's attitude proved so powerful, and so capable of resisting a well-provided opposition. His is a poetry of exile, even of what Mary, in an early draft of *The Family Reunion,* called "perpetual exile."[14] This is most obvious in *Ash Wednesday,* where exile has to be accepted with patience as the human condition, and in order that the prayer "Salve regina" may be prayed: "And after this our exile . . ." The spiritual exile, the separation, requires that "I renounce the blessèd face / And renounce the voice / Because I cannot hope to turn again . . ." The poem of Cavalcanti he echoes here, *Perch'io non spero di tornare mai,* is a poem of exile, and *tornare* really means not "turn" but "return."

Cavalcanti is far from being the only exile whose voice is heard in Eliot's poetry. We may think of Joyce, whom Eliot so much admired, if not for the right reasons, as some say, then for reasons of his own work; of Baudelaire, a spiritual hero; of Henry James, in some ways closest to himself, who wrote in "The Jolly Corner" a story of American exile and return that meant a lot to Eliot; Harry mentions it in that partly confessional play, *The Family Reunion*. And we must not forget Dante at Verona, or the wounded Tristan; or Beckett, who returned from exile to meet his death; or the voice in *The Waste Land* of one who weeps, like Israel in exile, by the waters of Leman; or Coriolanus, whose two most celebrated remarks are "There is a world elsewhere" and "I banish you."

It is easy to imagine Eliot, in certain moods, making both of these remarks on his own account. The world elsewhere was the remembered or imagined world of the past. The world of the present was a world of separation, heresy—an experiment in godlessness, a civilization that the saint and the intelligent man must banish, a time that must be redeemed. From such a deathly world one might seek relief in a mutual banishment; or in a vision, fantasy or memory, of a world elsewhere. But the relief is momentary; exile is to be accepted and the other, the habitable world of memory, renounced. Renounced are "the lost sea voices" and the voices of the children, "containing laughter," belonging to "our *first* world"; the "blessèd face" is "this face, this life / Living in a world of time beyond us," of "Marina," or, in darker mood, the "face still forming" of the familiar compound ghost of "Little Gidding." All are perceived in separation; the lady to whom one prays "Suffer me not to be separated" is "spirit of the river, spirit of the sea," the two spirits, in whatever mood, which return in "The Dry Salvages" as the separating Mississippi and the margin of the ocean at Cape Ann.

Exile, becoming the dominant trait of a personality, may take many forms. There is a metaphysical exile, the separation described in the famous quotation from Bradley at line 412 of *The Waste Land,* where it is given more concrete expression in the reference to Dante's Ugolino; "I have heard the key / Turn in the door." There is the exile from eternity, to be spent in the desert of time. Time must be redeemed—either by sitting still, or by right action. But the full redemption of time comes from elsewhere, at "the intersection of the timeless / with time"—of which that "moment in and out of time," which is all that we who are not saints can expect to experience, is, we are told in "The Dry Salvages," only a hint or guess. Such moments may occur in "England and nowhere, / Never and always"—the place and the moment always stand not only for themselves but for their absence. Wherever you are in time or space, the condition is exile: "and where you are is where you are not." You are merely a transient, a tenant, as you "stiffen in a rented house." "One is still alone / In an overcrowded desert, jostled by ghosts," says Harry in *The Family Reunion,* speaking as if for Eliot himself, walking in the city where, as in the city of Baudelaire, the specter in full daylight accosts the passerby.

And it is the city that must give us our final clue to the nature of Eliot's exile. In finding it we find also a reason for calling Eliot "the last classic," as I do in the title of this essay. I have given some rather humdrum reasons for Eliot's fascination with cities: with St. Louis, whose inhabitants forget their river, forget the brown god, now "only a problem confronting the builder of bridges," though "his rhythm was present in the nursery bedroom"; with Boston, where the slums of Roxbury are ignored by Aunt Nancy Ellicott, and by all who, like Cousin Harriet, read *The Boston Evening Transcript,* though not by the poet of "Preludes"; with Paris, and the Montparnasse of Bubu; with the Venice of Burbank; with London, "Unreal City, / Under the brown fog of a winter dawn," where each man fixes his eyes before his feet, where Mr. Eugenides makes his immodest proposal, and where with the fishmen, lounging at Billingsgate in the shadow of the splendor of St. Magnus Martyr, one may hear "the pleasant whining of a mandoline," some sort of exile's consolation. This city, and the other unreal cities, mime the *urbs aeterna,* but are also versions of the apocalyptic city:

> Falling towers
>
> Jerusalem Athens Alexandria
>
> Vienna London
>
> Unreal

Each is a place where people real or unreal make their homes, yet each is a place of exile, of isolation; each its own desert, its own lack.

The ideas of the city and of the province are inseparable, and while provinciality is clearly a version of exile, that condition can also exist in the city, just as traces, imitations, relics, parodies of metropolitan culture are to be found in the province. Within the *limes* or boundaries of empire there will be simulacra of Rome that are not Rome, that do not speak its language or even a derivative language. They are associated with the Ovidian *tristia* as well as the Virgilian *imperium*. Hugh Kenner, in a fine essay on the manuscripts, has stressed the Virgilian elements in *The Waste Land,* saying that Eliot, impressed by Joyce's use of Homer, "may well have had in mind at one time a kind of modern *Aeneid*."[15] And it has been pointed out that the Virgil of the early poem is not quite the figure represented in Eliot's later essays about him, with their emphasis on his relation to Dante and the Christian world. Aeneas was an exile, and he never did found a city. The cities in which we see him, Troy and Carthage, are cities famous not for the manner of their foundation but for the completeness of their destruction, just as those catalogued in Eliot's poem have been or will be; so that Augustan Rome is an example not solely of a glory to which other capitals may aspire, or with which their ignominy may be contrasted, but also of the apocalyptic terrors Virgil associates with the eternal city and its empire.[16]

It may be that after his conversion Eliot read Virgil by the light of Dante, and in a long tradition of interpretation which included the *pax Augusta* and the idea of Christian Empire. He developed his rich and complicated idea of the classic on this basis; he settled for a vernacular and provincial Catholicism (the Reformation, too, was a sort of exile) as the world had settled for vernacular versions of the classic.[17] But in so doing he did not forget the metropolitan terrors, nor that what the province took from the metropolis—images of the center entertained at the periphery, pride in partaking of the values of the *urbs antiqua,* and the classic authority—it repaid with the inescapable idea of exile; the more so now that the modern metropolis was itself deviant from the central image of Rome, and so itself an exile.

The sense of perpetual exile, doubtless in its origin very personal, is thus associated with a religion and with a theory of history and culture; and we can see that the St. Louis and Boston, the Paris and London of the poetry are logically connected with the idea of the classic, and of the more or less perpetual exile of literature from the classic. It would be hard to discover a poet or critic now living who shared these views, or held to any that even slightly resembled them; they are more likely to say to the classic "I banish you." And that is why we may think of Eliot as the last classic, at any rate until some new civilization should construct its own idea of the classic, and its own canon.

So here we confront yet another form of exile. Eliot was conscious of it, so often meditating the classic, so suspicious of its apparent opposite, the romantic, with which he nevertheless had such interesting relations. The more extreme modernisms were programmatically anticlassical, and Eliot knew and was affected by them. Later varieties assumed some connection between classicism and oppressive political prescription, in short, between classical and fascist order. With many aspects of these modernisms, though of course not with all, the early Eliot had a wary sympathy; they coexisted with a classicism he would not abandon, however its political implications might be deplored. The times seemed to insist on so many conflicting tendencies: the reconstruction of the past, the destruction of the past; the modernism of Dada that destroyed, or of Surrealism, associated with psychoanalysis, with what Hulme called "spilt religion," and a classicism that deplored everything that had happened in the world since the Renaissance. Both were of the city, the city as the political emblem of civility and the classic, but also the *immonde cité* of Baudelaire; a spiritual desert, yet the symbol of the *urbs aeterna.* In consciously holding together, as *metoikos,* these diverse ideas of an ideal eternity and a decadence in time, Eliot was unique among modern poets—and again an outsider, an exile from easy opinion, banished and banishing, honored and deplored.

To speak in this way of the so-much-honored poet as a Coriolanus may seem too high-flown, or excused as centennial rhetoric. One may think that William Carlos Williams was quite right to complain about the academics, who did and are doing so much to procure and preserve that honor. Given the nature of the efforts of Eliot and the other early modernists, it was in any case inevitable that they should fall into the hands of people with leisure to expound them—Joyce said he would keep the professors busy for years, and indeed the correspondence of the literary journals is currently proving, as if proof were needed, that he has done so; nor were the problems set by the others much less exacting. Some were opposed to conventional pedagogy and scholarship—Pound, for instance; Eliot had some respect for it, or pretended he had, when discoursing in that august *TLS* manner he so carefully acquired. But they also had very large educational aims. They wanted, consciously or not, to produce encyclopedias for the fallen modern world. The result might be ironic; a heap of comic *disjecta,* like *Bouvard et Pécuchet,* the preparation of which cost Flaubert years and years of severe but distasteful reading. Or it might be the *Cantos,* a disordered poem about the causes of disorder, of the world's usurious exile from justice; or Musil's strictly interminable study in the corruption of empire, or Eliot's fragments and ruins and shadows of the empire laid up in heaven. These are the encyclopedias of exile, the great and hopeless attempts to get a world into a book, not a world or a book like Dante's, to be bound up in one volume of exactly one hundred cantos, but a world of heresies and exile, as seen by a privileged and tormented minority and got into books of strange fragmentary shapes, dreams of an order hardly to be apprehended. To be avant-garde, to be elite (and Eliot very strongly believed in elites) is to be in opposition to whatever simply *is,* whether you are exiled in Paris or London, Rapallo or Trieste.

It is moreover to confront the corrupt world with messages, mostly about its corruption, which it will not, of its own will, even try to decipher. Yet some vestige of an old civility will ensure that the exiles or their shades are again welcomed into this actual world, the world they banished, with its collapsing imperial cities, its suburban provinces. They return to a world where the idea of the classic is dying or has died, to be celebrated only in doctoral theses and the books of professors. They come as if from classic center to vulgar periphery, no more than shades, still exiles, and still, even for their spectral existence and the tenuous survival of their dreams of order, dependent on the professors they openly or secretly laughed at. We provincials offer our civil respect to a great metropolitan classic, whom we exile and by whom we were ourselves banished.

But disparate, banished ideas can be held together—about past and present and exiles—and we should give our exile the last word, written when, an Englishman of many years standing, he thought about his American origins, which as time went on he did more and more. Perhaps, because one spirit animates the whole, that past was not lost but transformed, and the absent is somehow made present, the exile momentarily at home in his memory, or rather, in his poem:

See, now they vanish
The places and the faces, with the self which, as it could,
loved them,
To become renewed, transfigured, in another pattern.

CHAPTER 5

# *William Empson*

## THE CRITIC AS GENIUS

William Empson died in 1984, and his admirers on either side of idolatry have been glad to learn that a considerable body of his work survived for posthumous publication. Empson had strong views on the purposes of literary criticism, disagreed with almost all the assumptions of his contemporaries, and said so in a unique tone of genial asperity, so that *Argufying,*[1] the big collection of his shorter pieces, is notable not only as the record of a rare critical intelligence but also for the variety of Empson's targets and his rapid rate of fire. Often wild but never dull, he wrote much more of value than his published books contain, and all the posthumous collections, including the two I here discuss, are accordingly more than merely welcome extras. Over the years it has often been said that the premature end of his career as a poet was a big price to pay for the rest of the work, splendid though it is; so particular interest attaches to *The Royal Beasts,*[2] a remnant, though of substantive importance, of the more "creative" early years.

The volume contains "The Royal Beasts," an unfinished story, together with a short play, a ballet scenario, a batch of early poems, and a valuable seventy-page introduction and useful notes by John Haffenden, who has arranged the material in roughly chronological order. The play or melodrama, *Three Stories,* was written when the poet was twenty, and performed, with him in the cast, by the Cambridge Amateur Dramatic Company (ADC). Long supposed to have been lost as Empson pursued his career in the East, it somehow turned up, and is certainly worth having. The poems mostly belong to the late 1920s. Some appeared in Cambridge magazines but were excluded from the first collection of 1935. A dozen had never appeared in print before the publication of *The Royal Beasts*. The novel was written in China in the immediately prewar years; the ballet belongs to 1942, when Empson was working for the BBC and writing propaganda for Chinese consumption.

Between Cambridge and the BBC he had published *Seven Types of Ambiguity* (1930), *Poems* and *Some Versions of Pastoral* (both from 1935), and a second volume of verse, *The Gathering Storm* (1940). He also wrote many reviews and—as we learn from Haffenden's Introduction to *The Royal Beasts*—a book on the faces of the Buddha, obviously the product of intense research and imaginative energy, but totally lost.[3] He had been a professor in Japan from 1931 to 1934, and in 1937 joined the faculty of Peking National University in Hunan, where the northern universities had retreated before the Japanese advance. These were the years when he taught English literature without the aid of books, at the same time getting on with his writing. *The Royal Beasts* has a whole library behind it, but he must have carried it in his head. (It is said that he wrote down the text of *Othello* from memory; his version would be highly interesting, but unfortunately it did not survive.) He was the only non-Chinese around, and obviously enjoyed the whole dangerous and uncomfortable enterprise. He returned to England when the European war began, but went back to China afterwards, coming home finally in 1952. By that time he was already a legendary figure, partly because of the precocious *Seven Types* but also for the poems, which enjoyed a revival of attention around 1950. *The Structure of Complex Words* had come out in 1951, *The Collected Poems* in 1955. Now a professor at Sheffield University (he had wanted to work in Yorkshire), he published *Milton's God* in 1961.

During his years at Sheffield, and afterwards, Empson entered with spirit into the life of the literature professor and took part with idiosyncratic vehemence in the professional controversies of the day. But although he didn't mind being a prof, there was an element of suspicion or mistrust in his dealings with other profs. He wished they could all be different and often suspected them of holding detestable and smug views on Intention or God. In his critical writings one sees again and again that he is trying to deal justly with these contemporaries, but sooner or later exasperation at their dullness takes over. I think he was very conscious of the breadth and variety of his own experience and so thought us all narrow and tame, venturing our pathetic little audacities from positions of bourgeois security. "It is not human to feel safely placed" is a line that expresses a deep conviction.

Not being fully human, the professors frequently missed the simple meaning of the great literature they were supposed to know about. What they admired in Empson was his extraordinary subtlety, his sometimes shocking novelties: but although he was properly proud of such powers, I think he came to set even more store by his access to quite simple truths about literature and life that were being overlooked. There is a famous page about Gray's "Elegy" at the beginning of *Some Versions of Pastoral*[4] which shows how the cleverness and the simplicity worked together. Commenting on the stanza beginning "Full many a gem of purest ray serene . . ." he points out that it means eighteenth-century England had no *carrière ouverte aux talents*.

> This is stated as pathetic, but the reader is put into a mood in which one would not try to alter it . . . By comparing the social arrangement to Nature, he makes it seem inevitable, which it was not, and gives it a dignity which was undeserved. Furthermore, a gem does not mind being in a cave and a flower prefers not to be picked; we feel that the man is like the flower, as short-lived, natural and valuable, and this tricks us into feeling that he is better off without opportunities. The sexual suggestion of *blush* brings in the Christian idea that virginity is good in itself, so that any renunciation is good. (*SVP*, p. 3)

And so it goes on, one of the texts that taught a generation to read well and feel good about it. Here we feel we are really seeing through Gray; his poem has a "massive calm," but it doesn't take a Communist to see that it is a political cheat; "the 'bourgeois' themselves do not like literature to have too much 'bourgeois ideology.'" Splendid: but it is the sentence beginning the next paragraph that gives the Empsonian surprise: "And yet what is said is one of the permanent truths; it is only in degree that any improvement of society could prevent wastage of human powers; the waste even in a fortunate life, the isolation even of a life rich in intimacy, cannot but be felt deeply, and is the central feeling of tragedy" (*SVP*, p. 4). One hears rather little about permanent truths in modern criticism; to Empson it was obvious that they existed and that it was dishonorable (another word he didn't mind using) to "wince away" from them.

Watching everybody wincing away made him more and more peppery and also, on occasion, less reasonable. He was the cavalier and the wincers mean-minded puritans. The authors he venerated he went on listening to very carefully, but there was a sort of boisterous uncharitableness in his treatment of their expositors. He was not an easy man to argue with; he liked to say he was only the *animal méchant,* and it is true that he had to put up with some fairly ferocious attacks in his time: but there was a touch of Prince Rupert also, a feeling that *à outrance* was the only way to fight. Of course a man can't go on charging all the time, and what one remembers mostly is a morose geniality of manner, an amiability isolated and wary. But above all one thinks of him with affection and deep respect, the one genius that the modern explosion in the critical population has produced. So it seems, at any rate, to my generation. Recently Christopher Norris has been meditating, with his usual tact, the resemblances and differences between the Empson of *The Structure of Complex Words* and the Paul de Man of *Allegories of Reading*—a sign, perhaps, that the most neglected (and most theoretical) of Empson's books will have something to say even to the young, who may suppose that really serious rhetorical analysis only got going in the late sixties.

However, *The Royal Beasts* is not criticism, though it shows the intellectual force of the critical books of the thirties, and sometimes reminds us of them. It is striking, for instance, that the play *Three Stories* should, at such an early date, show Empson experimenting with elaborate double plots. The main plot is about a young man who serves as secretary to an old novelist, and as lover to the old man's young wife. There is some good rather "brittle" dialogue, some bright talk about sexual morality; and the old man gets shot for patronizing the young one. In between the two halves of that plot there occurs an apparently unrelated scene about a man named Smith, who is the captive of Dracula. Some of this scene is written in that free-associative style Empson used in his first published poem, "Poem about a ball in the 19th century," and in another printed in *The Royal Beasts,* called "Address to a Tennis Player"; the notes to the poems express some doubt about the virtues of this manner, and they seem justified, but he kept the first poem in the *Collected Poems* and perhaps rightly, for some of his best works ("It is this deep blankness is the real thing strange . . .") have put the half-awake, entranced style to better use.

The formal experiment in *Three Stories* is not just the Dracula sandwich: as the title says, there are three stories. The other is a framing romance, a mythical induction and epilogue in heroic couplets: in this story the wife is in chains, the young man comes with a sword to slay the dragon; he does so and they live happily afterwards, as they don't in the verismo version. It is admittedly a curious affair, properly admired in the Cambridge of its day. Haffenden quotes the *Granta* review, which smartly praises the author for achieving "an almost complete mastery of his Oedipus complex" and using it "for very intelligent purposes . . . If we interpreted it rightly, it amounted to something like this: that the ethical problems of life differ from the scientific problems only if one conceives them romantically, and even then, the apparent romanticism achieved, they become scientific again." Much later, Empson told Martin Dodsworth that the structural idea had been "to take a story and interpose a scene of apparently total irrelevance in the middle":[5] we can now confirm the accuracy of that recollection as well as offering belated congratulations to the *Granta* reviewer.

In the chatter about sex the name of A. M. Ludovici is mentioned, a writer now remembered, if at all, for having infuriated T. E. Hulme by writing a little book on Nietzsche ("Mr. Ludovici, writing on Nietzsche, might be compared to a child of four in a theatre watching a tragedy based on adultery . . . The most appropriate way of dealing with him would be a little personal violence")[6] and patronizing Epstein. Ludovici was also a feminist. Haffenden provides an interesting note from a diary Empson kept in 1926 which says that despite "the grave national crisis" (the General Strike) what he wants to talk about is Ludovici and his creed of Heterosexual Healthiness. Against this doctrine the young poet argues that natural man really wants only a honeymoon; he will impregnate a woman and then "swing back to the homosexual . . . A purely heterosexual man is dangerously uncivilised." We shall see the relevance of this observation to *The Royal Beasts*. The note goes on to remark that Freud had shown how "to make sure of the family . . . we took sex aside and turned it Oedipose." One can see that Empson at twenty had a lot going for him, and there is abundant testimony to the fame he enjoyed in what he called, after they kicked him out, "that strange cackling little town."

This collection includes more of the poems that contributed to his early reputation. He remarked in a letter to Ian Parsons, who was to publish his first books, that "there is a rather portentous air about compact poems without notes, like a seduction without conversation," and of course he wrote notes fairly freely, though claiming to believe that what made them necessary was weakness in the poems. We could certainly use some notes to these unpublished poems. There is a pretty piece he wrote at thirteen and a rueful one about being sent down from Cambridge. "Letter vi" is instantly attractive, an epithalamion:

> Never to be thrust on your unwilling notice
> Still less before the public, annotated.

Yet here it is, though unannotated. There is as usual a lot of astronomical troping. "Insomnia" feels like a good poem; it is one of those where for a while you congratulate yourself on hanging on to the sense, but then fall off, or look for notes.

There is one theme which often appears with variations: a move into unintelligibly vast space, or downwards in a cave, or in a labyrinth:

> Simply we do not know what are the turnings
> Expound our poising of obscure desires,
> What Minotaur in irritable matched burnings
> Yearns and shall gore her intricate my fires.

Haffenden has some useful remarks on the poems, not unlike those of the *Granta* reviewer on the play: they try to solve the contradictions between the world of science and the feeling of being human; in the circumstances of the late twenties it seemed the way to do this was to "build . . . with slow labour and a due regard for fame, a private cosmos," as Empson put it. He always believed the main reason for writing poems was to be rid of psychological tension, though there was a social obligation to be intelligible: so it is not surprising that the poems are so tormented, and look down long vistas of possibility, moving from one metaphor to another in an attempt to express a meaning that cannot be literal. Yet Empson always insisted that there was nothing in the poem for you if you couldn't follow the argument; and if his "audience within himself" couldn't, the poem failed in its therapeutic function, which was to save the poet's sanity. All this is very clearly stated in Empson's interview with Christopher Ricks in *The Review* (June 1963). Presumably the audience, within and without, needs to get some notion of how it felt to have to write the poem, and then to write it. This is a clue to much that goes on in the criticism; it explains Empson's lengthy campaign against W. K. Wimsatt, the aesthetician of the New Criticism, and it also explains why American critics, who tend to class Empson as a New Critic, are sometimes unable to believe that he wasn't "anti-intentionalist." In fact, he is the most convinced of intentionalists, and although he does a certain amount of unfair sneering at his opponents, his most ravishing, as well as his most wrong-headed, interpretations are always meant to be about what happened in a poet's head. Later on I shall give some instances I myself think important or weird.

The strangest of these works is the ballet scenario, "The Elephant and the Birds," with Empson's comments on it and some interesting ancillary material supplied by Haffenden. Empson worked on it in 1942, when he was at the BBC, and seems to have gone on thinking about it for some time after that. The ballet combines two quite different stories, the Greek myth of Philomel and Procne and an Indian legend about the Buddha's incarnation as an elephant. As Haffenden says, the idea was to ask a double-plot riddle: what does the tale of rape and cannibalism in Thrace have in common with the Buddha's self-sacrifice in his animal incarnation?

Empson knew a lot about Buddhism, which he saw as representing a stage of religious development from which Christianity, with its equation of love with torture, was a regression. Moreover he had argued, in his lost book *Asymmetry in Buddha Faces,* that by giving each of the Buddha's profiles a separate expression the sculptors produced a sort of icon of unity in dissimilarity, and of the way in which "one arrives at two ideas of dealing with things which both work and are needed, but which entirely contradict one another," as he remarked in a review of 1928. He was also interested in the Gandhara sculpture and the argument as to whether or in what degree the eastward penetration of Alexander gave a Greek form to images of the Buddha. The ballet has something to do with holding East and West in a single thought.

Empson worked it out in great detail, not only the conduct of the narratives but the stage settings and music. He seems to have got Leslie Hurry—a stage designer associated with the Sadler's Wells Ballet—to show interest, and sent a copy to John Hayward for comment. Hayward was used to this kind of request: he advised Eliot on his *Quartets,* especially "Little Gidding" and a few years later Auden on the libretto of *The Rake's Progress;* and for somebody who professed no expert knowledge of ballet he acquitted himself rather well. It occurred to him that elephants were not very balletic; or, as he put it, there might be "some difficulty in finding adequate symbolism for the Elephants' weight, majesty and dignity." And he made a number of practical suggestions: though dumpy in real life, the nightingale need not appear so on stage; swallows should be accompanied by violins, and so forth. Empson's reply is in his familiar tone of cheerful insult: "My dearest Hayward, I was much shocked by your kind letter . . . Your views on my little ballet show I think the appalling corruption into which European ideas about ballet have fallen." He had seen Japanese dancing in the Noh plays, and the Cambodian *asparas* at Angkor, and much preferred them to occidental galumphing.[7]

One may ask why he should have spent so much energy on this recondite project when he knew that in the unlikely event of the ballet ever being danced it could only be danced absurdly. However, he did think the European ballet—he mentions *Swan Lake* and *The Firebird*—had the power of restoring mystery to already known legends; and he wanted somehow to bring that kind of thing into contact with Eastern legend and Eastern dance, as in the double profiles of the Buddha. At this distance of time it may seem that it was pretty fantastic to hope for the realization of such a project in the dreary middle of the war: yet the old Sadler's Wells Ballet was not unadventurous and it might just have come off, however disappointingly. In any case, it enlarges one's idea of the man to have a sight of this rather weird enterprise.

We learn even more, I think, from "The Royal Beasts." It is a philosophical fable of great ingenuity and much charm, though it is easy to see why it was never finished. Empson wrote what there is of it on a Chinese mountain, without the aid of books, and although he presumably did some reading for it before leaving England (Zuckerman on apes, at least), it is remarkable how, under such conditions, he disposed of so much considered information.

Swift invented reasonable horses to show what a rational animal would be like. Empson invents an animal distinct from man and the higher apes, which nevertheless has strong affinities with man: for instance, it uses language. It is fur-covered, with a long tail and lemur-like eyes. But probably the most important difference is that the Wurroos have a breeding season. The questions that come up when a representative Wurroo (called Wuzzoo) is brought together with a British colonial administrator are many and profound. Formerly the Wurroos had kept to themselves, beating and expelling intruders: but a prospector finds gold in their territory. Wuzzoo brings some; his people don't want it, but they do want protection from the evils that could follow its discovery. Not wishing to be treated like the native human populations, they ask to be regarded as beasts belonging to the King, feeling sure that he treats his animals better than his human subjects. So the immediate question, are they men or not? acquires some political urgency.

This is where their breeding season becomes important. Haffenden quotes a long unposted letter to Zuckerman in which Empson says that his Wurroos "have become rational without the Freudian machinery." A month of orgiastic copulation, with special rules, special music, obscene drawings, and so on, and then back to sexless fur-picking, which goes on for the rest of the year. Wuzzoo volunteers the information that he once had the same female for three seasons, but says this was thought odd. One sees here a resemblance to the ideal arrangements suggested in the younger Empson's notes on Ludovici, but the main point is that the family is an arrangement unknown to the Wurroos, who therefore are not Oedipal, and need a civilization that can be established without the creative energies born of sexual repression.

George Bickersteth, Empson's colonial administrator, is an intelligent human and sexually quite ordinary; he gives up a native mistress and brings out a wife from a rectory. She is attracted to Wuzzoo, whom she teaches English, and he has to explain what is possible between them and what not. This helps to show that the Wurroos are both very similar and very different from humans; and there are other related boundary problems, such as the visitor's sleeping place (indoors, or outside with the dogs?), and, in the megapolitical realm, jurisdiction over territories with vague frontiers controlled by obscure treaties. Empson is surprisingly calm on the colonial question, if one thinks of the sort of thing the Left Book Club was saying about it at the time: his interest is more abstract; he is trying to think about Man.

Wuzzoo is friendly but knows he is not a man and, as he

mildly tells Bickersteth, he thinks very badly of men. But the administrator has to warn him of the possibly severe consequences of not being human, such as being hunted for one's fur. Empson mentions more than once the decision of the Church in the matter of the natives of Tierra del Fuego: it proclaimed them human. And here he sets up a big court scene in which counsel argues the case of the Wurroos. This starts brilliantly with a plea for their non-humanity, very legal and scientific: humans cannot copulate with Wurroos, as experiment had shown, and any further attempts along that line would be liable to the charge of bestiality. Moreover, blood transfusions between men and Wurroos fail. Counsel further argues that the case is unprecedented, since previous history records no instance of a species to be inserted in the space between animal and man. (This is untrue, as *homo selvaticus* filled this space, though it is true that, like Caliban, he could copulate with humans and wanted very much to do so; nor did he have a breeding season.) The legal arguments in favor of the humanity of the Wurroos seem much weaker, and it is with the philosophical and practical issues arising from their rational non-humanity that Empson is concerned. Were they capable of redemption? Should missionaries be sent? The Archbishop of Canterbury contributes a good speech. The Buddhists make a strong claim that in their religion the Blessed One is open to the entire animal kingdom. Wuzzoo himself thinks Christianity fine for men, and also likely to be more creative, because more repressive, than Buddhism. But the main theological problem raised is one that had a permanent interest for Empson. The Archbishop remarks that if we got to Mars and found it inhabited, we should certainly want to convert the natives. Empson is thinking, not for the first time, about the plurality of worlds, and the need for multiple redemptions. Was Christ to be crucified all over the universe? If it became necessary, would he be recrucified here? Granted this sacrificial versatility, could he even appear under many guises, so that one might think of a particular person (Donne's Elizabeth Drury, for example) as Christ?

Although Empson has a lot of fun inventing a system of

music appropriate to a "sexless" species, and imagining the Wuzzoo attitude to babies ("Do your women *like* having to look after these things? Of course they are only raving lunatics for a year or so, but then they only get on to nagging and whining. Is that why women have to be kept under, because otherwise they wouldn't let you breed the things at all?"), and although the whole performance is notably high-spirited, this matter of plural worlds and redemptions was a serious one. Empson pondered it often: so, as it happens, did C. S. Lewis around the same time, but the emphasis was different. Perhaps Empson's interest in the theological implications of Bruno's plurality of worlds (which he sees as very complex) really stems from his almost obsessive interest in Donne, whom he regarded as the poet of the New Philosophy as it was circulating around 1600, the year of Bruno's execution, and for a while after that. In fact, I think, the religious issue and the poetry of Donne were deeply involved with each other in Empson's head, and the effects of the involvement are odd and important. "In the twenties, when my eyes were opening, it was usual for critics to consider that Donne in his earlier poetry held broad and enlightened views on church and state, that he was influenced by the recent great scientific discoveries, and that he used the theme of freedom in love partly as a vehicle for those ideas . . . I was imitating this Donne, the poet as so conceived, in my verse at the time with love and wonder, and I have never in later years come across any good reason for the universal change of opinion about him at the start of the Thirties."[8]

The inhabited planet stood for a place where lovers could be free, independent, in a world of their own. Identifying so profoundly with Donne (so that he was sure he knew what had been going on in the young poet's mind), Empson had a deep quarrel with others who could not share this view, a quarrel which developed alongside his quarrel with the supreme torturer who required Satisfaction from his Son in all the worlds that otherwise stood for human and poetic freedom.

Though it may take a bourgeois professor to say so, Empson was wrong about Donne and the New Philosophy. Donne knew about Copernicus and made jokes about Kepler and Tycho Brahe and Galileo, but he habitually thought about the world in pre-Copernican terms, and treated the New Philosophy as further evidence that all human knowledge was extremely fallible, a point sufficiently proved by the failure of the old philosophy and of all human philosophies; only in heaven will you see things "despoyl'd of fallacies." But Empson knew a lot about the New Philosophy, so in an odd way he assumed that Donne must regularly have put it into his poetry, or his poetry would not be as like Empson's as the latter thought. Others thought so, too, including Dr. Leavis. And yet it is not true. The mere difficulty of following the arguments of Donne's poems (which in any case did not stem from his frequent use of new scientific ideas) has steadily diminished since the Grierson edition of 1912 did so much to purge the text and make the allusions available: but nothing can really make Empson's poems easier because they use metaphor quite differently.

For example: Donne's "Nocturnal upon St. Lucy's Day" is certainly a difficult poem, but if you know, or get up, the elements of alchemy and a bit of quite antique cosmology you can hold on to the argument; that is not, of course, all you need to do, but it is a prerequisite to the rest. The following lines, which come at the beginning of a poem called "New World Bistres," seem to me quite different:

> The darkest is near dawn, we are almost butter.
> The churning is fixed now; we have 'gone to sleep'
> In body, and become a living pat;
> It is then that the arm churning it aches most
> And dares least pause against the ceaseless churning.
> I am sure he will soon stumble upon the gift,
> Maypole his membranes, Ciro be his eyes,
> A secret order, assumptive distillation;
> Fitting together it will be won and seem nothing,
> Mild artifact, false pearl, corpse margarine.

Here one can get most of the jokes and allusions, even the general run of the thing: but not, so far as I can see, the unbroken thread of argument. Even the title is baffling, and becomes even more so if you look up "bistre" in the *Oxford English Dictionary*, as the poet is likely to have done. To put it coarsely, he was imitating a Donne of his own imagining.

However, Empson was quite unwilling to budge on such points, and once showed me a copy of the *Kenyon Review* containing the long essay "Donne the Space Man" with copious annotations and additions strengthening his position, and so striking at those who by doubting it dishonored Donne. At the time of Donne's quatercentenary in 1972 he and I found ourselves trying to collaborate on a stage piece for the Mermaid Theatre. I can no longer remember how Bernard Miles came up with this very bad idea, or why we both agreed to try it. I had known Empson a bit since his return from China—we had lunch and sometimes met as neighbors in Hampstead—but there was an element of unease in the relationship, which I think he accounted for by including me in a blacklist of neo-Christians, a charge difficult to deny, since one's protests could be thought to be evasions or distorted admissions. There was trouble from the start, since Empson wanted it made perfectly clear that in "The Good Morrow" the man and woman had been making love on the planet Venus, a reading he characterized as belonging to an older and more reliable school of thought about Donne: by wincing away from this view I was meanly trying to make the poet less interesting. We had the devil of a time trying to get something together that would work, and then he had to go to Canada before the show came on, adjuring me not to meddle with his share of the script. Two or three days before the first performance the actor playing Donne—Alan Dobie—walked off; he had done a lot of work but was perhaps sickened by certain contradictions in the script. The piece was hardly a success, and I am glad to think the Empson scholars are unlikely to trace *that* manuscript. The point is that the preservation of his lifelong view of Donne was really self-preservation; he reacted like a wicked animal if anybody seemed to disparage his scientist-poet.

The measure of this virtuous *méchanceté* can be got from the ferocity with which he attacked Helen Gardner's edition and, almost at the end of his life, John Carey's critical biography. According to Empson's review,[9] Carey's book says "no one need bother any more about Donne," and the tone is fiercely contemptuous; the main argument is about the Elegy "To his Mistress Going to Bed," and especially the line "Here is no penance, much less innocence," or "There is no penance due to innocence." The second of these is the reading of the first edition, held up on moral grounds till 1669; the former is the reading of some good manuscripts. The choice of reading does make a difference to the sense of the whole poem. Empson is certain that the "due to" reading is the right one, and he gives reasons for this, though the main reason is that he wants a young poet to be saying, with the utmost cleverness of course, that this sexual encounter is innocent in itself. Carey's version of what was going on in the poem (and many are possible) required him to adopt the other reading, and Empson thought that reading exceedingly base. What is extraordinary is the combative rancor of Empson's comments. Helen Gardner joined in to say, quite reasonably, that the 1669 version means: "Why wear this last white garment? It symbolises penitence or virginity, and neither is appropriate." Empson's reply is that her reading is textually "impossible." When another correspondent points out that in the course of his review he misread some of Carey's commemorative verse, Empson allows that the reading now proposed is right, but that the wrong one was there all the same, and the passage would have been heard "as an adroit piece of double talk." This is as defensive as he ever gets. When he castigates Carey's version of the poem as sadistic ("panting, bug-eyed Carey") he uses words like "malignant" and "ignorant";[10] I myself think Carey has got the poem wrong, but his version is no more fanciful than Empson's, in which the girl is an upper-class person who has left her husband drunk at some city banquet and hurried round to the poet's rooms. Claiming to know too much weakens the claim to knowing the important thing.

Empson's quarrel with the God of the Christians is also associated with his views on the young Donne, but got its fullest airing in *Milton's God*. There is, in that remarkable work, an excursus on Pascal which above almost anything else in this writer gives one an impression of the genuine moral power of his criticism. He is assaulting the professors who cannot see that Satan, in his initial address to the troops, speaks out of a conviction that his cause is just. He finds their attitude "confidently low-minded," and it reminds him of Pascal's Wager:

> He argued, while more or less inventing the mathematics of Probability, that, since the penalties for disbelief in Christianity are infinitely horrible and enduring, therefore, if there is any probability however tiny (but finite) that the assertions of the religion are true, a reasonable man will endure any degree of pain and shame on earth (since this is known beforehand to be finite) on the mere chance that the assertions are true. The answer is political, not mathematical; this argument makes Pascal the slave of any person, professing any doctrine, who has the impudence to tell him a sufficiently extravagant lie. A man ought therefore to be prepared to reject such a calculation.[11]

"If you win, you win everything," says Pascal; "if you lose, you lose nothing." Empson has many more subtle points to make, but it does warm the heart to hear this line of argument dismissed as simply dishonorable. He associates it with that "unpleasant moral collapse" which he thought had during his own lifetime struck "our literary mentors"—neo-Christians with "no sense of personal honour or of the public good."

You can see how a man who was willing to rough up Pascal, not to mention God, as dishonorable and rather low-class would not worry about calling "our literary mentors" disgusting, malignant, horrible, and so forth. Critics have to prove that they aren't the literary version of Evelyn Waugh's Hooper trespassing on Brideshead. The examination of their credentials came to occupy more of Empson's time than writing about poetry as such, and although the result can be entertaining and even heartwarming, there must surely be a sense of loss.

That is why the Shakespeare collection is not likely to be thought one of his major works. His fondness for a good row, and for working out difficult puzzles, give the book much interest, and the whole thing is manifestly a product of his great veneration for Shakespeare, so it is a pity there is so little about the poetry. He had come to think that much criticism was too fancy, took far too little notice of basic story and plot, character, theatrical conditions; he was in reaction against the anti-Bradleyanism of his Cambridge days, the time of L. C. Knights' *How many children had Lady Macbeth?,* as well as against the more highfalutin criticism that poured out in his later years, the product of academic market pressures or perhaps a corrupt neo-Christianity. People had stopped understanding what poets actually do; Empson would dogmatically explain this, dwelling on what seemed to others minor issues like the supposed marriage of Marvell to Mary Palmer or the way some manuscripts were filched.

The Shakespeare essays,[12] written over twenty-seven years (the latest, a review of Harold Brooks' edition of *A Midsummer Night's Dream,* appeared in the *London Review of Books* in October 1979), share these characteristics. The racy manner almost prevents one from questioning the confidence with which we are told Shakespeare or the Archbishop of Canterbury would or must have done this or that; or that in "The Rape of Lucrece" Shakespeare says nothing about the subsequent fall of the Roman monarchy because, as anybody who knows what it is to live under political censorship would be aware, he couldn't. Here, in the essay on the poems, I thought he was so busy making this sort of point against the Hooper-critics that he failed to register the Troy tapestry episode as a rich bit of double-plotting, finding it hard to excuse except as "a substitute for dangerous thoughts about royalty."

And those "would's" and "must's" change easily into "did's": "I think a visitor was left to wait in a room where a cabinet was unlocked . . . he saw at once that they would sell . . . Thumbing through the notebook, he . . ."[13] On "The Phoenix and Turtle" he is so involved in the mysterious story of how the compilation in which it figures was got together that he writes, on the poem itself, what must be the weakest of all his criticism. No wonder he wonders how Shakespeare went straight on from this to his great tragic period.

The fifty-page essay on Falstaff and the seventy-page essay on *Hamlet* are as much as anything a running commentary on John Dover Wilson, who is treated with as much respect as Empson ever offers, but gets a lot of ribbing as well. Their difference concerning Falstaff is, crudely, that Dover Wilson thought he must choose one of the two options that seemed to be on offer, whereas Empson, claiming the support of the first audience, saw that you had to take both: the audience would certainly be all for political order, good kingship and so on, and against Riot, but they would also be for Falstaff—"the first major joke by the English against their class system; he is a picture of how badly you can behave, and still get away with it, if you are a gentleman." This seems acceptable, but it is argued at length and in that tone of ferocious facetiousness which can sometimes be tedious. Sometimes he seems to want all the good tunes. First he turns down Dover Wilson's parallel between the deaths of Socrates and Falstaff, saying it could not have been intended; but on second thought he takes the parallel into his own argument and credits Wilson with an "eerie flash of imagination." However, there is no doubt that anybody who feels like writing about Falstaff should work through this piece.

Of *Hamlet* Empson, who certainly had a smack of Hamlet, rightly remarks that it "opened up a new territory to the human mind." Again he tries to receive it as the first audience might. Shakespeare was required to rewrite an old play for an audience which remembered it only as a joke, and would now ask questions they hadn't in their simpler days. The solution was to make the question of delay very conspicuous instead of pretending it didn't exist. "The only way to shut this hole is to make it big. I shall make Hamlet walk up to the audience and tell them, again and again, 'I don't know why I'm delaying any more than you do; the motivation of this play is just as blank to me as it is to you; but I can't help it.'"[14] This of course helps to explain the new self-conscious theatricality of the play. Empson goes into all the famous problems with great patience and vigor: the sheer length of the piece, the relation between the three texts, *Der Bestrafte Brudermord,* the complicity of the Queen, the odd placing of the soliloquies, especially "How all occasions" (which he says was only played when an encore seemed called for), and so on—a sort of *What happens in Hamlet* in miniature. Among the good things he says about Hamlet himself is this: "Hamlet never loses class, however mad. He keeps also a curious appeal for the lower classes in the audience as a satirist on the upper classes":[15] perhaps one of the ways in which one can say that he himself has a smack of Hamlet. It also seems characteristic that when he says he thinks the madness in Elizabethan drama, of which there is a lot, probably derives from Hamlet, he apologizes for producing irritating guesswork, though this conjecture has a much more solid basis than many that aren't called guesswork at all.

The commentary on Dover Wilson continues in a briefer essay on *Macbeth,* but in a sixty-five-page essay on the Globe he turns his critical gaze on others. He pins his faith on J. C. Adams, whose book on the Globe is over forty years old, though updated in 1961. Empson wants to amend Adams, and does some close work on theatrical structures, scorning much scholarship that came later and running a special campaign against Glynne Wickham. There is some rousing stuff about the staging of the opening battle in *Coriolanus,* but to say anything very useful about this essay one would have to be more up to date about the whole big controversy than I am. The essay on *The Dream,* and another on the last plays, are more eccentric than interesting. The last has a go at Derek Traversi and a milder one at me: I mention this in case some keen reader accuses me of wincing away from the charge of being at least Christian and possibly even an advocate of slavery.

The Shakespeare book is likely to be thought of as second-rate Empson and read more for its manners—the bulldog-like hanging on, the Hamlet-like flyting—than for its content. He was a great deal more than a tough controversialist, but he was certainly that, and he always found it hard to change his mind. In *Seven Types* he remarked that it was only in *Don Juan* that Byron escaped from his infantile incest-fixation on his half-sister, "which was till then all he had got to say." Later he added a note to say he now understood that Byron did not meet

Augusta till he was grown up (till he was twenty-four, in fact). It seems very like him to have owned up but not to have altered the text. It is very much the attitude he would take toward God. He never loses class. And take him for all in all, we shall not look upon his like again.

# CHAPTER 6

# *Freud and Interpretation*

Those who honored a complete outsider like me with an invitation to give the Ernest Jones Lecture must have been well aware that the last thing I had to offer was instruction in psychoanalysis. In what follows I shall discuss several intellectual disciplines, psychoanalysis being one of them—a sort of wide-angle view in which neither psychoanalysis nor anything else can hope to be displayed to the satisfaction of the expert. The only justification for doing this is that to see one's subject in relation to some of its neighbors may, in spite of distortions in the presentation, provide a view of it that is useful only in so far as it is slightly unfamiliar.

In its origins psychoanalysis depended upon certain assumptions, not inherent in it, about the past. Having the support of the powerful natural sciences, nineteenth-century geology and biology, these assumptions were not even recognized as such; and so they were, for a time, inescapable. They controlled many other kinds of inquiry, for example, linguistics, biblical criticism, history generally and art history in particular. But well within the lifetime of Freud these assumptions came into question. Others began to replace them. There were new notions as to what constituted valid interpretation. The criteria appropriate to natural science no longer seemed so obviously and unproblematically appropriate to the human sciences. In particular, the relations between past and present became vexatious. Once upon a time it seemed obvious that you could best understand how things are by asking how they got to be that way. Now attention was directed to how things are in all their immediate complexity. There was a switch, to use the linguist's expressions, from the diachronic to the synchronic view. Diachrony, roughly speaking, studies things in their coming to be as they are; synchrony concerns itself with things as they are and ignores the question how they got that way.

More about that later. Crudely, then, my subject is this switch of attention from explanations assuming a very long and rather simple past to explanations focused rather intensely on the here and now, with the past either ignored or given a new and difficult role as a sort of hinterland, in which fact and fiction are not readily distinguished, and perhaps do not need to be. This raises the further question, on which I shall, like Milton's Satan, gloze but superficially, of the relation between historical fact and fiction in historical constructions, a matter to which Freud gave some attention. Like him, we still have a troublesome remnant of a conscience in such matters, though it is a very long time since St. Augustine remarked that "not everything we make up is a lie"; a fiction may be *figura veritatis,* a figure of the truth. Perhaps, in the end, we shall find some comfort in that observation.

A lot has been written lately about "the archaeology of knowledge"—about period systems of discourse which put invisible constraints on the *kind* of thing that can be said at any particular time. Only later, in a new period, can we identify the constraints of a former one; we cannot do it for our own.[1] But it seems extravagant to maintain, as some do, that these epochs are necessarily discontinuous. With psychoanalysis, anyway, one may surely speak of an origin in one epoch and a development in the next. Freud himself, though the most important herald of a new era of interpretation, was formed under the old regime, at a time when it seemed right to give most things a historical explanation, and to be suspicious of explanations that did not appeal to objective historical truth. Science, especially geology and botany, had enormously extended the past of the planet and its occupants; and this new past provided a space for previously unthinkable explanations of how things came to be as they are. In such a climate it would have been extremely difficult to prefer explanations of another kind; that would have been to show less than the proper respect of historians and scientists for fact.

The reader might here wish to remind me that Freud did, on occasion, give some thought to the relation between fact and fiction, truth and the figure of truth. "In my mind I always construct novels," he told Stekel.[2] He called his Leonardo piece "partly fiction," and "Moses and Monotheism" had as its working title "The Man Moses: An Historical Novel." He seems always to have felt the attraction of the storyteller's ways of making sense of the world. The case histories, and especially that of the Wolf Man, have often been thought to show a regard for narrative values—for coherence, development, closure—not entirely consistent with simple factual record. Even "Beyond the Pleasure Principle" has been plausibly studied as a fiction, a masterplot for psychoanalytic narration.[3]

Yet, so far as I know, Freud, when he considered these matters, always reaffirmed the criteria of truthfulness he inherited from science, and from an idea of history deriving from science—an idea that took no account of its fictive qualities. As we shall see, there were, during Freud's lifetime, new approaches to such problems; but he seems to have taken very little notice of them. His own amazingly original work was founded in an older tradition. For example, when he decided to abandon the simpler version of the seduction hypothesis, he got out of the resulting dilemma not by appealing to some theory of fiction but by making use of the extended past. When he says in his "General Theory of the Neuroses" that neurotics are "anchored somewhere in their past," and that their symptoms repeat the past as distorted by the censorship, he does add that the *Kinderscenen* thus recovered are not always *true*—they can be phantasies disguising childhood history, much as nations use legends to disguise their prehistory. But he goes on to claim that psychoanalysis is a technique that can be applied to transindividual subjects such as the history of civilization; and the next step is to explain the phantasies of the individual as inherited by means of genetic memory traces. So, talking of anxiety, he maintains that its "first state" has been "thoroughly incorporated into the organism through a countless series of generations."[4]

By these means it was possible to extend the history of a neurosis beyond the bounds of an individual life, and so to confer upon phantasy the status of historical truth. That the case history of the Wolf Man depends equally upon this move is so obvious as to need no elaboration: the analysis had to proceed as though phantasies were true recollections, and could not otherwise succeed. Patients believe in the reality of the primal scene, and their conviction "is in no respect inferior to one based on recollection."[5] And later Freud remarks that while it would be agreeable to know whether a patient was describing a phantasy or recollecting a real experience, the point is not of much importance, for in either case what is being described has objective historical reality. The phantasies "are unquestionably an inherited endowment, a phylogenetic heritage."[6] Here he found himself in agreement with Jung, with the important qualification that correct method requires one to exhaust ontogenetic explanations before going on to phylogenetic ones. One goes behind the individual history only when historical validation is not to be found there.

The formula *ontogeny repeats phylogeny* thus provides Freud with the means to extend indefinitely the past of the individual, and so create space for acceptably historical explanations. "Totem and Taboo" (1913) clearly depends on the formula. Even more enthusiastic applications of it are to be found in Ferenczi, who mapped the findings of psychoanalysis onto the biological and geological record with much boldness and assiduity. Haeckel's idea had been around for quite a while, and as it happens he was a Darwinian. But Freud and Ferenczi, though keen on the idea of recapitulation, associated the formula not with Darwin's evolutionary biology but rather with the earlier theory of Lamarck, who believed much less ambiguously than Darwin in the inheritance of acquired characteristics. Lamarck suited psychoanalysis much better; it seemed to need what Ferenczi called a "depth biology" that would explain how phylogenetic memory-traces accumulated in the germ plasma, imprinting there "all the catastrophes of phylogenetic development."[7]

Freud's own adherence to an outmoded evolutionary theory, strongly expressed in his letter to Groddeck in 1917[8] and lengthily expounded by Sulloway,[9] was a source of distress to Ernest Jones;[10] but he never gave it up. From his remarks in "The Future of an Illusion," twenty-five years after the event, one sees that he was quite unperturbed that the ethnology of "Totem and Taboo" was said to be out of date,[11] and he obviously felt the same about condemnations of Lamarck. It was important to be able to map neurosis, genitality, and so forth on to an indefinitely protracted past, or, as he himself put it, to "fill a gap in individual truth with prehistoric truth."[12] Actual historical occurrences are somehow genetically inscribed in the individual. Behind the idea of "prehistoric truth" we detect the immense authority of nineteenth-century science and its new explanations of the planet's history.

I shall come back to Freud on this point, but it is now time to ask how this idea of a hugely extended past affected other disciplines outside the natural sciences, and how it began to be given up. The most striking case is probably that of linguistics, because here the twentieth-century break with the historical approach was so decisive, and so clearly marked by the publication of Ferdinand de Saussure's *Course in General Linguistics,*[13] posthumously assembled from students' lecture notes and first published in 1915. It is to Saussure that we owe the distinction between synchronic and diachronic. Hitherto the prevailing mode of linguistics had naturally been historical; languages were studied along a chronological axis. From their interrelations one could construct prehistoric states and parent languages from which they descended. This kind of linguistics was fully warranted as a science, and we know from the early essay on antithetical primal words, and from "Totem and Taboo," that Freud respected it. He shows no signs of having read Saussure, and it is not difficult to guess that had he done so he would have felt little sympathy with the new approach. For Saussure argued that although there is nothing wrong in studying language historically, the investigation of language here and now has clear priority. The speaker of a language is confronted not with a history but with a *state*. "That is why the linguist who wishes to understand a state must discard all knowledge of everything that produced it, since what produced it is not a part of the state"; at this stage he must ignore diachrony.[14] He must look at the systematic interrelations of a language *as it is;* other studies must be subsequent to that one. The questions how things are, and how things got to be this way, are therefore sharply separated.

I should perhaps add what everybody knows, that modern semiology and structuralism grow directly from Saussure's emphasis on state or system, and accept his critique of diachronic assumptions. Freud had an inveterate suspicion of system, which he associated with magic, and with the prescientific, so it is conceivable that he would have thought Saussure's methods regressive. But Saussure never came to his notice, and the direct impact of synchronic linguistics on psychoanalysis was delayed until the advent of Lacan.

The authority of a single person can, it is clear, affect the rate of change in this way; and there is also, more vaguely, a kind of inertia, say of stubbornness, which also tends to slow it. I myself was taught pre-Saussurian linguistics in the 1930s, and the reception of Saussure's ideas did not happen everywhere all at once. So one should not make these changes seem quite as sudden as the importance of the date 1915 suggests. Nor, of course, should it be thought that the move into the here and now was wholly the work of Saussure, or that it always took precisely the same form. And here the example of biblical criticism may be useful.

The historical criticism of the Bible was an eighteenth-century development, but its flowering in the nineteenth century is rightly thought of as among the greatest intellectual achievements of the period. The Bible came to be thought of less as a divinely instituted unity than as a collection of miscellaneous documents, each with a prehistory of change and redaction and conflation over very long periods of time. What had been treated synchronically, as a homogeneous canon, was now to be explained diachronically, as a set of independent documents brought together by editors who did not manage to conceal every trace of their activities.

The Old Testament was sorted into various strands that had been put together in a way that left visible joins. Behind the written versions were oral sources, the subject of prehistoric constructions. The magical view of the Torah as a book somehow coextensive with creation, uniformly inspired, faded away. Something of the sort happened also in New Testament scholarship. It was established, to the satisfaction of most, that Mark's was the earliest Gospel, and that Matthew and Luke used it as a source. But where did they find the material in their books which was not in Mark's? The question is typical, and so is the answer: there must have been a sayings-source, a document having historical existence though now lost, which was labeled Q. But Q, thus constructed, cannot account for the material in Matthew that is not in Luke, and vice versa. So each had to have a private source, called M in one case and L in the other. And this was by no means the end of it.

Now it so happens that this practice of constructing historical precedents came in at about the same time as the discovery of an extended geological past. Now there was *time* for such things to happen; time became a space for interpretation to work in. What validated interpretation was history. The parallel with psychoanalysis seems obvious. The new biblical criticism was of course strongly contested, but it prevailed, and has still not lost its potency. In recent times, however, the grip of history has been somewhat loosened. The historical events of the New Testament themselves command a much less simple kind of assent, as we know from the existentialist theologians. The biblical canon, split, as I have said, into separate books, is once again studied synchronically, as a *state,* in Saussure's word, of which the internal relations may be considered without regard to actual or conjectural chronologies. In a different though related tradition, structuralist anthropology treats the Bible as it would any other corpus of myth, that is, synchronically rather than diachronically, as something that developed through time.

An obvious question now is how this shift of interest affected the writing of history in the ordinary sense. It is a large question, and I shall begin to answer it by giving an example from a subdepartment of the subject, namely art history. German art historians were attracted by theories of transindividual memory, with archaic traces in art that could by research be found to originate in prehistoric events; ancient terrors, according to Aby Warburg, were transmitted by the cultural memory to reappear as sources of energy and delight, as when a girl in a fresco by Ghirlandajo recapitulates, in a beneficently distorted form, the image of a primitive Maenad.[15] The cultural transmission of such "mnemic traces" or engrams is parallel to the genetic survival of prehistory in Freud's individual patient. We may remind ourselves that similar notions were still extant in practitioners of the more exact sciences. The American neo-Lamarckian E. D. Cope, for instance, proposed a doctrine of mnemogenesis, which said that the recapitulation by the embryo of phylogenetic history is made possible by the existence of unconscious memory-structures in the organism.[16]

Warburg continued to think along these lines until his death in 1926; some of the methods he devised for the study of recurrence are still in use, though detached from his theories. He found support wherever he could for his mnemic traces, for instance in the work of Semon, which had much to say about memory traces. It is worth noting that only a few years later, in 1932, there appeared F. C. Bartlett's *Remembering,* a work remembered when other books on memory are forgotten, yet which has no ancient traces or reactivated engrams. Bartlett prefers to speak of personal interest in the here and now—adaptation and response to an immediate stimulus. Once again it seems that the older historical assumptions are set aside.

Indeed they were under question as early as the 1870s, when Nietzsche called history "the gravedigger of the present";[17] and among other inquirers it would seem that a characteristically modern philosophy of history began to develop. Where does history happen? One answer was, in the historian's head, now. The related question, what does it mean to do history? required of the historian a new effort of self-reflection. He could no longer claim to be merely arranging objective and verifiable facts. And the problem was to find new ways of talking about what now appeared to be the obscure relation of past to present. It fell within the domain of the revived discipline of hermeneutics.

Hermeneutics, as understood in our time, owes much to Wilhelm Dilthey (1831–1911). Dilthey distinguished between the natural and the human sciences *(Geisteswissenschaften),* and this distinction was later to be important for psychoanalysis and indeed to all the other interpretive sciences. Freud seems to have ignored Dilthey; he would probably not have liked the philosopher's insistence on taking into account the historical situation of the observer as well as that of the observed; which is to complicate something Freud insisted was simple. According to Dilthey, understanding is subject to time and change; no past is fixed, and no present is to be thought of as somehow outside time. We survey the past from within our own horizon, and that horizon is always changing. That is why, as a matter of course, we lose faith in world views formerly taken to be beyond controversy—in "any philosophy which attempts to express world order cogently through a series of concepts."[18]

Dilthey's line of thought, much transformed, has persisted into our own time, and hermeneutics has spread itself over the whole body of philosophy. But it continues to hold that meaning changes, including past meaning; and that the past is inextricable from the present of the interpreter. *There and then* cannot be detached from *here and now,* and objectively inspected. The past becomes, at least in part, a construction of the present. Thus Lévi-Strauss can say quite flatly that historical narratives are "fraudulent outlines" imposed on the data, which are of course synchronic.[19] Most hermeneutic claims are less nihilistic, but still fatal to the old idea of the past.

And with that I conclude this extremely superficial account of altered attitudes to the past in some of the human sciences with which psychoanalysis must acknowledge kinship. Before I return to psychoanalysis with the object of seeing how it looks in this changed context, I should summarize the summary. The new long view of the past provided by natural science was imposed upon and in various ways exploited by the interpretive disciplines. In psychoanalysis individual histories were projected onto a longer phylogenetic scale, so that a present neurosis could be interpreted by reference to a remote "prehistoric" catastrophe; thus phantasy acquired the status of historical (scientific) fact. Linguistics, biblical criticism, and historiography also made use of these new time scales, accepting that historical factuality was the ultimate source of authentic interpretation. However, we thought we could see in these studies a shift into a new set of assumptions—rather dramatic in the case of linguistics, where Saussure explicitly affirmed the primacy of the synchronic, but no less certain, though more gradual, in the other disciplines. The interpretive emphasis, in short, was shifting away from that long past, so receptive of narrative explanations, and into the actual moment, the here and now. It would be easy enough to provide more evidence of this shift, say from the various kinds of formalism practiced in literary and other sorts of criticism, as they developed in different ways in Russia, America, and England; all were more or less dismissive of the historical dimension, all were concerned with synchronicity, the words on the page, the verbal icon.

To some who experienced this shift a particular problem must have grown more vexatious, namely the exact demarcation between historical truth and fiction, and, as I have remarked, it sometimes occurred to Freud to give the matter thought. How he dealt with it we may perhaps see from a single example. In 1911 Hans Vaihinger published his *Philosophy of "As if,"* though in fact he had written it twenty-five years earlier. It is, roughly, a Nietzschean philosophy of fictions. It was often reprinted, and came to Freud's attention. Vaihinger's explanation of the heuristic value of "as-if" thinking seems at first to have impressed him; but he soon dismissed it with the Johnsonian observation that this was an argument "only a philosopher could put forward."[20] For it was not philosophy but hard science that was in touch with the truth. When, in "The Future of an Illusion," Freud defines illusion as the conformity of a belief with a wish,[21] he obviously implies that psychoanalysis is saved from illusion by its observational basis. He allows the carping critic set up as a kind of Aunt Sally in that book to complain that Freud has set up his own system of illusions in place of another; science is neither system nor illusion, and psychoanalysis is a science.

At the same time, and with some inconsistency, he commends "Totem and Taboo," despite its outdated ethnology, for the way in which it brought a number of disconnected facts into a coherent whole.[22] Of course he knew very well that a capacity to be represented as whole and self-consistent does not guarantee theories against illusion. When he condemned Adler's theories as "radically false" he said that their very consistency constituted a distortion comparable with those introduced by secondary revision in dream theory.[23] In short, Freud would have agreed with the poet Stevens that "to impose is not / To discover." Whatever theory imposes on observation is likely to induce distortion and illusion. The doctrine which holds that the innocent eye sees nothing would not have been acceptable to Freud. He affirmed, indeed, that the foundation of science was "observation alone";[24] and he held this to be as true of psychoanalysis as of physics.

Everybody is now much more skeptical about the possibility of context-free observation, and most are much more ready to allow that the criteria for valid interpretation in the human sciences are different from those obtaining in natural science. In particular, the notion that historical facts exist in simple and accessible objectivity has become hard to hold. And in the present climate few could be as calm and certain about the nature of historical constructions as Freud was. In the late essay entitled "Constructions in Analysis" he is still saying there is nothing delusive about the contact of such constructions with historical reality.[25] And he denied that the issue was of much practical importance because all the relevant material, whether fact or phantasy, had *some* historical reality, however archaic and however distorted in transmission. He would have thought rather ill of the argument that everything relevant belongs to the here and now—that what occurred in the transference was not, in some perfectly real and genuine way, a recapitulation of actual events. To think in that way he would have had first to abandon the foreunderstanding he had inherited from the dominant science of his formative years.

Possessing a degree of hindsight, we may think it inevitable that psychoanalysis should one day break its bond with natural science and move into the more congenial context of the *Geisteswissenschaften*. I don't know if he was a pioneer in this, but I learned that in 1939 Kroeber suggested that it was a mistake to treat the Oedipus complex as historical in origin. More recently Jerome Neu (from whom I gained this information) has asked "Must actual remorse for an actual crime be an essential step in superego formation?" replying that it need not be. Freud's account of the matter would be unobjectionable, says Neu, only if Lamarckianism were true, which it isn't.[26] For this as well as other reasons psychoanalysis might want to reconsider its position among the disciplines.

A rapprochement between psychoanalysis and hermeneutics was proposed in Ricoeur's monumental *Freud and Philosophy*.[27] Ricoeur maintains that the proper questions to put to Freud are those one would put to Dilthey, Weber, or Bultmann rather than those one would put to a physicist or a biologist. "It is completely misleading," he says, *contra* Freud, "to raise the question [of theory in psychoanalysis] in the context of a factual or observational science."[28] And he stresses the uniqueness of the transference, its unpredictability and its here-and-nowness, as the distinctive characteristic of psychoanalysis considered as a hermeneutic.

To treat it thus is to avoid the Popperian charge of pseudoscience by taking psychoanalysis out of the arena in which Popper's criteria apply. The move once made, it is possible to think of psychoanalysis not merely as a hermeneutic science, but as the paradigm of all such sciences, and this is what Jürgen Habermas has argued. The interpretive disciplines differ from natural science in that they cannot yield demonstrative certainty, and depend on different procedures. In outlining them Habermas follows Dilthey. He adds that Freud took no account of all this, but stuck to the view that psychoanalysis was fundamentally a positive science, though with certain peculiarities.[29] For Habermas the distinctive characteristic of psychoanalysis as hermeneutic is that it deals with discourses the authors of which are deceiving themselves; that is, it is concerned more with distortion of meaning than with meaning, or, as he says, with the intrusion of an at first incomprehensible private language into everyday language games. Analysis seeks to cure these linguistic deformations. Its explanations are not, as is supposed of those proper to the natural sciences, determined by context-free laws, for here interpretation is a formative part of the discourse; its aim is "the reintroduction into public communication of a symbolic content that has been split off."[30] Psychoanalysis, unlike the sciences which pretend to context-free observation, is necessarily self-reflexive, always making its concern as to what it is doing a part of what it is doing.

And here we may recall that it was during Freud's most active years that poets and novelists discovered, or rediscovered and exploited, the possibilities of reflexivity, the values of systematic distortion, and the benefits of what is sometimes called "spatial form"—a detemporalizing of narrative which, accompanied by all manner of dislocation, overlaps, gaps, condensations, displacements, called for a quasi-synchronic reading and heightened interpretive awareness on the part of the reader. Works so composed can be seen only as wholes, and can be made sense of only by a collaborative act on the part of the reader; all reading is of course collaborative, but now the reader's share of the work is quite deliberately increased. The analogy between psychological and fictional interpretation was there *in posse* from the earliest days of psychoanalysis, but the forces which bound Freud to objective history, and many novelists to the conventions of "secretarial" realism, prevented, and in some degree continue to prevent, its exploitation.

However that may be, it is now quite usual to speak of Freud's historical constructions as delusive.[31] One commentator will lament Freud's "limited epistemology," which prevented him from understanding that historical truth, or the appearance of it, is entirely the product of the analytical session. "The reality tested and the reality created . . . claim no authority outside the analytic process. What authorizes the process is immanent in the process."[32] Let us leave aside the question whether Dr. Schwartz has considered the possibility that he too has a limited epistemology, and remark that self-authorization of this sort is also commonly credited to poems and novels—to works of fiction. Skura, indeed, says that the analyst can now teach critics how to attend to details apparently too trivial to bear the weight of interpretation; but he can only do so because he has given up the "referential fallacy" and come to see "the psychoanalytical process as a self-conscious end in itself."[33]

Such commentators take the death of the psychoanalytical past as a *fait accompli*. According to Merton Gill the analysis of transference ought to be "content-free," and the analysand's references to the past are to be interpreted as indirect, resistant allusions to the here and now.[34] And Donald P. Spence[35] attacks many aspects of psychoanalytical practice which seem to him to derive from mistaken assumptions governing the aims and techniques of traditional analysis: the partnership between free association and evenly hovering attention, thought to create the conditions for an interpretive recovery of the past, is nonexistent. Pasts, indeed, are not reconstructed; they are constructed here and now. Moreover, since the analyst inserts fictions into the discourse, he might be more usefully thought of as a kind of poet rather than as a kind of archaeologist. What psychoanalysis does is construct "truth in the service of self-coherence . . . It offers no veridical picture of the past." Like the poet, the novelist, and the historian, the analyst creates under his specific conditions a past that is really here and now, a fiction appropriate to the present. Any interpretation is true "only in its own analytic space."[36] Moreover, it is pointless to call an interpretation erroneous; it works by contributing to narrative intelligibility, and is neither true nor false but only a means to an end.

Spence and Viderman (who seems to have originated the analogy with the poet) have been accused of seriously misrepresenting the analyst's role, which, says one critic, is less like that of a poet than like that of a detective breaking an alibi.[37] This analogy might have a certain appeal to all who would rather deal even with a policeman than with a poet, but it simply assumes the old historical dimension Spence and the others reject. As so often, old assumptions linger on, wearing the guise of common sense.

It is of course part of the premise that what is new will become old, perhaps lingering for a while as common sense before sinking into disuse or being revived and given a new dress. The most appealing thing about the hermeneutic approach is that it forbids itself to suppose that it can stop all movement at exactly the right place, namely one's own moment, or that it has achieved an interpretive apparatus that is permanently valid. And of course the sort of paradigm change I have been discussing can only be represented as a matter of history, which at least to that extent is not dead at all, as linguists, theologians, and historians of the most modern sort perfectly well understand. But this is second-order history—the narrative not of events or linguistic change or whatever, but rather the narrative of such narratives. Anyway, the shift seems to have happened, and it is hardly a surprise that psychoanalysis, with its roots in one epoch and its branches in another, should demonstrably have been caught up in it.

There is, I think, one more thing to be said. The most radical theologians, some of them atheist to all intents and purposes, are still Christians. Philosophers eloquent in their distrust of history and system—as nowadays some influential thinkers are—remain for all that philosophers. The art-historical methods of a Warburg have become the possession of scholars who may think his theories of small concern. And all the critics of the Freudian concept of the past to whom I have referred in this essay are either psychoanalysts or friends of psychoanalysis.

Nietzsche remarked in *The Use and Abuse of History* that every past is worth condemning; and it is possible to believe in psychoanalysis without thinking that any of its past pasts are exempt from this general rule. Nevertheless, certain values seem to survive the conceptual forms in which from time to time they have been—*have* to have been—embodied. The certainty that present structures of belief will also change is therefore not a reason for supposing that psychoanalysis will cease to figure among the arts or sciences of interpretation, or even that it will not dominate them, in times when they will probably be defined in ways quite unforeseeable by us.

For my own part I am happy to think that psychoanalytic interpretation may hold commerce with the theory of fiction. The theologians are interested in a similar concordat, having lost confidence in objective history. I promised comfort at the end: it is this, that we may all, under the special conditions of our trades, claim to be dealing with *figurae veritatis,* figures of the truth.

# CHAPTER 7

# *Divination*

My subject is divination, and I had better give a hint as to what it means. The *Oxford English Dictionary,* I'm afraid, is unhelpful, concerning itself largely with the primary sense (prophecy and augury) and coming close to me only in treating what it calls the "weaker sense"—"guessing by happy instinct or unusual insight; successful conjecture." Now that everybody finds literary theory so much more interesting than literature, we must expect a certain amount of imperialist rapine. A recent issue of *Critical Inquiry* has an article on information-processing in reading poetry, and deals, it claims, with "variant readings" of a poem, always an absorbing subject. But I soon saw that "variant readings" now means not what it used to mean, namely *variae lectiones,* conflicts of textual testimony, but rather the different ways in which various people read the same poem. My complaint is not that this matter is not worth the writer's time, or mine; merely that a new interest, supported by all the modern armaments of phenomenology, Gestalt psychology, information theory, and so forth, has usurped an expression that has had for centuries a perfectly plain and very different meaning. Let us, while we may, use the old sense of *varia lectio;* it reminds us of an old, yet still current, sense of the word "divination." It may be weaker, but it is strong enough for me. For divination, *divinatio,* is a power traditionally required by those who wish to distinguish between variant readings, and to purge corrupt texts.

I shall add at once that nobody can suppose divination is

*merely* inspired guesswork. Freedom to divine, in this sense, has been restricted since the Renaissance, and especially since the early eighteenth century, by the advance of what might be called science. Philology has always claimed to be so called, and especially in the nineteenth century aspired to the rigor of even more fashionable sciences. Indeed, in its modern forms it still does so. And the truth is, that much knowledge has been progressively acquired. How texts are transmitted through time, what are the habits and failings of scribes and compositors, the paradoxes of history which make it possible that the earliest is not the best manuscript or edition—all this lore is now quite well understood. The liberty to divine is reduced by this understanding of the possibilities, and even geniuses are no longer allowed the freedom enjoyed by, say, the great Bentley.

All the same, it would be wrong to think of science as the enemy of divination. All it does is to define its limits. I doubt if one could find a Shakespearian who would deny the proposition that Charlton Hinman's vast book on the printing of the First Folio[1] is one of the essential contributions to the study of Shakespeare's text; yet as far as I can tell Hinman never so much as proposed an emendation. What he did was to define more precisely than had been thought possible where and how the text is likely to have gone wrong. The way of the editor is by this means made clearer and narrower. But he will still have to divine.

Some great diviners like to affirm that divination is a gift you are born with, that it cannot be taught. George Steiner recently quoted A. E. Housman's famous words to this effect.[2] I doubt if they are wholly right, but they're not wholly wrong, either; history supports them, up to a point. For, as L. D. Reynolds and N. G. Wilson observe in their book *Scribes and Scholars,*[3] "while general principles are of great use, specific problems have a habit of being *sui generis.*" And we need to remember also that some, perhaps most, of the most impressive emendations made in texts of every sort were provided by scholars who had never heard of stemmatics, or of Hinman's ingenious optical machine—who were ignorant of principles and information now available to everybody—what went on in scriptoria, what were the habits of Elizabethan compositors, and lots of other things.

However, we must not suppose that divination is something only textual scholars do. In the early years of the last century Friedrich Schleiermacher, generally remembered as the founder of modern hermeneutics—the science of understanding texts—took over the term *divinatio* for something rather different. Schleiermacher needed a word for a moment of intuition which was necessary to his theory, and also, probably, to any commonsense view of what it is we accomplish when we interpret a text. We understand a whole by means of its parts, and the parts by means of the whole. But this "circle" seems to imply that we can understand nothing—the whole is made up of parts we cannot understand until it exists, and we cannot see the whole without understanding the parts. Something, therefore, must happen, some intuition by which we break out of this situation—a leap, a *divination,* he called it, whereby we are enabled to understand both part and whole.

Much has happened since Schleiermacher's day. In our own time we hear a lot about the "reader's share" in the production of sense. For every act of reading calls for some (perhaps minute) act of divination. We may content ourselves with obeying clear suggestions and indications in the text—as, for example, to setting, character, what we ought to be thinking about the action described or enacted. Every competent reader can do that much, and there is in consequence what is called an "intersubjective consensus" about the meaning of the text. But we may have to do rather more; there are works, especially modern books, which may frustrate such responses, or at least suggest a need for going beyond them. And it is quite usual to attach more value to such complex works, and to feel that our relating of part to part and parts to whole is the only means by which anything like the sense of the whole can be achieved. In other words, our power of divination is necessary to the whole operation—without it there will be no sense, or not enough.

It follows, I think, that we can distinguish between normal and abnormal divinations. The first kind we refer to the "intersubjective consensus"—we expect the agreement, without fuss, of competent, similarly educated people. Then there is the second kind, which we also submit to our peers. But this time they will not simply nod agreement, but either reject it as preposterous, or hail it as brilliantly unexpected, a feat of genius. For although there is no guarantee whatever that the institutional consensus will always be right, it knows the difference between the valuable normal and the abnormally valuable. Though it will condemn divinations that run counter to its own intuition, the institution will tend to admire most those divinations which cannot be made by the mechanical application of learnable rules. Divination, in other words, still has the respect of the bosses.

What I have been doing so far is this: I have been suggesting that divination as the whole concept applied to the correction of texts is a special form of a more general art or skill, which we all employ, at one level or another, in the interpretation of poems and novels. The difference is merely one of degree; for in *all* cases divination requires, in its treatment of the part, an intuition of the whole. It would be possible here to introduce a related topic of much interest and difficulty: the relation between the reader's act of divination and the process by which authors compose the texts in the first place. The poet's drafts may show him preferring one word to another, even sometimes substituting a word of which the sense is the opposite of the original, as better in relation to the yet undetermined whole of the poem. The novelist, who may or may not have a Jamesian scenario, but who will have some probably indistinct intuition of the whole as he labors through the parts, can be found making the most drastic changes to the part as that intuition fluctuates, or discovers itself. But that would be another essay, and a harder one as well. I shall stick to lower forms of divination, using examples.

The devil answers even in engines.

The first example, as a matter of fact, is a sort of warning. A word once favored among critics was "sagacity." Dr. Johnson had a great respect for "critical sagacity," and we may take it as representing, under another guise, the power to make acceptable divination. Johnson admired one emendation made by Thomas Hanmer in the text of Shakespeare so much that he said it almost set "the critic on the level of the author." One day he gave Boswell a test. He pointed to a paragraph in a book by Sir George Mackenzie, and asked Boswell whether he could spot what was wrong with it. "I hit it at once," says Boswell. "It stands that the devil answers *even* in *engines*. I corrected it to '*ever* in *enigmas.*' 'Sir,' said he, 'you're a good critic. This would have been a great thing to do in the text of an ancient author.'" But James Thorpe, from whose learned and amusing book[4] I borrow the example, is inclined to think that Boswell is wrong, at any rate about *engines,* which can be held to make perfectly good sense. It can mean "snares, devices, tricks." "If so: poor over-clever Boswell; alas, poor over-knowing Johnson," says Mr. Thorpe. To be truly sagacious you have to know when divination is not called for.

Diviners had best be prepared to be called over-clever, over-knowing. In the days of Richard Bentley, the "modern" skill in emending ancient texts met with a lot of opposition of this nature from people who favored this "ancient" side of the quarrel. Bentley's self-assurance was assaulted by Swift and ridiculed by Pope. The notes to the *Dunciad* are full of such mockery.

> lo! a Sage appears
> By his broad shoulders known, and length of ears

says the text, and the notes call "ears" a sophisticated (that is, a corrupt) reading. "I have always stumbled at it," says the annotator Scriblerus, "and wonder'd how an error so manifest could escape such accurate persons as the critics being ridiculed. A very little Sagacity . . . will restore to us the true sense of the Poet, thus,

> By his broad shoulders known, and length of *years.*

See how easy a change! of one single letter! That Mr. Settle [the Sage] was old is most certain."[5] Such unkind responses to divination not only remind us of the risk it involves, but also cause us to reflect that the task of the diviner may often be very difficult. Indeed there are problems for the solution of which it is safe to assert that nobody has ever had, or will ever have, sufficient sagacity. All one can do is to award them what is known as a *crux desperationis,* a cross of despair, a sign that they are beyond human ingenuity.

(A) a nellthu night more
(B) a nelthu night Moore
(C) come on bee true
(D) come on

My second example offers a sample pair of hopeless cases. (A) is from the 1608 Quarto of *King Lear,* (B) from the second Quarto of 1619. It is obvious that nobody could have made head or tail of them, had not the true reading survived in the corrected state of Q1 and in the Folio text of 1623: "He met the night-mare." (C) and (D) come from the same scene (III.iv), the first from the uncorrected Q1, the second from the corrected Q1. So if Heminge and Condell hadn't put together the First Folio in 1623 we should not have known that Lear, tearing off his clothes in the storm, says "Come, unbutton heere." He is raving, and might have said either or neither of the things preserved in the Quarto; and no diviner could have done anything about it.

> Then the stars hang like lamps from the immense vault. The distance between the vault and them is as nothing to the distance behind them . . .

However, the diviner's problem may arise from difficulties less obvious than those, for example when he has first to divine that, contrary to appearances, there is a need for his services. The third passage is from the beautifully composed opening chapter of E. M. Forster's *A Passage to India*. Let me play Johnson to your Boswell: what's wrong with it? Well—isn't the distance between the vault and the stars the same thing as the distance behind the stars? Could it be that a typist or compositor has accidentally repeated the word *vault* instead of what the author wrote? (This is called *dittography* by the experts.) Yet the fact is that between 1924 and 1978 nobody noticed there was anything wrong. Now we know that the manuscript reads not the second *vault* but *earth;* and the typescript also survives, so we know it was the typist who made the mistake, and that Forster set a good precedent for all who study him by not noticing it for the remaining half-century of his life. Perhaps some genius a thousand years hence might have been smart enough to see that somebody had gone wrong, and bold enough to risk the conjecture *earth*. Perhaps not. Anyway, he was forestalled. The moral may be: don't burn your manuscripts, diviners can't be trusted in every case.

> She was praising God without attributes—thus did she apprehend Him. Others praised Him without attributes, seeing Him in this or that organ of the body or manifestation of the sky.

The fourth extract is also from *A Passage to India*. Boswell should find this easier; obviously the second *without* should be *with*. Forster's editor, Oliver Stallybrass, who loved his job, once went through my copy checking conjectures against the manuscript, and this one was right. But although the balance of the sentences ("Some . . . Others") to say nothing of the fact that the second *without attributes* is followed by a catalogue of attributes, makes it obvious to the meanest diviner that something has gone wrong, the right reading appeared in no edition before Stallybrass's, in 1978, more than fifty years late.

We must conclude from this that attentiveness is necessary to divination; reading novels, we are all too ready to skip over interruptions in the flow of words, and in so doing miss many opportunities; for the texts of many standard novelists are much worse than Forster's. Our laziness has important implications; if we miss such manifest errors, we may also miss less manifest subtleties. By under-reading we fail to divine the larger sense of a novel. But I shall come a little later to that kind of divination.

> In the offing the sea and the sky were welded together without a joint, and in the luminous space the tanned sails of the barges drifted up with the tide and seemed to stand still in red clusters of canvas sharply peaked, with gleams of vanished spirits.

Here is one more instance of a famous text with an obvious corruption, from the opening paragraph of *Heart of Darkness.* There is something odd about *vanished spirits;* everything else has to do with the shapes and colors of the natural world. You can argue that Conrad, who was anyway rather keen on ghosts and spirits, is preparing us for the talk about the London river centuries ago, when the Romans used it, and you can supply other explanations of that sort—indeed there are ingenious explanations on record. If you are more skeptical you may look at other versions of the text, and find *varnished spirits,* which doesn't help much. What Conrad himself wrote was *varnished sprits;* I have only to say it for you to think it obvious. Yet if some Boswell had guessed it, that would, as Johnson said, have been something; and there would have been no doubt that he was right. But the answer was got by looking back to the first edition. The other readings are progressively corrupt, as the texts of all novels are, for the next edition repeats the mistakes of the previous one, and adds more.

*Heart of Darkness* is more or less intensively studied in the classroom by hundreds of experts and thousands of students every year. Unless they use the Signet edition, they all meet this corrupt reading instantly. (The Signet is the only popular text I can lay my hands on that has it right. The *Oxford Anthology,* I regret to say, has it wrong.) Nobody, so far as I knew, ever divined the true reading. This tells us among other things that there may be something wrong with the way we focus our attention on texts. Of course it doesn't amount to much: "one single letter," as Scriblerus remarked, and *vanished* replaced *varnished;* then somebody thought *vanished sprits* looked queer, and added another single letter to *sprits.*

> You are a Counsellor if you can
> command these elements to silence,
> and worke the peace of the present, wee
> will not hand a rope more . . .

Sometimes it seems that we will do almost anything rather than get the right answer. The sixth extract is from the opening scene of *The Tempest.* The Boatswain wants to get rid of the courtiers, who are getting in the way of the sailors as they cope with the storm. "The peace of the present" is an unusual expression, but it might just pass—"bring the present moment into a peaceful state," or something of that kind. Still, it is odd; and if you read *presence* (supposing that Shakespeare wrote *presenc* and the scribe mistook the *c* for a *t*) you have a known expression. It means the area occupied by the king and his court; within it peace is kept or preserved or "worked" by his officers. This conjecture, by the late J. C. Maxwell, seemed right to me, and I put it in the text of my edition of the play,[6] where it has been on view for over thirty years without attracting the slightest notice. It makes sense; the explanation in terms of graphic error came after the divination, as Housman says it should; but the world remains content with *present.* There are some interesting implications. First of all, there is in all guardians of sacred texts a profound conservatism. Erasmus edited the Greek New Testament, not very well; in fact by later standards very badly. But it became the received text, and for three hundred years scholars who knew perfectly well that it had many obvious mistakes did not dare to change it, and smuggled the right readings into the footnotes. So with Shakespeare, whose texts are riddled with error. In the eighteenth century there was much liberty; but in spite of an occasional plea for boldness, it is now normal to give sage approval to the claim that a text is very conservative. The diviner is not a popular person; he is constrained by professional skepticism and by our veneration for the received text (as if the merits of the Bible and Shakespeare rubbed off onto scribes and printers) as much as he is by the formidable growth of editorial "science."

> Oh Sunne, thy uprise shall I see no more,
> Fortune and *Anthony* part heere, even heere
> Do we shake hands? All come to this? The hearts
> That pannelled me at heels, to whom I gave
> Their wishes do dis-Candie, melt their sweets
> On blossoming *Caesar:* and this pine is barkt
> That over-top'd them all.

That is why I have to look back to the eighteenth century for an example of divinatory genius at work on Shakespeare. Look at the extract above, which is from the original text of *Antony and Cleopatra*. Antony is nearing the end; he has lost, his followers have left him. Something is wrong, though, and it must be the word *pannelled*. Thomas Hanmer, in 1744, said it should be *spanielled;* and we have most of us accepted this (or *spannelled*) ever since. It is one of the finest emendations in the whole text of Shakespeare and one of the most certain—it is indeed the one commended by Dr. Johnson, as quoted earlier in this essay—though Hanmer didn't know the first thing about Shakespearian bibliography. If we ask ourselves why it is so admirable we shall have to start using words like intuition or divination. Another matter of which Hanmer probably had no conscious knowledge, though it is now well known, is Shakespeare's tendency to associate dogs, melting candy, and flattery. Of course he must in a sense have known about it, to see what was needed in place of *pannelled* was a doggy sort of word; it also had to be a verb in the past tense.

The importance of this point is that such divinations depend on knowledge (of course you can have the knowledge without the power to divine). Hanmer's familiarity with the whole body of Shakespeare's work gave him a place to jump from. He would not be alarmed that if his conjecture gained acceptance we should have to admit that Shakespeare makes hearts turn into dogs, then melt (*discandy*—a word used, for example, of ice melting in a brook or a lake); that the intransitive *discandy* generates the transitive *melt* and the noun *sweets;* that *melt* becomes *melt on,* with its strange suggestion of the erstwhile cold hearts dropping slobbered sweetmeats on a tree (dogs and trees go together) but a tree called Caesar, which is in turn contrasted with a less lucky though originally more upstanding and attractive tree called Antony. Even *barkt*—referring to the manner in which this tree was spoilt—reminds us of the dogs. Hanmer must have known this strange piece of language was perfectly Shakespearian; he knew the manner of his poet.

Also, of course, he knew *Antony and Cleopatra,* at that moment, with the peculiar intimacy of an editor. A little earlier in the play there is a scene in which Antony, smarting under defeat, is enraged to find Cleopatra treating a messenger from Caesar with what he thinks to be rather more than due civility. He who had, at the outset, dismissed with magnanimous impatience the superstitious notion that a messenger should suffer because he bears bad news, now has this messenger whipped, rather in the style of Cleopatra herself. He then turns on Cleopatra in a fury of disgust; then there's a sort of detumescence of rage, while Cleopatra waits patiently for him to finish. ("Have you done yet?") His reproaches grow more pathetic, and there follows this remarkable dialogue:

> *Antony:* Cold-hearted toward me?
> *Cleopatra:* Ah (Deere) if I be so,
> From my cold heart let Heaven ingender haile,
> And poyson it in the sourse, and the first stone
> Drop in my necke: as it determines so
> Dissolve my life, the next Caesarian smite,
> Till by degrees the memory of my wombe,
> Together with my brave Egyptians all,
> By the discandering of this pelleted storme,
> Lye gravelesse, till the Flies and Gnats of Nyle
> Have buried them for prey.

Cleopatra speaks in a very elaborate figure of which the basis is Antony's word *cold-hearted*. Let her heart be thought cold; let it also be thought poisoned, so that the heart's hail will be lethal when it melts. Let these deadly hailstones kill first her; then her son; then all her posterity ("the memory of my womb"), until all the Egyptians are dead and consumed by the insects of the Nile, "melted" by them. We cannot help noticing all the synonyms for "melt": *determine, dissolve, discandy*. There is a contrast between Egyptian heat and the supposed unnatural cold of Cleopatra's heart, with the words for rapid melting mediating between them in such a way as to enforce the absurdity of the whole hypothesis ("*If* I be so . . ."). The play has made us familiar with the notions of Cleopatra's fecundity and sexual warmth, and related the same qualities in the Nile. This great lover cannot have a cold heart; coldness belongs to Rome. The Nile floods annually, and melts its banks; and when Antony says, "Let Rome in Tiber melt!" he is invoking the impossible for merely rhetorical purposes.

I couldn't help making a few of the many possible comments on this wonderful passage; but my real purpose is to draw attention to its connections with Hanmer's emendation. For Antony's "cold-hearted" here develops into very elaborate figures of melting, and the word *discandy* is used among others. The cold hearts and the melting pass magically over into the later speech, this time attended by a dog. Noting that the melting cold hearts seemed for some reason to be at Antony's heels, Hanmer put the spaniel in. This part called for a very active knowledge of the whole of the play, and perhaps of the greater whole, all the plays.

After all that we are in a better position, I hope, to see how the addition of "a single letter" may truly be called an extraordinary act of interpretation, and how it calls for knowledge, knowledge which must be drawn from a greater whole yet bear down with all its weight on the smallest part, a word or a phrase. I will now try, with the aid of the eighth extract, to drive home the point that the rightness or wrongness of a particular reading may be a matter of enormous consequence; and that a preference for one reading over another may inescapably involve great decisions about the whole text in which the crux occurs. Divining is often a matter of choosing, as it is in this brief sentence from St. Mark's Gospel.

(i) Egō eimi
(ii) Su eipas hoti egō eimi

We have here two versions of the words spoken by Jesus at the Sanhedrin trial, when the Priest asks him, "Are you the Christ, the son of the Blessed?" The first means "I am," and the second, "Thou hast said that I am." The first is positive, the second is noncommittal. The Jesus of Mark is nowhere else positive in his reply to similar questions, and only a short time afterwards declines to make a straight answer to Pilate when he asks, "Are you the king of the Jews?" *Su legeis,* says Jesus, which amounts to the same thing as *su eipas*. And such a reply would in this case be much closer to the run of the reader's expectations; for Jesus, in Mark's Gospel, has consistently refused to make public any messianic claim. Which reading is the right one?

Now it often happens that editors of the New Testament have to choose between a shorter and a longer version of the same passage. Has something dropped out of one version, or has something been inserted in the other? Long experience has evolved a rule: *brevior lectio potior,* the shorter reading is the stronger; all else being equal, scribes are more likely to leave things out than put things in. On the other hand, texts could be altered for doctrinal reasons; and scribes, looking at other manuscripts than the ones they are copying, sometimes reintroduce errors previously corrected. Also, copying Mark, they may alter him to conform to Matthew, who was thought to be more authoritative. Anyway, there is no rule of thumb strong enough to enforce the shorter version. We have to consider many other matters, some of them of very great importance.

For example: if the shorter version is right, we have to allow that its effect is to confound rather than comply with our expectations. Is Mark the kind of text in which the unexpected ought to be expected? In other words, what *kind* of book is it? Mark inserts into his account of the Sanhedrin trial the story of Peter in the courtyard denying Jesus. Peter was the man who first named Jesus as the Messiah, and here he is denying him at the very moment when for the first time Jesus himself is making the claim. If we read it that way we are virtually saying that this is a text so subtle that we can read none of it without expectations of similar subtlety. Our reading of the whole is profoundly affected. Matthew, whether he had the choice or not, used the longer version; the problem does not arise in that Gospel, which is not concerned with what is called "the Messianic secret." We have to choose—and not between these two different versions merely, but between two different *books*.

The difference between *homoousia* and *homoiousia,* "of the same substance" and "of like substance," divided the fourth-century church; one iota; "but a single letter," as Scriblerus remarked. The choice involves a whole theology, the pressure of a whole institution rejecting heresy. Christians who declare every Sunday that they believe in Jesus Christ, being of one substance with the Father, do so because of a learned controversy sixteen hundred years ago. A single letter can make a difference.

> Tōi agapōnti hēmas kai { lusanti / lousanti } hēmas ek tōn hamartiōn hēmōn en tō haimati autou.

That is why I included the ninth extract, another curious instance of a choice, this time purely editorial, that has had endless repercussions upon people's behavior and beliefs. It is from Revelation 1:5, and it means either (a) "unto him who loved us and freed us from our sin in his own blood," or (b) "unto him who loved us and washed us from our sin in his own blood." There are defenses available for the second version, which is the one preferred in the King James Bible and the Vulgate *(lavit).* Allusions to regeneration by washing are common enough in the Jewish Bible, and so, of course, are blood sacrifices; but the idea of washing in blood is not. All the evangelical tropes about being washed in the blood of the Lamb depend largely on the reading "washed." However, *lusanti,* loosing or freeing, is now almost universally preferred, not only, I think, because it is the reading of the better manuscripts, but also because the washing in blood is un-Jewish and un-Greek. Thus a whole strain of evangelical imagery may depend on a scribal lapse; those who preferred *lousanti* divined wrong, though with interesting results.

Let us return for a moment to Mark. We have there, I think, a clear demonstration that when we attend to a minute particular of interpretation, we must do so with a lively sense of the whole text in which it occurs. The consequences of our choice may not always be so momentous, of course. And here I want to introduce a new notion, namely that it may sometimes be necessary to good divination that the practitioner should decide to *minimize* the relation between the part and the whole.

> Whose yonder,
> That doe's appear as he were Flead? Oh Gods,
> He has the stamp of Martius, and I have
> Before time seen him thus.

Look at the tenth extract, which is from the first act of *Coriolanus*. There is nothing wrong with the text, so far as I know— which gives us another new notion, namely that divination is not merely a matter of correcting texts. In the swirl of battle Cominius has some difficulty in recognizing Coriolanus, or rather Caius Martius, as he emerges from the enemy city; he is wounded and covered in blood. He appears "as he were flayed . . . He has the stamp of Martius." Is Cominius merely recognizing Martius at last, or is he also saying that the hero looks like Marsyas? Marsyas was a satyr who stole a divine flute, challenged Apollo to a musical contest, lost, and was flayed alive. Though only a satyr, he tried to behave like a god. Coriolanus is sometimes thought of as a beast-god, his conduct depending upon a particularly bleak form of presumption; he behaves toward them as if he were "a God, to punish; not a man of their infirmity." "He wants nothing of a God but eternity and a heaven to throne in." Shall we, having divined the presence of Marsyas in Martius, collect all the figures which speak of Coriolanus as a beast, remember that he tried to behave like a god, and announce that we have discovered some previously unnoticed key theme of the play? I think not. Marsyas, in my opinion, is present in the text; but only as a momentary glimmer. Good divination stops there; it recognizes a necessary constraint. Bad divination drives out good, which is why Richard Levin's amusing book *New Readings versus Old Plays*,[7] which concerns itself mostly with unconstrained divinations, has an excuse for being so wrong about the art of interpretation. It is true that people are always looking for new thematic keys to very well known plays, and that they often behave foolishly; but it does not follow that they are wrong to look. What calls for discussion (not here, not now) is the nature of the constraints. Meanwhile it is enough to say that this tiny part of *Coriolanus* seems to have no extensive relationship with the whole, and testifies simply to the extraordinary intellectual vivacity and freedom of association—the peripheral vision, as it were—that make the late verse of Shakespeare so inexhaustible a source of surprise.

We are now no longer talking about divination as a branch of emendation; so it is important to emphasize not only that there continue to be constraints, just as there are in emendation, but that the existence of constraints should not be misunderstood as a virtual ban on new interpretations of old texts.

> "What a strange memory it would have been for one. Those deserted grounds, that empty hall, that impersonal, voluble voice, and—nobody, nothing, not a soul."
>
> The memory would have been unique and harmless. But she was not a girl to run away from an intimidating impression of solitude and mystery. "No, I did not run away," she said. "I stayed where I was—and I did see a soul. Such a strange soul."

I shall try to illustrate this point from the last of the extracts. It is quite long because I had to get in the two expressions "not a soul" and "I did see a soul." The source is Conrad's *Under Western Eyes;* Natalia Haldin is telling the narrator what happened when she visited Peter Ivanovitch, the great anarchist revolutionary, in his villa at Geneva. She stood around in a dusty hall, listening to the great man's voice in another room; and she might have left without seeing anyone, without seeing a soul. However, the *dame de compagnie,* the oppressed Tekla, turned up, so she did see a soul. It would be possible to say that Conrad's control of English idiom was never perfect (there are undoubtedly unidiomatic expressions in this as in the other novels), and that he wrongly supposed that if you can say in English "I didn't see a soul" you can also say "I saw a soul." This would be a way, in effect, of writing the awkward expression out of the text. But to my mind that is an illicit act; it is conceivable that a native English speaker would have intuitively avoided this locution, but it is fortunate for us that Conrad did not feel himself disqualified from writing in English because he was Polish. Nor do we resent the other forms of alienness his misfortune of birth enabled him to import into our fiction.

The word *soul* (with a great many variants such as "specter," "phantom," "spirit," "ghoul") occurs many dozens of times in Conrad's novel, very often with an unidiomatic quality which serves to draw attention to it. It is, in fact, a characteristic of many long passages of the book, especially in dialogue (we must remember that it is mostly Russians who are doing the talking, Eastern behavior under Western eyes), that it takes a considerable effort of specialized attention on the part of the reader not to see and hear the language employed as extremely odd. Conrad, who wanted to sell his books, was always willing to cater to the kind of reader who has been brainwashed into the right kind of narrowed attentiveness, but he wanted to do other things as well, and a good reader will certainly divine, particularly at such moments as the one I am discussing, that several apparently incompatible things are going on at once: that the word *soul* is here overdetermined, belonging not merely to a colloquial dialogue but also to a "string" or plot of soul references that only very occasionally appears relevant to the simple action of the piece, and in fact constitutes an occult plot of its own. In cases like this the best emblem of the diviner is the third ear of the psychoanalyst; if Conrad is committing a parapraxis when he says "I did see a soul," then that slip is of high analytical importance. And it is worth adding that given the kind of book one is reading, a book in which some measure of divinatory activity on the part of the reader is actively solicited (a *good* book, in our normal view of the matter), all occult relevances count; the question of intention does not arise.

I am now talking about divination on a rather larger scale. There are constraints upon it, certainly; but one must not be deterred by the skepticism, sometimes the ignorant contempt, of one's peers. On the other hand, there is a difference, which the diviner himself must judge, between Shakespeare's Marsyas and Conrad's "soul." In simpler cases one may depend more on a professional consensus. I should add that there is great satisfaction to be had from solving the sort of problem most unprejudiced people can see to be a problem, and to offer a solution that can command assent straightforwardly, as a matter of evidence. If I may be autobiographical for a second, I got as much pleasure out of explaining the presence of the chickens in *The House of Seven Gables* as from any more high-flown divinatory attempt;[8] the explanation had the merit of being falsifiable; it involves a leap of some kind, but a leap anybody can take, then check whether he lands in the same place. Of course he had better not do it in ignorance; but then, as I have argued, no divinatory leap can really be taken in ignorance, however inspired, any more than it can be taken by somebody who has devoted all his study to the theory of leaping.

Intuition, that is, needs support from knowledge, whether we are editing a text or simply reading a novel. We need it even when we are reading undemanding books. We are required to do something, our share, even if that share is deliberately kept to a minimum. Coding operations are called for, even as they are in ordinary conversation. More difficult books reduce their audience by calling for a degree of competence higher than that. Some books we are inclined to think of as great very often make enormous demands, and may also contain fewer indications as to how they are to be read. Such books call forth interpretations which go beyond the consensus; they will probably *include* that consensus and then vary according to the predispositions and perspectives of the individual interpreter, who will nevertheless hope to have them accepted, though there is a high risk that they will be dismissed as counter-intuitive. When we are reading these great books with a proper regard for their complexity, with a sense that we, like their authors, are exploring labyrinths of interpretative possibility, we are diviners (good and bad) just as certainly as Bentley or Housman. Housman once remarked that if a manuscript read just *o* he would have no hesitation in reading *Constantinopolitanus* if he divined that to be the true reading;[9] I think we ought to take similar risks, though remembering that Housman really did know a great deal, and so must we.

We may well believe, then, that there is some continuity between the skills of the old *divinatio* and those of modern reading. Schleiermacher was quite right to borrow the expression for a different sort of interpretation. If you look once more at the second extract, you will have once more a sense of interpretative chastening. No two people could come up with the same answer, or if they did they would both be wrong. There are, it is conceivable, texts which similarly defy the reader of longer discourses; they would be what Roland Barthes calls *scriptible* texts, quite *illisible,* a sort of aconsensual utopia. In other cases an editor makes a reasoned choice, and we can do that also, appealing to the institutional consensus of comparably qualified persons. In still others, one may make a sensible conjecture (which might get us back from *vanished spirits to varnished sprits*). In others we need to be peculiarly attentive before we see that divination is called for anyway, as in the first Forster piece, and this is commonly our position when reading novels, which have a traditional duty to be clear and explicit. For all the operations I have touched upon in the editorial activity are paralleled on a grosser scale in the reading of long texts. Interpretation in that large sense still calls for the kind of skill and courage we associate with a Housman.

For, finally, there is something all we diviners ought to remember. Long after Hermes began the affair, long after Schleiermacher, there was a revolution in the analysis of long texts and in the interpretation of narrative; we correctly associate with it the name of Freud. Since his day we have learned to attend (to screw ourselves up into the posture of attending) not only to what is explicitly stated and conveniently coded, but to the condensations and displacements, the puns and parapraxes, to Shakespeare's Marsyas and Conrad's "soul." In fact it seems we are taking our time about learning the lesson; we are rather slow to pursue occulted senses, evidences of what is not immediately accessible. It is the mark of what I call a classic text that it will provide such evidence; if it were not so the action of time and the accumulation of interpretations would exhaust it or make it redundant. When we admit that something more remains to be interpreted we are in fact calling for divination. It may be very refined, it may be very silly, and in either case it will probably be rejected by other interested parties. But it has to continue. In a sense the whole future depends upon it.

That, in short, is our justification. Our kind of divination, like the older kind, contributes to the sense and the value of the inheritance. The great scholars, sure of their inspiration and often full of vanity, liked to say the gift was innate; whether it is or not, nobody will claim that it can be effective without learning, without competence, without a knowledge of books and methods that can be acquired by labor. Without the science there can be no divination; without the divination the science is tedious. So here is my last word: as to divination, see first that you are born with it. Then, by disciplined labor (whether it is described as philological or hermeneutic, or whether it is simply the acquisition of a perfect knowledge of a text or a corpus of texts), make yourself able to use the gift.

# CHAPTER 8

# *The Plain Sense of Things*

My title is taken from a poem by Wallace Stevens:

> After the leaves have fallen, we return
> To a plain sense of things. It is as if
> We had come to the end of the imagination,
> Inanimate in an inert savoir.
>
> It is difficult even to choose the adjective
> For this blank cold, this sadness without cause.
> The great structure has become a minor house.
> No turban walks across the lessened floors.
>
> The greenhouse never so badly needed paint.
> The chimney is fifty years old and slants to one side.
> A fantastic effort has failed, a repetition
> In a repetitiousness of men and flies.
>
> Yet the absence of the imagination had
> Itself to be imagined. The great pond,
> The plain sense of it, without reflections, leaves,
> Mud, water like dirty glass, expressing silence
>
> Of a sort, silence of a rat come out to see,
> The great pond and its waste of lilies, all this
> Had to be imagined as an inevitable knowledge,
> Required, as a necessity requires.[1]

This is a late poem by Stevens, but it continues a meditation that began much earlier. In its own very idiosyncratic way that meditation echoes a central theme of modern philosophy. The plain sense is itself metaphorical; there is no escape from metaphor;

univocity in language is no more than a dream. The position is familiar, and the interest of Stevens' poem is that he is not so much affirming it as suggesting the movement of mind that accompanies its consideration. He is especially conscious of the extraordinary effort required even to imagine, to find language for, the plain sense of things and hold the language there for the briefest moment: worth trying, he seems to say, but impossible, this attempt to behold "the nothing that is not there and the nothing that is." To make the attempt, he said in the earlier poem I have just quoted ("The Snow Man"), is "to have a mind of winter" (*CP,* p. 9). Only such a mind, a snowman's mind, could attend to the frozen trees without adding to them some increment of language, of humanity, even if that increment is misery.

Such a moment, of unattainable absolute zero, is anyway only to be imagined as a phase in a cyclical process. Language, always metaphorical, falsifies the icy diagram, corrupts by enriching the plain sense, which can only be thus corruptly or distortedly expressed. "Not to have is the beginning of desire" ("Notes toward a Supreme Fiction," *CP,* p. 382); and so metaphor, like spring, adorns the icy diagram; only when that desire is satisfied do we grow tired of summer lushness and welcome the fall and winter again. So the plain sense continually suffers change, and if it did not it would grow rigid and absurd. It must change, or it will simply belong "to our more vestigial states of mind" ("Notes," *CP,* p. 392). But change is inevitable anyway, since the effort we make to attend to plain sense itself takes away the plainness. That this is the case may distress philosophers who want to be able to distinguish the literal from the metaphorical, but it is nevertheless a source of poetry: "Winter and spring, cold copulars, embrace, / And forth the particulars of rapture come" ("Notes," *CP,* p. 392). The imagination's commentary is a part of the text as we know it—that is, distorted by metaphor, by secondary elaboration. This is what Stevens means when he speaks of the effect of the gaiety of language on the natives of poverty ("L'Esthetique du Mal"): the games, fictions, metaphors which accommodate the plain sense to human need.

Without such "makings," as he calls them, the world is just "waste and welter" ("The Planet on the Table," *CP,* p. 532). And the makings are themselves part of a reality more largely conceived, of a whole which is not merely or not always poor; the words of the world are the life of the world.

In the poem at the opening of this essay there is a winter, a due season, a world stripped of imaginative additions, so cold that it resists our adjectives. The summer world made by our imagination is now a ruin; the effort has ended in failure. So, difficult though it may be, one tries to find an adjective for blankness, a tropeless cold. But to say "no turban" is to introduce a turban, something exotic, a gift of imagination; the floors, though lessened, are still fully there; the structure is still a house. Imagination wants a decrepit greenhouse, a tottering chimney; blankness itself becomes a pond, and the pond has lilies and a rat. "The absence of the imagination had / Itself to be imagined." The pond has reflections, leaves, mud, as real a pond as imagination at the best of times could imagine. All these things have to be added to the plain sense if we want it; it is not to be had without comment, without poetry.

It may seem that I have begun this essay at a great distance from any topic that might be thought appropriate to the occasion of its writing, for I was asked to write about the Jewish interpretative practice of *midrash* and its relation—if any—to the interpretation of poetry more generally. In poetry there is often a plain sense and also senses less plain: we might risk saying, a sense corresponding to *peshat,* and others corresponding to *midrash*. But we know that *midrash* and *peshat* are also an intrinsic plural; that the play, might one say even the gaiety, of the one is required to give a human sense to the inaccessible mystery of the other. And it is on the other instances of this collaboration that I shall be expatiating. So it seems sensible enough to begin with a poet who saw so well the relations between plain sense and human need—saw it not as a philosopher or a hermeneutician, but rather as his own major man might, though the major man would understand wholly the supreme fiction in which plain sense and trope, truth and fiction, are finally apprehended as a unity, and the world stops. (Stevens sometimes thought of this major man as a rabbi.) For him the kind of poetry Eliot said he wanted would be a part, but only a part, of poetry: "poetry standing in its own bare bones, or poetry so transparent that we should see not the poetry, but what we are meant to see through the poetry."[2] Note that in speaking of this impossible nakedness or transparency the poet has to imagine a skeleton and a window. The most arduous effort to express the poetry of plain sense brings with it its own metaphors, its own distortions. There are, as Freud would have said, considerations of representability, there are secondary elaborations, there are fortuitous inessentials, day's residues; he might have agreed with Augustine that some things are there for the sake of the sense but not constitutive of the sense. And our only way to catch a glimpse of the sense is by attending to the inevitable distortions.

Northrop Frye remarks that the literal sense of a poem is the whole poem.[3] And the whole which constitutes the literal sense may not be a single poem; nor need that whole be the same for everybody. A canon may define the whole, and the same parts may figure in different canons. For Christian commentators the Psalms belong to a whole different from the whole to which they belong for Jewish commentators; they may agree that there are messianic psalms, but the plain sense of such psalms must be different for each, since the whole text of the Christian shows the fulfillment of the messianic promises. Herbert's poem "The Holy Scriptures (II)" compares the separate texts of the Bible to a constellation, and remarks on the remote interactions of the verses:

> This verse marks that, and both do make a motion
> Unto a third, that ten leaves off doth lie . . .

But for some, though they might accept the principle, those ten leaves are not in their copies. The expression *Son of man* occurs in Psalms 8:4, and modern scholars agree that it means simply "man," and that it ought not to be thought of in relation to the apocalyptic sense of the phrase in Daniel or the passages in the

New Testament which seem to derive from Daniel. But, as John Barton says, the case would be different if the New Testament had happened to cite the passage from the psalm for christological purposes;[4] and in any case it seems unlikely that less scholarly Christians, coming upon these words or hearing them sung in church on the first day of the month, will quite exclude from their thoughts the resonances of New Testament usage.

So the whole, by which the sense of the part is to be determined, varies between the religions and the canons. And there is a further extension of context, which, since it will recur in my argument, I shall mention now. The Roman Catholic Church affirms the authority of the magisterium over all interpretation, and the Church is the custodian of a Tradition; so that to the two parts of the Christian Bible one adds a third contextual element, and the whole that determines the plain sense of the part is thus extended.

However, we need not confine the question thus: for it is clear that different people at different times will form their own notions of the relations between parts, and between parts and wholes. For example, some will maintain that christological interpretations of Old Testament texts are valid only when they have been made in the New Testament; others, a great army of them over the centuries, think otherwise. And the language in which each person or party expresses the sense of the text will necessarily be figurative. The plain sense is not accessible to plain common sense. That is why it has been possible to say, "The plain sense is hidden." Luther believed that "the Holy Spirit is the plainest writer and speaker in heaven and earth," but we may well sympathize with Erasmus, who wanted to know "if it is all so plain, why have so many excellent men for so many centuries walked in darkness?"[5]

The expression *plain sense,* as I am using it, covers the overlapping ideas of literal sense, grammatical sense, and historical sense. It is also a usual translation of *peshat.* The most obvious indication that the plain sense is not a universal and unequivocal property of mankind is that it resists translation from one language into another. A well-known example is John Lyons' demonstration of the difficulty of finding a French equivalent for "the cat sat on the mat"; the nouns are troublesome but the verb is worse, since English does not adjudicate between the senses, in French, of *s'assit, s'est assis(e), s'asseyait.*[6] I shall return to the cat in another connection, but the present point is that plain senses can be tricky to translate. Bruno Bettelheim laments that Freud's English translators alter his sense by refusing to use the word *soul.*[7] But the senses of that word in English are very different from those of its German cognate; *soul* would often be wrong in English. Bettelheim is especially bitter that the translators of the Standard Edition have smuggled in a new word, very technical sounding, to translate *Besetzung,* namely "cathexis." But would "occupation" or "investment" really do the work? And how should we deal with *Überbesetzung?* No doubt "hypercathexis" gives a different idea, but it is probably closer to Freud's sense than "overinvestment," and the same must be true of "anticathexis."

These minor discrepancies are perhaps emblematic of much larger ones. Psychoanalysis changed when it moved from the Viennese into other cultures, and it can never again be what it was in prewar Europe; like other religions it was fissile even in its early stages, and different sects and individuals have always found different plain senses in the original deposits of doctrine. There are obvious parallels in Christianity. Jerome began it, offering *hebraica veritas,* and Greek truth also, but in Latin. Thereafter *logos* became *verbum,* and *verbum* became so firm a part of the theological tradition that when Erasmus, with good philological justification, translated *logos* as *sermo* he got into trouble; for *verbum* seemed to match the required plain sense as *sermo,* a surprising novelty, could not. On the other hand More attacked Tyndale for giving "love" instead of "charity" for *agape;* but now "charity" has changed its contexts and "love" is preferred.[8] The naive desire of the New English Bible translators to provide plain-sense equivalents for the Hebrew of the Old Testament sometimes leads them into what can fairly be called mistranslation, as in their version of the rape of Dinah by Shechem (Genesis 34:3): "But he remained true to Dinah." The sense of the Hebrew *nefesh* is lost, though the King James version, which has "And his soul clave unto Dinah," conveys, as Hammond observes, the intensity of Shechem's erotic feelings. "'Remained true' is exactly the wrong phrase since it implies fidelity and honour; the point of the story is that Shechem's lust is not fulfilled by one act of rape."[9] No doubt this view could be disputed, since *nefesh,* according to the Lexicon, is a tremendously complicated word, and no translation could do it justice. But King James wins by not seeking a commonplace equivalent.

When whole systems of belief are involved, as in the case of the Bible they always are, the difficulties are multiplied. Christianity decided to reject Marcion and keep the Jewish Bible, and thenceforth the question of the nature of its relevance to a non-Jewish religion became a permanent problem, with much bearing on the matter of plain sense. If the Law was abrogated the relevance of the Old Testament lay primarily in its prefigurative relation to the New; it became, more or less, a repository of types. But it contained other elements not easily given up—moral instruction and a history of God's providence and promises. And from quite early times there was some resistance to the copious allegorizing of the Alexandrian tradition, some respect for the *sensus historicus.* The school of Antioch limited allegorical interpretation to the sort of thing licensed by Paul, for example in his reading of the story of the sons of Sarah and Hagar. Theodore of Mopsuestia sought to understand the Old Testament historically; for instance, he rejected the usual (and, in the circumstances, obvious) reading of the Suffering Servant in Isaiah 53. But Theodore was posthumously condemned, and the majority of Antiochenes were in any case less rigidly historicist, as D. S. Wallace-Hadrill explains.[10]

And yet, despite the success of allegory, the importance of the literal sense was habitually affirmed, most influentially by Augustine, a contemporary of Theodore but working in a different tradition. Augustine was a historian, and as an exegete he held that an understanding of historical reality must be the foundation of any attempt to provide spiritual interpretation. His emphasis on Jewish history as continuous with Christian was influential. But he also ruled that no interpretation should transgress against "charity": any literal-historical sense that was inconsistent with virtuous conduct and the true faith should be treated figuratively. And he provided for the frequent occurrence of texts that appeared to have no particular Christian relevance; they were there for the sake of the others, as ploughs have handles.[11] Thus the typical quality of the historical sense is maintained, and the position is as J. S. Preuss describes it: the plain sense of some of the Old Testament is edifying in itself, but the remainder has value only because it means something other than it seems to be saying; the literal, grammatical, and historical senses include what should not be figuratively interpreted and also what must be so interpreted. But that which is edifying is so only because it already conforms with the New Testament, and the unedifying has to be made edifying by figurative reading in New Testament terms. Thus the extended context determines the plain sense, which, in the case of the Old Testament, resides effectively in the text of the New. There was a Jewish or carnal sense, to which one might attribute more or less importance; but the true sense was Christian and spiritual, and that sense could be represented as the plain sense. The figurative becomes the literal.

So, although the warning that the *sensus historicus* must be the foundation of exegesis was frequently repeated, it appears that a really active concern for the historical sense of the Old Testament did not recur until the later years of the eleventh century, when it was in large part the result of intercourse between Jewish and Christian scholars. It was at that moment that *peshat* entered, or reentered, Christian thought. Erwin Rosenthal has explained with great clarity the position of Jewish scholarship after Saadya Gaon; how the distinction between *peshat* and *derash* now grew sharper, how *peshat* served as a weapon against christological interpretations, and how Rashi, by his more correct understanding of the relation between the two, influenced not only his Jewish but his Christian contemporaries.[12] The conflict between extreme adherents of *peshat* and *derash,* between the literal sense and the tradition, the literal sense and the mystical kabbalistic sense, continued within the Jewish tradition. But meanwhile a new respect for the Hebrew text and the *sensus Judaicus* was once again altering the context of Christian interpretation.

Beryl Smalley established the influence of Jewish scholarship on the work of the Victorines.[13] Relations between Jewish and Christian scholars were never wholly cordial, but they were productive, for the "Hebrew truth" of Jerome was now taken back into its own language. Hugh of St. Victor had some Hebrew, and he consulted Jewish scholars and reported their interpretations. There was a new emphasis on the historical sense as Jews understood it. Hugh anticipated Aquinas in arguing that to be ignorant of the signs was to be ignorant of what they signified, and so of what the signified, itself a sign, signified. It will, however, be noticed that this formula does nothing to alter the position that a true understanding of the Jewish Bible depends upon and is subsequent to a true understanding of the New Testament; for the Jewish reading, though it accurately carries out the first stage of the process, the establishment of literal, grammatical, and historical sense, plays no part in the second, which is to determine what the signified signifies. The Jewish sense is still the carnal one, and preliminary to the spiritual reading.

It would seem that Jewish scholarship was bolder, in that it sometimes risked everything on the plain sense. Joseph Kara, early in the twelfth century, could remark that "whosoever is ignorant of the literal meaning of the Scripture and inclines after a Midrash is like a drowning man who clutches at a straw to save himself."[14] Masters of Haggadah may mock him, he says; but the enlightened will prefer the truth. Nevertheless, we are told, he himself frequently inclined after midrash. It was the next generation of Jewish scholars, contemporaries of Andrew of St. Victor, the hero of Beryl Smalley's research, who installed the literal sense more firmly. Andrew ecumenically devised a dual method of interpretation, giving the Vulgate text with a Christian explanation, and the Hebrew text with a Jewish. The literal sense was that of the Jews. For example, on Isaiah 7:14–16, "Behold, a virgin shall conceive," Andrew cites

Rashi to the effect that the literal sense is this: the bride of the prophet will conceive a son to deliver Israel. Though he rejects this interpretation with some vehemence, Andrew allows it the title of the literal sense.[15] But Christians live by the spirit, and their reading of the passage, based on the *virgo* of the Vulgate, is the true if not the literal one.

In using the Jews, to quote Smalley, as "a kind of telephone to the Old Testament,"[16] Andrew naturally annoyed some contemporaries. He was accused of "judaizing." But judaizing gave a new turn to the speculation about literal sense and its relation to spiritual sense. Henceforth the argument of Hugh of St. Victor, as restated and given authority by Aquinas, prevailed. The words mean one thing only; but that thing may be a sign of other things, and it is from those second-order things that the spiritual sense derives. The historical sense, the sense of the human author, is what he says; but there is a divine author whose intentions are other than his. "Truly, the literal sense is that which the author intended; but the author of sacred Scripture is God, who comprehends in his *intellectus* all things at once."[17] So the spiritual or symbolic or typical interpretation is more faithful to the *mens auctoris* than the literal; and regardless of what is properly to be called the literal sense, the true sense is to be found in the New Testament.

There were various attempts to resolve the ambiguities of this position, as when the extremely influential commentator Nicholas de Lyra also spoke of the literal sense itself as dual; the symbolic interpretation was to be regarded as the literal one if expressly approved by the New Testament (a partial return to the Antiochan doctrine). When God says of Solomon (1 Chronicles 11): "I will be a father to him, and he will be like a son to me," the application to Solomon is literal; but because the author of the Epistle to the Hebrews uses the text to show that Christ is higher than the angels, it has a second literal sense, which is also mystical. Preuss thinks this is the "first time . . . a New Testament reading of an Old Testament passage is dignified with the label 'literal'"; though the general idea is of course not new.[18]

It seems, then, that throughout this period there grew up a desire to narrow the gap between the Christian and the literal sense. But since the literal sense could still be referred to the New Testament, some Jewish scholars now abandoned their own messianic interpretations and clove to the *sensus historicus,* in order to avoid any suggestion that might give support to the christological reading, for example of Psalm 2. Once again it is apparent that the Christians, however devoted to the *hebraica veritas,* could not be so bold as the Jews; for their interpretations were always subject to censorship by the custodians of an infallible tradition that was partly independent of Scripture. Of course Jewish interpreters had to steer a course between the fundamentalism of the Karaites and the allegories of the Kabbalah; but the institution controlling Christian interpretation was very powerful, and the authority of the tradition, which in some ways stood to the New Testament as the New Testament did to the Old, could be enforced by the Inquisition; these were not merely erudite arguments.

By the fifteenth century the matter of literal sense called for formal discussion, as in Jean Gerson's *De sensu litterali sacrae Scripturae* of 1414, which decided that the Church alone had the power to determine the literal sense. It derived its authority to do so from the promise of Christ in the New Testament; that is, the literal sense of the New Testament confers on the Church the right to declare the true sense of any text. Preuss comments on the importance and timeliness of this pronouncement. Heretics claimed that their doctrines were founded on the literal sense of Scripture; but if the literal sense is by definition the "literal sense of the Church," and not anything more generally available, then merely to affirm a different sense from that of the Church was proof of heresy. "The possibility of argument from Scripture against the *magisterium* is for the first time . . . programmatically and theoretically eliminated."[19] There would no longer be any point in asking Jews about the plain sense of an Old Testament passage; that sense was first revealed through Christ and the apostles, then protected and studied by the Church, and subsequently enforceable with all manner of sanctions.

So the lines were drawn for the struggle between Luther's plain sense, his *sola scriptura,* and the authority of Rome, only possessor of the sense of Scripture. Luther was speaking no more than truth when he accused the Popes of setting themselves up as "lords of Scripture"; that was exactly what they had done. Of the religious, political, and military consequences of this hermeneutic disagreement it is unnecessary to speak. Curiously enough, in our own time it is a Protestant hermeneutics that has insisted upon the necessity of understanding tradition as formative of the horizon from which we must seek some kind of encounter with ancient texts, denying at the same time any immediacy of access to those texts. It seems that Gerson and the popes had grasped an important point, namely that all interpretation is validated in the end by a third force, and not by the unaided and unauthoritative study of isolated scholars; and they wished to be sure that the third force was the Church.

Luther, as a matter of fact, opposed enthusiastic reading also; as far as he could see Müntzer and the Pope were both arrogating to themselves an improper authority over Scripture. But in the next century the Council of Trent made equivocation and compromise impossible by giving renewed emphasis to tradition and authority. The subsequent history of the Catholic view was determined by the Tridentine decisions.

It seems reasonable to conclude this brief anthology of disputes about plain sense by glancing at some exegetical problems which had to be settled at the time of Catholic Modernism. The intellectual atmosphere of the late nineteenth century, including the success over a generation or so of Darwinism and, perhaps even more threatening, the achievement and the fame of German Protestant biblical scholarship, made both Authority and Tradition subject to question. There arose within the Church scholars who thought the official position needed revision. An early hint of the new kind of hermeneutic understanding recommended to the Church is to be found in the work of the Tübingen Catholic theologian Johann Evangelist von Kuhn. He agreed with the Protestants that the Bible is privileged over all other documents, but said that they failed to understand this: Tradition, as distinct from traditions, is the preaching and consciousness of the Church *in the present moment*. "Tradition is the *kerygma* of the present; Scripture, the *kerygma* of the past, is the *doctrina*-source of the present."[20]

This new formulation places the sense of Scripture firmly in the here and now; it denies that application can be divorced from understanding. A related idea, very characteristic of its time, is that religion has undergone an evolutionary development, and that the old texts and forms might be thought of as types of later doctrine, an idea prevalent in the thought of the period, and given expression in literature (by Hawthorne, for instance) as well as in Catholic theology (by Newman, who said that "the earlier prophecies are pregnant texts out of which the succeeding announcements grow; they are types").[21]

Such views were condemned in 1870, but a generation later they appeared again in a rather different form with Modernism proper. Its proponents favored Tradition over Scripture, seeing Tradition as a process of inspired development. The reflex of the Church, inevitably conservative, was to retreat to a scriptural position. This is not surprising; it must have been rather horrifying to hear Von Hügel, a man of impeccable piety (Yeats praised him because he accepted the miracles of the saints and honored sanctity) proclaiming that even if the Gospel narratives were unrelated to historical events they would still be true as "creations of the imagination"—a position not really very far from that of some modern Protestants. The English convert George Tyrrell was shocked to find in the Roman Church the sort of bible religion he had thought he was leaving behind. He believed that God was the First Cause, and so the author of Scripture only in the sense that he was the author of everything. He was aware of the difficulty of steering a course between the two positions, one holding that the deposit was perpetually valid, the other that doctrine developed progressively. Here again is the hermeneutic problem about original and applied sense. Tyrrell failed to solve it and was disgraced. In France Alfred Loisy expressed similar views and with more force, remarking in a very modern manner that a book absolutely true for all times would be unintelligible at all times; he too saw the danger of reading back a modern idea of religion into the Scriptures. Caught between these positions, he too fell foul of the Church and was excommunicated.[22]

The plain sense of Scripture, as of anything else, is a hermeneutical question, and we have seen how different are the hermeneutics of Augustine, the medieval Jewish scholars, Gerson, and Loisy. One concept that was rigorously developed was that of the role of authority, the institutional power to validate or to invalidate by reference to Tradition; but when Tyrrell and Loisy were purged authority was acting as it were politically, for to the outsider it might have seemed that they were trying to give the idea of Tradition new force. Their proposals, like those of von Kuhn, offered the Church a plausible modern hermeneutic, with an acceptable view of the relation between the origin and the here and now; but the idea of development, though supported by the whole history of dogma, was too frightening.

Modernism was revived in a modern form in the 1940s and partly endorsed by Vatican II. The principal effect has been to allow Catholic scholars to engage in the sort of historical research formerly associated with Protestant scholarship; and this may seem belated, for elsewhere there is a strong shift away from the objectivist assumptions of that scholarship and toward a newer hermeneutics. It is now often maintained that the plain sense, if there is one, must be of the here and now rather than of the origin.

One thing is sure: the body of presuppositions which determines our notions of the plain sense is always changing, and so is the concept of the validating authority. As the new canonical criticism demonstrates, there are new ways of establishing relevant contexts, and new extratextual authorities, like the idea of canon in this case. And a hermeneutics that allowed for possibilities of change and adaptation might have suited the Church, as the defender of Tradition, very well, as—or so it appears—the Jewish tradition has accommodated change and adaptation without sacrificing the original deposit. What the Modernists saw was that if Tradition entailed change, there was a need for a theory of interpretation which could close the widening gap between doctrine and text and require newly licensed plain senses. In practice the means has always been available; the dogma of the Assumption of the Virgin, promulgated in 1950, depends on Tradition and not on Scripture, and on a tradition that can only with difficulty be traced back as far as the fourth century. It would have been particularly surprising to St. Mark. But if we think of Tradition as the third part of the Catholic canonical context it is possible to suppose that the Assumption is part of the plain sense of the whole; and, after all, assumptions occur in both the other parts.

My purpose has been to suggest that the plain sense of things is always dependent on the understanding of larger wholes and on changing custom and authority. So it must change; it is never naked, but, as the poet says, it always wears some fictive covering. Time itself changes it, however much authority may resist. It must, of course, do so. And it cannot do so if it fails to preserve its foundation text; and, short of keeping that text out of unauthorized hands, it cannot prevent readers from making their imaginative additions to the icy diagram.

Finally, the plain sense depends in larger measure on the imaginative activity of interpreters. This is variously constrained, by authority or hermeneutic rules or assumptions, but it is necessary if the text is to have any communicable sense at all. Given plausible rules and a firm structure of authority, change may not be violent. One recalls Raphael Loewe's magisterial essay on "The 'Plain' Meaning of Scripture in Early Jewish Exegesis."[23] The word *peshat* itself is metaphorical; its plain senses have to do with flattening, extending, and derivatively with simplicity and innocence and lack of learning, with the popular, the read-once-only, the clear, the generally accepted, the current, and so on; but the central sense, Loewe maintains, is authority. It is used to describe readings by no means literal, and applications "entirely arbitrary." Loewe concludes that the best translation of the word, at any rate up to the end of the period of the Talmuds and the midrashim, is "authoritative teaching," which covers both traditional teaching and teaching given by a particular rabbi of acknowledged authority. And, says Loewe, "the conventional distinction between *peshat* and *derash* must be jettisoned." In times later than those of which Loewe speaks, the identification of *peshat* with plain sense became firmer, with important results. But its historical association with authority, and its inescapable association with *derash,* point clearly enough to the conclusion that our minds are not very well adapted to the perception of texts in themselves; we necessarily provide them with contexts, some of them imposed by authority and tradition, some by the need to make sense of them in a different world.

It is possible for some philosophers of language to speak of a "zero context"—to maintain that "for every sentence the literal meaning of the sentence can be construed as the meaning it has independent of any context whatever." In expressing his dissent from this opinion, John Searle argues that the meaning even of "the cat sat on the mat" depends upon "background assumptions"; there is, he believes, "no constant set of assumptions that determine the notion of literal meaning."[24] Some of these assumptions are silently at work when we make the statement about the cat. Its plain sense depends, among other things, on the assumption that the cat and the mat are within the gravitational field of the earth; and Searle is able to fit out the sentence with speculative contexts which give it quite other senses. But this fascinating sentence invites other potentially interesting considerations. For example: the sentence is felt as somehow infantile, as belonging to a reading primer, perhaps; it owes its memorability to a triple rhyme—a phonetic bond which solicits our attention to the code rather than the message. That the procedures are metaphoric rather than metonymic gives the sentence a poetic quality and more potential intertext (so long as we have it in the original language). There is the further consideration that the sentence must almost always have a citational quality—Lyons and Searle both cite it as an example, and I have cited them citing it. Since it lives in such rarefied contexts its simplicity is certainly bogus, and its use variously colored by pedantry and archness. It has no plain sense; it merely serves as a lay figure, like the poet's icy diagram, his lake with its shadows, rats, and lilies.

And that takes me back to the imaginary zero context where

I began. There is no "inert savoir"; to speak as if there were is already to speak "as if." Metaphor begins to remodel the plain sense as soon as we begin to think or to speak about it. If Stevens is right in saying that the words of the world are the life of the world, then metaphor runs in the world's blood, as if *derash* and *peshat* were the red and the white corpuscles, intrinsically plural.

I have taken most of my examples from exegesis as practiced in religions which maintained over very long periods an extreme veneration for their sacred texts, and which certainly abhorred the idea of deliberate interference or distortion. The place of rule-governed imagination was clearly established in *midrash*. In the Christian tradition, with its basic belief that the sense of the Jewish Bible must be sought in another book, there is a quite different imaginative challenge. All such result in *Entstellung*, not *Darstellung*. Among the thousands of commentators there have been literalists of the imagination and also extravagant poets. But all have in their measure to be creators, even if they wish to imagine themselves at the end of imagination when the lake is still, without reflections; there may be silence, but it is silence of a sort, never zero silence.

CHAPTER 9

# *The Argument about Canons*

Except when the true ecclesiastical canons are their topic, people who use the word *canon* usually have in mind quite practical issues. They may, for example, be stating that there is for students of literature a list of books or authors certified by tradition or by an institution as worthy of intensive study and required reading for all who may aspire to professional standing within that institution. Or they may be disputing the constitution of the canon, or even the right of the institution to certify it. And now the issues grow more theoretical. For some maintain that the very concept of "literature" as a way of discriminating between more and less privileged texts is an illicit one; so, *a fortiori,* further discriminations between texts that have thus been set apart must also be improper.

There are arguments of this kind now actively in progress in the humanities, and especially in literary criticism, but it is presumably acknowledged by all parties that the analogy which permits them to speak of secular canons is an imperfect one. The ecclesiastical canons are, allowing for a small measure of sectarian variation, fixed; and their fixity, however come by, is a matter of principle or doctrine. Secular canons need to be more permeable; new works are occasionally added, old works, now held to have been neglected, are revived and inserted; now and again something may be excluded. Still, even allowing for these differences, the concept of a secular canon has real force, and may even be necessary to the preservation of our disciplines.

However, that is not my present subject. I want rather to see if laymen have anything to learn from listening in to a current dispute over the true character of the ecclesiastical canon, on the ideas of which their own notions of canonicity are founded.

I shall not attempt to give a detailed account of what is inevitably a complicated matter, or to provide a history of the whole contention. It will be quite enough, I think, to explain the nature of the differences between the champions of the two parties that now oppose each other. What is called "canonical criticism" can fairly be represented by Brevard S. Childs of Yale, and the most powerful enemy of this new style is James Barr of Oxford.

Childs, in his *Introduction to the Old Testament as Scripture* (1979), says that the Bible should be treated as a "collection with parameters" (p. 40). That is, of course, the old way of treating it; but Childs says that the traditional concept of canon, weakened already by the Reformation, suffered progressive collapse under the pressure of the historical criticism that has flourished over the past two centuries. Attention was diverted from the wholeness of the Bible and directed instead to the study of individual books and segments. To criticism of this kind the canon was interesting, if at all, because of the peculiar, historically irrelevant, and inevitably misleading way it was put together. No time or energy was left for what came to be seen as a merely pious or archaic study of this fortuitously assembled collection as a unity, as the singular Bible that evolved out of the plural *biblia*.

Consequently, says Childs, there is a "long-established tension between the canon and criticism" (meaning the "traditio-historical" variety so long dominant). He wishes to reduce this tension; he will try "to understand the Old Testament as canonical scripture [that is, to see it as a literary and presumably theological unit, 'with fixed parameters'] and yet to make full and consistent use of the historical-critical tools" (p. 45). He is not, that is to say, proposing a primitivistic return to the prehistorical mode of criticism, which could afford to treat the canon as all of a piece, and divinely instituted exactly as it was; for proper attention to the integrity of the canon need not preclude historical study of the interaction between the developing corpus and the community as it changes through history. It is important to Childs that the canon was the product of many successive decisions, not of some belated and extrinsic act of validation. The history of the formation of the canon is important. Nevertheless, the canon as it is, in its full, valid form, ought, in his opinion, to be the prime object of attention.

Perhaps one can best illustrate the desired interplay between this kind of history and this kind of canonical criticism by citing the well-known demonstration by James A. Sanders, in his pioneering book *Torah and Canon* (1972), that the intrusion of Deuteronomy between Numbers and Joshua decisively affected the tradition and gave a new cast to subsequent understanding of the Jewish Bible as a whole. Similar observations have been made, though with less confidence, concerning the decision to put St. John after St. Luke, thus dividing the two-part work Luke and Acts.

The suggestion, then, is that historical and canonical criticism can live together and cooperate. But priority is still to be accorded to the canon. That, however, is a decision unacceptable in principle to historians who think the canon a late and arbitrary imposition with no bearing on the true (that is, the original) import of its members. Hence the tension Childs seeks to resolve. On the one hand it is necessary to maintain that the canon is not just an opaque wrapping that must be seen through or removed if one is to get at the contents and achieve a true sense of each of them. On the other, it has to be acknowledged that the constituents of the canon have their own histories, and that all the work devoted to the recovery of their original precanonical sense has not been entirely wasted.

It can of course be said that in canonical books there are words addressed to an original situation that are intended to have relevance also to later ones, and later ones that derive from, or relate more or less directly to, earlier ones, so that for some purposes at least it is only sensible to think of the canon as a whole. Moreover, the preservation of old writings and the habit of venerating them happen not primarily because they are witnesses to a merely historical state of affairs, but because that state of affairs has consuming relevance to later times; so that it is their capacity to be *applied,* and the practice of applying them to situations other than the historical circumstances of their origin, that saves them. In a closed canon this position is generalized, and the entire body of scripture is endowed with a potential of perpetual and prophetic applicability. Before closure it was possible to obtain this necessary modern application by rewriting or adding to the body of sacred texts, but as soon as you have an enclosed canon you can no longer do that, and indeed the unalterability of the words becomes an essential aspect of its sacredness. Henceforth all interpretation, all modernization, has to be in the form of commentary. Indeed this sequence of events is in a way repeated, since there accumulates an Oral Torah which acquires its own kind of canonicity when it is written down: and so forth. Thus in the Jewish tradition the Torah is always accompanied by its shadow, the commentary that will presumably go on forever; and yet they are thought of together as the Torah, a syzygy of that which is fixed and that which changes in time.

Such considerations do not appear to be part of Childs's case, but he does argue that the formation of the canon was a decisive moment in the history of Jewish religion; for after that moment it was possible for Israel, no longer possessed of a Temple cult, to define itself instead in terms of a book. Its existence made possible all succeeding "actualizations" of the religion. And by minimizing the importance of the canon, historical criticism has destroyed or damaged our ability to understand the process by which scriptures which were once of temporally restricted significance became one Scripture, normative for a community throughout its history.

Behind Barr's objections to Childs there is a wholly different idea of what it is to read a book, especially a book that claims or seems to claim the property of historical reference. To Barr it appears obvious not only that the individual books are much more important than the enclosure into which they were eventually herded, but also that what the books are *about* is much more important than the books. It is not the canon that gives the books their authority; it is the events and persons the books report. Indeed the habit of venerating writing for what it is, and for its relation with other writing that has got between the same covers, strikes him as simply dishonest, and he says so with impressive vigor. His book, *Holy Scripture: Canon, Authority and Criticism* (1983), is indeed an exceptionally strong polemic against the position taken by Childs, and against Childs himself as its leading exponent.

Barr thinks it worth notice that the interesting persons represented in the Bible got along perfectly well without a canon. Those of the New Testament, happy with their oral kerygma, were quite unaware that they were writing books that would later be made canonical. Childs had argued for a connection between the self-identity of a church and its possession of a precisely limited canon; Barr declares this connection to be illusory. How much difference, he asks, would it make to the Roman Catholic church if the book of Wisdom were struck out of the canon, and how much to the Protestant churches if they had to admit it (pp. 41–42)? Barr maintains that the extreme canonical position—that sixty-six books are inspired and nothing else is—has no scriptural support; and indeed he finds offensive the implication that there are no truths outside them, when on any sane view there are. And he points out, correctly, that to privilege books by establishing them in a canon is to confer great and in his opinion undeserved advantages upon them; for example they belong automatically—whatever their intrinsic quality—to a class above the *Confessions* of St. Augustine. Success in these matters is determined simply by getting inside; Jude is in and Augustine isn't; as with the Order of the Garter there's no damned nonsense about merit. Serious scholars should avoid such foolishness.

In any case it makes little sense, Barr believes, to speak of the Old Testament having a canon at all. The textbooks, with some support from the Talmud, will tell you it was established at the council held at Jamnia toward the end of the first century of the present era. Barr inclines to the view that if anything at all happened at Jamnia it had nothing to do with canons; perhaps there were "academic discussions about legal questions" (p. 56). Moreover, he is suspicious of the so-called "Alexandrian canon," the larger canon that makes up the Greek version of the Jewish Bible. It was merely the Torah plus a number of other books. In any case, if one is really looking for the true source of authority in Judaism one will have to admit that it is not identifiable with scripture but with Torah and Talmud together; so that even if a canon were fixed at Jamnia or anywhere else, "this was a less important and less decisive fact than would seem natural to those who have seen the notion of the canon through the glass of the Calvinistic Reformation" (p. 61). It will be seen that Barr has little use for canons in general. They are, if taken seriously, impediments to the real business of history.

However, his strongest objections to Childs arise less from disagreements about the history of the canon than from the claim that "canon and criticism" can be put to work as partners. This is tantamount to saying that truth and falsehood can be yoked and plough together. And the difference between Childs and Barr now presents itself in this manner: for Childs the final meaning—the meaning established by the formation of a canon—is the true one; but for Barr the true meaning is the *original* meaning, to be ascertained as far as possible by progressive historical research. Here, then, is the root of this matter: the argument is between "objective" history and a hermeneutic approach to truth.

According to Barr, "canonical" criticism entails a "decontextualization" (the stripping away, he means, of the real historical context) comparable to that effected by midrash—which updates by adaptive commentary the text that time has made obscure or apparently irrelevant—or the selfishly limited interpretative techniques used by the Qumram community, techniques which applied scripture exclusively to the modern moment of the sect (p. 80). Such decontextualization entails falsehood. Truth lies in the historical method; it is therefore dependent upon scholarly methods and techniques discovered in the past couple of hundred years. Barr allows that its discovery was belated, but holds that it has nevertheless its basis in "an ultimate datum of faith" (p. 101). These methods give us access to the important persons and events described in the books of the Bible; and to be interested in them is to be interested in the truth. But scholars whose training has been oriented toward hermeneutics, especially in the adulterated versions of the German originals he says are current in the United States, are not interested in the truth. He blows them all away with an epigram: "The final criterion for theology cannot be relevance; it can only be truth" (p. 118).

This is the position expounded by Barr in a long and acrimonious appendix. That the "final" meaning can be the true one he rejects on instinct. That "appropriation" or application is inseparable from understanding, that the most learned and conscientious historian is still restricted by his own historical situation, a situation of which he cannot be so fully conscious as to transcend it by an effort of will and intellect—these are just the arguments Barr most deplores. He says there are grounds for thinking "this philosophy"—attributed to Bultmann and his epigoni—"a wrong one" (p. 143), but he does not, at any rate in this book, say what those grounds are. It was presumably enough to notice that the consequences of behaving as if this philosophy were a right one are absurd and repellent. What, for instance, is one to make of a way of doing biblical scholarship that treats Amos as of no more importance than his redactors? Or, more generally, that regards the Bible as a "separate cognitive zone" (p. 168)? The position is so ridiculous as to require no confutation.

Whether or not Barr is right about the absurdity of this view of the canon, he is surely wrong to call it a twentieth-century innovation. For example, it is stated dogmatically by Milton's Jesus in *Paradise Regained,* and would have seemed familiar to all who defined *curiositas* as the quest for useless knowledge, meaning knowledge not conducive to salvation: a very large number of people over a very long period. However, that is not the important issue, which I take to be, inevitably, hermeneutic. Barr asserts that it is untrue to claim that understanding and application are simultaneous; but that is the belief of the opposite party. Strong in the conviction that common sense supports only his own view, Barr simply denounces theirs. But there is more to be said.

One could reasonably say that some modern criticism is "holistic" and "appropriative"; which of course is not to say that these are exclusively modern qualities. Indeed such criticism bears an obvious resemblance to some ancient modes of interpretation. It is rather important to understand this, though it is equally important to take account of the differences between old and new. Probably the most important (as this dispute demonstrates) is that the modern variety has a strong antithetical relation to the tradition of "objective" historical scholarship which it wishes to modify or oppose. Childs of course knows that very well, and Barr accordingly scolds him for his ambivalence toward historical criticism; but it would surely, even on his view, be a worse error to forget or ignore that kind of criticism altogether and really write like the Qumram sectaries.

That there are rote denunciations of historical criticism by persons unqualified to make them, as Barr alleges, may well be true. There are always people around who think it would be a good thing to abolish the past. Barr remarks, and plausibly, that Rudolf Bultmann, the godfather of hermeneutics as understood by most American theologians, would have been disgusted by such facile condemnations of the sort of work on which he spent so much of his life. Evidently Barr thinks better of that side of Bultmann's work than he does of the hermeneutics. In fact Bultmann cannot have thought of the two as quite so easily separated; indeed the relationship between his historical work and his hermeneutics, like the argument between Childs and Barr, is inescapably a hermeneutic issue, and one that already has a very long history.

The problem declared itself, and was duly discussed, as soon as the historical criticism of the New Testament began with the work of Semler and Michaelis in the eighteenth century. Michaelis saw that to subject the separate books of the Bible to historical analysis implied the view that the canon was not uniformly inspired. He did not think this change of attitude harmful to religion; indeed he tried—by historical research!—to establish which books were truly inspired and which were not. But the consequences for later scholarship were very great, and the inferences drawn were different. Scholars were able to behave as if inspiration were none of their business, and the tensions between history and faith, reflected sometimes in controversy between historian and theologian, and sometimes within one man who aspired to be both, became a permanent problem.

Almost a century before Barr we find Wilhelm Wrede confidently stating that objective scholarship has no concern with the canon. It must simply seek "to recover the actual state of affairs"; what theology makes of the results is another business altogether. The vocation of the scholar calls for complete disinterest: "He must be able to distinguish his own thinking from that alien to it, modern ideas from those of the past; he must be able to prevent his own view, however dear, from exerting any influence on the object of research, to hold it, so to speak, in suspension. For he only wishes to discover how things really were." The words echo Ranke, and the practice of historical scholarship continues to do so. Wrede expressly asserts the consequences of this doctrine for the canon when he says that the New Testament writings are not to be understood "from the point of view of a subsequent experience with which they *originally* had nothing whatever to do" (my italics). There must be no difference between the ways in which one treats canonical and noncanonical documents. The assembly into a canon of certain favored documents is at best evidence for the quite obsolete presuppositions or desires of canon-makers, trapped in their own historical moment; and the assumption is that by using modern historical methods the scientific scholar is exempted from any such historical limitation, and may make direct contact with the past as it really was.[1]

That there can be no distinction between sacred and secular hermeneutics—that biblical texts are susceptible to exactly the same treatment as any other ancient documents—was early declared to be a rule in biblical interpretation. But it is a position easier to assert than to maintain. If you treat the sacred book exactly like any other you must ask, for example, what was the nature of the now blurred original? What were the local constraints, the historical needs, the intentions of the human author? These are matters for the historian. The theologian, on the other hand, will have to consider the canonical New Testament as the source of his interest and the object of his inquiries, the very *donnée* of his religion. Yet the historians are, for the most part, clerics, and wish to reconcile with their scientific historical project the religious foreunderstanding they possess as Christian preachers. And even if these theologians are not historians they can scarcely dare to ignore the extent and import of centuries of historical research and speculation.

Such was the dilemma of Rudolf Bultmann. He was an eminent practitioner of that branch of historical inquiry known as form-criticism. He believed that the historical was the only scientific method of research. But as a theologian, working in the shadow of Barthian existentialism, he needed to reconcile his practice as a historian with the assumption that faith was immediate, modern, and personal. He summed up his attitude thus: "Historical and theological exegesis stand in a relationship that does not lend itself to analysis, because genuine historical exegesis rests on an existential confrontation with history and therefore coincides with theological exegesis."[2]

Bultmann was therefore, it seems, committed to these opinions: (1) that "the interpretation of biblical writings is subject to exactly the same conditions of understanding as any other literature," a view he shared with many precursors; (2) that their interpretation depended upon foreunderstandings between the reader and the text. There has to be previous acquaintance with the material—an understanding not acquired directly from the text in question, a presupposition. But what is presupposed is, at least in part, a relation between the interpreter and God. Bultmann's foreunderstanding of biblical texts is therefore unavoidably theological, as of course it would not be if he were reading a secular text or indeed uncanonical religious writings. He seems, by a very tortuous route, to have got himself back into something like the position of Augustine; and the formula he uses to get out of that position will not convince everybody.

The effect of such foreunderstanding as Bultmann speaks of is an easy one to illustrate. A Jew may share with a Christian the presupposition that he is concerned with the question of God, and the presupposition that the Old Testament bears on that question. But their concerns are shaped by different notions of the truth; the Jew will not think the Christian correct in his interpretation of the Jewish Bible because he reads it in the light of assumptions concerning the New Testament. A Christian—St. Augustine for example—will hold that the faithful must read the Old Testament as typological, as containing latent truths the Jews have obstinately ignored. Foreunderstandings are obviously different for different religions, and they will be different again for the nonbeliever; but it is these foreunderstandings that determine the application which, for example in Gadamer, who uses the above illustration, determines meaning.[3] Of course foreunderstanding is not foreknowledge. It implies a certain provisionality in one's approach to a text, and the text will modify it; Bultmann is of course fully aware of that. But it remains clear enough that historical self-understanding (such as we get from dialogue with other people or with profane books) is, in his theology, a wholly different matter from the eschatological understanding of faith.

How then can it be that historical inquiry into sacred books should use methods identical with those proper for profane texts? Are the latter also to be read in some eschatological sense? The answer seems to be that the methods must in practice differ. There is a truth, Gadamer observes in the course of his remarks on Bultmann, which is a revealedness revealed historically to subjects historically situated; and this truth is not eternal. Bultmann wants truth to be what is understood within the existential possibilities of the interpreter, but also wants the historical facts to have a status independent of such considerations; to claim that the two positions are one is to claim more than common sense will allow. The "tension" spoken of by Childs is not so easily eliminated.

Gadamer also speaks of the "tensions" between historical study and hermeneutics. The historian is always after something *behind* the text. "He seeks in the text what the text is not, of itself, seeking to provide [evidence, for instance, of a pre-redactional state, direct testimony as to events and persons]. . . . He will always go back behind [the texts] and the meaning they express [which he will not regard as the inherently true meaning] to enquire into the reality of which they are the involuntary [*scil.* 'perhaps distorted'?] expression. Texts are set beside all the other historical material available, i.e., beside the so-called relics of the past." But the critic is interested in the *text* and *its* meaning. Hence the tensions, which of late—indeed for a long time—have been masked by the fact that literary criticism has allowed itself to be regarded as "an ancillary discipline to history."[4] (Note that for Gadamer it is the historical method that violates the intention of the *text,* whereas in recognitive hermeneutics it is held that the intention of the *author,* the sole donor of meaning, is the victim of the sophistries of Gadamer and his like.)

For Gadamer the only way to reconcile the two practices of history and criticism is to insist on the integrative role of application. And he makes in this connection a point of unusual interest. Both historian and critic assume, whether consciously or not, a need to relate individual text to a total context. The historian's foreunderstanding impels him to apply the individual text to a total historical situation (or, as Barr would probably say, to the true historical context). The critic's foreunderstanding makes him try to understand the text in the unity of its meaning, its total textual context (which will certainly entail intertextual relations limited only by the boundaries of a canon, if at all). In either case a prior supposition determines the application. Each such supposition has its own history and its own "situatedness." Each presupposes some sort of totality to which it must find its relation. Nobody, that is, will read only and exactly what is *there.* And of course nobody will ever again read exactly as Barr or Gadamer or anyone else reads.

Gadamer likes to say that he is only describing things as they are, merely saying what is the case or the truth of the matter (though since he thinks that truth is not eternal this leaves room for disagreement from the standpoints of different foreunderstandings than his, which is precisely part of the truth he is telling). And in the present instance it does appear that he is stating the facts of the matter—that either side of the Barr-Childs argument makes a large assumption about the context of its observations on texts. Gadamer, as he often rightly remarks, is not hostile to historical research, and he denies that he is opening the door to arbitrary interpretation, a common charge against him. But his view of what happens in historical research would not be acceptable to Barr. "It is part of real understanding . . . that we regain concepts of an historical past in such a way that they include our own comprehension of them. . . . There is no such thing . . . as a point outside history from which the identity of a problem can be conceived without the vicissitudes of the various attempts to solve it."[5] Moreover, he might add that the presupposition that one is free of presuppositions is the consequence of many former presuppositions, which are themselves a proper study for historians, who had better look out for their own.

Neither of our combatants shows much interest in Gadamer, but since I have brought him in as an adjudicator I had better say that on the whole Childs fares better in his judgment than Barr. Not that Barr would mind; for Gadamer belongs to a tradition of hermeneutics of which Barr would say, with E. D. Hirsch, that it has simply gone off in the wrong direction, taking the scenic route via Heidegger instead of the direct Schleiermachian road. Barr has stayed on that road, preferring the objective or recognitive highway, which is why he sounds like Wrede, and why he has so little time for the canon. The Bible is an unintegrated collection of *biblia*. Considered as a whole, it has no special claim on the attention of the historian. I don't think Barr ever says anything quite so confident—he seems clear that Christians have to treat the Bible, the book as assembled, differently from other books, as possessing authority—but as a man with an authoritative vocation to study history he need not, in his vocation, be disturbed by that belief.

And so it happens that Childs fares better with Gadamer. He might suffer criticism for presupposing that one particular historical act of application, namely the establishment of the canon, should be so privileged, but he could plausibly reply that the canon was not only the product of many former acts of application but the culmination of all that preceded it, and the foundation of all that were to follow; so that even in purely historical terms it is privileged.

Nevertheless, this assertion of privilege also proceeds from certain presuppositions. In forms less qualified than Childs's own but still related to his procedures, one might say that confidence in the integrity of the canon stems from a partly occult assumption that might for short be called magical. And something similar can be said of Barr. For the sake of clarity I will restate the character of the opposition between our champions in a crude and extreme manner. One party would really prefer to have the original documents, or perhaps even any oral predecessors, than the canonical texts. This, the Barr party, may be said to have a nostalgia for the pre-text, for the persons and events behind the books. Here is a touch of magic, the magical power of narrative as it is described in the opening words of *Adam Bede:* one may see in a drop of ink that which will "reveal to any chance comer far-reaching views of the past." Emulating "the Egyptian sorcerer," the author says that "with this drop of ink at the end of my pen" she "will show you the roomy workshop of Mr. Jonathan Burge, carpenter and builder, in the village of Hayslope, as it appeared on the eighteenth of June, in the year of our Lord 1799."

Persons and events will thus be made available to the reader, as if by magic. The other party is in general willing to use the history of the texts and their redactions, but only as prehistory of the text itself, a text that is fixed and calls for interpretation affirming its coherence and plenitude, with internal relations one can only with difficulty avoid describing as organic, and a complexity-in-unity inviting us to think of it as a world in itself. One side treats the text as a difficult means of access to historical truths which belong to the whole context of history; the other treats history as a precursor of a text which constitutes its own context. Each depends upon a magical presupposition.

It might be possible to argue for a third view. What about

treating the canon as a stage in tradition, and then considering it as an intertextual system only to the degree that it imposes its own measure of intertextuality? This would entail that one did not treat it as rigidly bounded, as confining the attention of serious interpreters to the "inside" books—rejecting, that is, the "fixed parameters" of Childs, but without denying a measure of canonical privilege. Such an approach would be congenial and familiar to secular critics, who cannot in any case have a canon of absolute authority and fixity, and who tend to behave as if a loose notion of canonicity were an accurate reflection of the way things are, at any rate for the present, in professional circles. But it is perfectly plain, even from this proposal for compromise, that neither the Childs party nor the Barr party could accept it, for it violates theological and historiographic beliefs on both sides. It is, moreover, much weaker magic: on the one hand it cannot make historical persons live again, or even show them as they were; and on the other it forfeits the advantages of that organic wholeness which is the concomitant of all doctrines of plenary inspiration. As a *via media* it simply won't do. Its rationality cannot compensate for the loss of magic.

Let me qualify the rather vague and possibly offensive term *magic*. In *Wilhelm Meister* Goethe says *Hamlet* is like a tree, each part of it there for, and by means of, all the others. Five hundred years earlier a Kabbalist said this of the Torah: "Just as a tree consists of branches and leaves, bark, sap and roots, each one of which components can be termed tree, there being no substantial difference between them, you will also find that the Torah contains many things, and all form a single Torah and a tree, without difference between them. . . . It is necessary to know that the whole is one unity." Thus Moses de Leon, perhaps the author of the main part of the Zohar, as quoted by Gershom Scholem.[6] Moses and Goethe seem to be saying very much the same kind of thing; certainly they have hit upon the same figure. We should be wrong, however, to make too much of the resemblance. The context of Goethe's remark is that of Romantic organicism and *Naturphilosophie*, of the philosophical and scientific proposals which interested him in his moment; and without some consideration of them as well as of more literary contexts we shall scarcely grasp the full quality of his saying about *Hamlet*. The beautiful excesses, if so we think them, of Kabbalistic commentary belong, despite the similarity of the figures, to a different world. One might get some measure of the difference by comparing the context provided for one by the scholarship of Scholem with that provided by the scholarship of M. H. Abrams toward the understanding of nineteenth-century organicism. The idea of the work as organism is ancient and powerful, but we do not suppose that it serves exactly the same purpose whenever it recurs; it will have a difference enforced by its position within a contemporary structure of belief (though that is yet another if less definite holistic notion). Potent critical myths may sleep and be rediscovered, but they do not return to just the same place. The Kabbalah had its organicism, and so did Romantic thought; we have legacies from both, though the latter is still the one that is more continuous with our own presuppositions, which may explain why most of us would think the Kabbalah the more "magical" of the two.

It is worth dwelling for a moment on these differences. To the Kabbalist, and even to the Talmudist, the text may be said to be coextensive with the world, and coeval with it; it is indeed, like ritual, out of time. Thus it does not prevent the kinds of problems that scientific philology was invented to solve, any more than it needs to adapt an idealist philosophy. There are no redactions, no contradictions, no errors even, that cannot be explained or explained away in terms of the text itself; there is perfect unity and inexhaustible sense. The closure of the text is obviously of great importance, whatever historians may say of its fortuity; it stimulated and governed commentary, and the commentary became part of the world of the text, an Oral Torah that articulated what had been there, latent, from the creation. For Torah was present on that occasion, though Torah is also called midrash of Torah. The application of the sacred text to all later times is only a continuation of a process that began when everything began, so that there is no divorce between application and understanding; the meaning is the meaning of both the original and the latest accepted interpretation. The tradition is continuous, and however novel the explanations they were part of a transhistorical whole; Scholem says of the ideas of Isaac Luria that "for all their glaring novelty" they were "not regarded as a break with traditional authority."[7] It was Luria who thought of the Torah as having 600,000 faces, each turned to only one of the 600,000 at Sinai. The officially fixed text could indeed generate any number of interpretations; individual letters and their numerical values have secret senses, new insights arise from the alteration of vowels within the consonantal stems; every conceivable device may be used to get at the white fire behind the black fire of the Torah. It is there to be read, but—wrapped in secrecy. Some say that the Israelites at Sinai heard only the first or the first two commandments before being awed into deafness by the divine voice, so that the rest were known only in the accommodated forms provided by Moses; or even that they heard only the first of God's word, "I," *anoki,* or perhaps only the first consonant, the *aleph,* so that the prophets continually explicate that hugely pregnant but silent consonant.[8] It is, to recall a line of Stevens, a world of words to the end of it; a world of written words, and of letters and the spaces between them.

Compared with all this, our way of talking about the world of a poem, or of the creative act of imagination—and in so far as we still do so we are harking back to Goethe—sounds self-consciously figurative and feeble. For here is the extremest and most magical form of application; the text becomes a type of its interpretations; it is prophetic of all futures and all readers, since in principle it contains them; its truth is concealed and revealed in words that constitute the world. The later organicism dealt in analogy rather than identity. Moreover, it grew up alongside the new historical philology, which was radically opposed to it. Out of that strife was born modern hermeneutics. As we have seen, the struggle continues; it is now a struggle between weaker, less confident varieties of magic, the canonical and the historical.

More precisely, it can be said that the new hermeneutics came into existence when historical criticism (begun as a secular activity and so not at the outset troubled by questions of faith) began to be applied to the scriptures. And each of them—history and hermeneutics, or by extension Barr and Childs—is the shadow of the other. The title of founder of modern hermeneutics is usually given to Schleiermacher, who was also a major New Testament historical critic. He believed in a universal hermeneutic but also said that "a continuing preoccupation with the New Testament canon which was not motivated by one's own interest in Christianity could only be directed against the canon."[9] This must mean that if you really treated it as you would any other ancient document you would be forced to dismantle it; therefore it must be given special treatment. The wish to resolve such difficulties gave rise to ever more subtle hermeneutic formulations, defenses against the dismantling historian. It is not really possible to understand them outside that context. Dilthey was a pupil of Ranke. Heidegger took on the entire opposing tradition, and made the world hermeneutic. Yet to speak of the anti-objectivist hermeneutics in this way is to study them historically, as Gadamer does. One approach becomes the shadow of the other. Whenever we think about writing history we face problems that are best thought of hermeneutically; whenever we think of understanding and application, or of the developing notion of the hermeneutic circle, we are obliged to take account of history.

We cannot escape this double, nor should we wish to, wherever our sympathies lie in such disputes as that between Barr and Childs. It does seem that we have to recognize that all historical knowledge has to be understood with an understanding that includes not only the facts, the events and persons, but our own limited comprehension of them; and that we must see that those conditioned understandings themselves have a history which confirms that, like all understandings, they are likely to prove transient. This does not mean we should not believe and act upon our understandings, a point neatly made by D. C. Hoy in his book *The Critical Circle:*[10] the belief that my belief will be shown to be wrong does not invalidate my belief. The view that there are no eternal truths does not entail that there is no truth.

The revival or redevelopment of canonical criticism, remote as it is from the Jewish variety or indeed from that of the early Church, mild and concessive as it is, strenuously opposed as it is by the historian, seems to me to be a matter of more than local interest. It has some bearing upon secular literary criticism. I cannot at this late moment enter into this tricky and rather fashionable subject, but it may be worth saying this much. The great modernist critics (and authors; sometimes they were the same persons) were inclined to holism. Eliot, for instance, had quite a magical view of the literary canon, though he thoughtfully provided for the possibility of adding to it. The New Criticism believed at least in the autonomy of works of art and explored their latent internal relations. Opposition came from literary historians; or it might come from Marxists, or from all who believe that to confer upon some works the special status implied by their description as literature is false in itself. Deconstruction, perhaps oddly, has its canon, and to some practitioners it seems that only great works, which are great because they have already deconstructed themselves, are worth deconstructing. But whether some version of the canon is endorsed, or whether all canons are anathematized, we can detect in each of the combatants presuppositions of which they may be largely unconscious. Their struggles are not unlike those of Childs and Barr, each side having to hear the other speak in order to complete its own argument; for example, orthodox literary history, thought by its practitioners to be the most natural and sensible thing in the world, has its own mythology of period, its own magical plot of history, regarded as beyond criticism. Finally, the argument between the theologians seems to illustrate a more general problem: history struggles with its hermeneutic shadow; hermeneutics with simple history. There is magic in both, and magic is no longer a powerful preservative, so that all we can be sure of is that the terms of the argument will change once again, and it will seem to no one that either party has laid a hand on what might be called the truth. At any rate, that is the truth as I happen to see it at the moment.

# CHAPTER 10

# *The Bible*

## STORY AND PLOT

To put the matter very simply, plot is what becomes of story when its internal relations grow complicated. Such complications arise most obviously from an emphasis on causality as against mere sequence, but they can take other forms, which call for a kind of attention not wholly unlike that which we give to poetry. In such cases the relations between the parts of the narrative may be of a kind that cannot be explained as a causal relation between the events narrated; they may be said to constitute a plot, but it is an occult plot; for the relations are not explicit and they do not imitate the relations between events in real life. Such plots do not work in time or as an imitation of time; they depend upon intemporal relations, and lack the more obvious kinds of narrative value.

The difference between these two sorts of plot has been expressed in various ways. There is, for example, St. Augustine's extraordinary meditation on time in the eleventh book of the *Confessions*. Ordinary plot exercises the mind in a manner appropriate to our temporal condition. In the middle of the narrative we speculate about our position in relation to its beginning, in order to move as best we can to some predictable though possibly surprising end, which will dominate the story and give it whatever fullness it has. These are familiar mental operations: Augustine calls them expectation, attention, and memory. He illustrates them by the example of a recited psalm. At first all is expectation, but the recitation progressively removes the psalm from that province, and it passes gradually into that of memory. Attention remains constant even when the whole psalm has passed out of time; and it is thus, he argues, that we may see not only a psalm but a life, or even the entire history of mankind, as freed of temporality—an image, however imperfect, of the created world and of the creator's understanding of that world. In that understanding there is no place for memory or for expectation, only for attention, for the world is a plot of timeless relationships, not of events foreseen and unforeseen. It is *sub specie temporis* that plots are characterized by consequence, by reversal and recognition; *sub specie aeternitatis* they are the occult structures of a whole, of a complete book, or a world.[1]

It may be helpful to put the point in a quite different way, and I do so with the aid of the Soviet semiologist Jurij M. Lotman. He also speaks of two types of plot, "primordially opposed": one is without anomalies and relates to a law "immanently inherent in the world." The other has its origin in incident, anecdote, news, in what he sometimes calls "scandal" or "excess." We might call it the plot of *faits divers,* or use Lotman's own expression and say an "archive of excesses." Anyway, the two plots which Augustine distinguished as intemporal and temporal are here called myth and scandal.[2]

So however we describe them, and however much we allow for differences of focus, we have here two plots, one primordial and metaphoric and related to the true design of the world, the other modern and temporal and concerned with superficial connections experienced in time. And it is with the relations between such plots that I am concerned. Modern literature, and in its wake modern criticism, have been increasingly concerned with the double plot, occult and obvious, the plot of time and the plot of intimate structural relationships. The rediscovery of that doubleness can be traced in all narrative forms; it is the concern of psychoanalysts and mythographers and structural anthropologists, as well as of novelists and their critics. "There is the story of one's hero," says Henry James in the Preface to *The Ambassadors,* "and then, thanks to the intimate connexion of things, the story of one's story itself."[3] There are hidden plots which the author, with immense labor and at great psychic expense, may suggest to you by various sorts of narrative parapraxis, as Conrad does.[4] You can puzzle about it in all sorts of ways; E. M. Forster struggled with the idea of a plot that moved forward and another, less conspicuous, that did not, but was made of "rhythms."[5] But however the matter is expressed, there are always these two plots, and one of them is always deeper, darker, and more primitive than the other; for it escapes time, whereas its companion is always in time, concerned with things that happen, with the apparently unpredictable sayings and doings of its agents, with anecdote and excess. And the value of this second plot will depend upon its fidelity to the first.

Now it will be part of my argument that our studies in the modern dialogue between these types of plot have given us new ways of thinking about the plot relations in the Old and New Testaments. The examples by which I try to make this point will be largely familiar to biblical scholars, but the familiar may have unfamiliar implications. My first example is of a secular character, so much so that the book from which I borrow it was for some years considered unsuitable for general distribution. We have changed all that. Then I shall give some biblical examples, with the caveat that I approach them without theological authority of any kind. The opinions I express are those of a secular critic with nothing to say about doctrine. I treat the relation between the myth or world-plot and the plot of excess as a problem for general literary criticism.

James Joyce's *Ulysses* has long since been promoted from the ranks of low realism; indeed it has been called a sacred book of the modern world; certainly it has served, more than half a century, as the *livre de chevet* of many readers. It was not always so. D. H. Lawrence called it "a stupid *olla podrida* of the Bible and so forth."[6] Even T. S. Eliot, who admired the book enormously, could not think of Leopold Bloom as a moral exemplar.[7] But Joyce himself said that Bloom was "a complete man—a good man,"[8] and the world, it seems, has come to agree with this estimate. Bloom and his book have been transformed into a guide to conduct and to the world in general.[9] *Ulysses* has been the subject of editorial attention as laborious and minute as any devoted to the Bible, and the problems are comparable, as the new edition with its five thousand changes in the received text seems to demonstrate. And the opponents of this new text have inveighed against it with true theological ardor. Nor have the commentators lacked zeal; *Ulysses* has been expounded with a devotion that might well, even in its occasional excesses, be called religious. We are talking about a spiritual encyclopedia.

The sixth book, chapter, or episode of *Ulysses* originally bore the title "Hades," and although Joyce dropped it, modern scholars continue to use it. The story of "Hades" is, in part, as follows: Bloom and some other Dubliners attend the funeral of Paddy Dignam. The somewhat erratic progress of their "creaking carriage" from Dignam's house to the cemetery is minutely described, and the conversation of the mourners is reported, along with the unspoken thoughts of Bloom. After a while the talk turns to the character of the deceased. "As decent a little man as ever wore a hat, Mr Dedalus said. Heart. He tapped his chest sadly. Blazing face; redhot. Too much John Barleycorn. Cure for red nose. Drink like the devil till it turns adelite. A lot of money spent colouring it." This last sentiment is Bloom's. Arriving at the cemetery, they find that the hearse has preceded them. "Got here before us, dead as he is," muses Bloom.

Considered simply as a representation of an hour or so in Bloom's long day, "Hades" is still a remarkably original piece of writing. The journey of the mourners takes them across a city that is registered with minute topographical exactness, as Bloom's movements always are. At the same time the occasion is such that Bloom is found to be quite naturally thinking of his dead father and his dead son, of the circumstances of his own life and marriage, and of the last things. The story, one might say, is both plausible and accessible. But what is going on is much more than story. Take the dead man's face, for instance: is it said to have been a drunkard's red until death made it gray-yellow simply because it was so, to produce an effect of reality?

For this is precisely the kind of detail used to produce such an effect. Or is there more to it, some mystery arising from its being part of a larger entity, some plot that does not immediately declare itself?

One thing everybody knows about *Ulysses* is that it exhibits, and was intended to exhibit, extensive parallels with the *Odyssey,* and that "Hades" is based on the eleventh book of that work, in which Odysseus descends into the underworld to consult Tiresias. From schemes drawn up by Joyce himself for the benefit of privileged translators or commentators, we know that when the mourners pass by two canals and two rivers, the Dodder and the Liffey, they are unwittingly encountering the four rivers of Homer's hell. We know that the mourners and others at the funeral are related to persons encountered by Odysseus in the underworld: Martin Cunningham is Sisyphus, always restarting the hopeless task of making a go of life after his wife's drunkenness has brought him down; Father Coffey is Cerberus; and Paddy Dignam is Elpenor. Homer's Elpenor has a red face. He breaks his neck in a drunken fall from the roof of Circe's house, and so has reached Hades before Odysseus, who tells him so: "thou hast come fleeter on foot than I in my black ship."

Now Joyce studied not only Homer but his explicators, and especially Victor Bérard, who wrote a book on the Semitic origins of the *Odyssey* and held that the name "Elpenor" derives from a Semitic root meaning "blazing face." So the plot thickens. All this, and a good deal more, has been known since Joyce's friend Stuart Gilbert wrote his book on *Ulysses* in 1930.[10] Gilbert believed that the Homeric correspondences were extremely important, and argued that the book could not be understood without them. But another close friend of the author, Frank Budgen, whose *James Joyce and the Making of "Ulysses"* appeared in 1934, paid far less attention to them. He knew they were important to Joyce, but thought the interest that fact conferred upon them was all the interest they had.

Indeed this difference of opinion on the importance of the Homeric parallels began even earlier, before the book was properly published, and among the very people who were doing their best to promote it. T. S. Eliot thought the correspondences essential, for they were the means by which Joyce used myth to give "a shape and significance to the immense panorama of futility and anarchy which is contemporary history"; and Eliot's opinion, that this "mythical method" might be "a step toward making the modern world possible for art," has a bearing on our understanding of much that was done in the name of the modern, including his own poem *The Waste Land*.[11] Joyce had found a way of seeing behind the accidents and confusions of the present a universally valid structure thought to have been lost. Yet Ezra Pound, Eliot's friend and co-promoter of Joyce, wrote that the Homeric parallels in "this super-novel" were "part of Joyce's mediaevalism and . . . chiefly his own affair."[12] The argument, begun thus early, has continued ever since.

No one, of course, denies that the correspondences exist. The question is whether they have any importance independently of their importance to Joyce. It should be said that to the ordinary eye the parallels with Homer are often very inexact. Bloom is clearly unlike Odysseus in many respects, even if they are thought to share a Semitic origin. In at least one way Molly Bloom fails to resemble the faithful Penelope. Nor is a day spent wandering about Dublin an obvious close parallel to the original odyssey. But closeness is not the only point. And Joyce in any case used the *Odyssey* to furnish him with an extraordinary amount of detail, often allowing it to determine character and incident, and in ways that call for the labor of commentators. For instance, as Hugh Kenner deftly notes, Paddy Dignam's home had to be placed a long way from the cemetery so that the carriage could pass the four "rivers." Then the mourners had to be driven at high speed to get to the cemetery in the time available, and they notice this: "God grant he doesn't upset us on the road, Mr Power said." Homer, then, often provides reasons why, in Bloom's world, things are so and not otherwise, though it remains true that many correspondences seem less than intrinsic. Kenner's mature judgment is that the larger ones are material to all sound interpretation, but of the lesser "many are trivial. Some, if we chance to know them, lend definition, some contrast. Joyce listed many, did not list many, and some we see he might not have thought of at all."[13]

Perhaps this is the general view, but it is not shared by at least one great authority. Richard Ellmann remarks that the parallels derive from Joyce's belief—seriously held and inextricable from his book—that Homer's narrative was a key to the world, or anyway to *his* world. The *Odyssey* begins on Calypso's island, Ogygia; and did not Plutarch call Ireland by that name? Were not the Irish, like the Greeks, of Phoenician origin? It has even been suggested that St. Patrick was the great-grandson of Odysseus. Homer, Joyce believed, was a very accurate author, for example in his topography; and his poem was a spiritual encyclopedia and the right model for another such. Ellmann will not regard all this as merely curious; he thinks it matters.

The fact is, I think, that when a book reaches the quasi-sacred status attained by *Ulysses* we assume that everything we can find out about it is valuable, including every possible parallel, whether intended or not; and whether we are baffled or not by this magical view of the world. Joyce advised a reading of Homer as preparation for taking on his book, but he refused to allow the correspondences absolute precedence. To inquirers who appeared to do so he would represent his book as a novel in the realist tradition. To others, who thought of it only thus, he stressed the Homeric element.[14] Before he had finished writing it he said that his intention was "to render the myth *sub specie temporis nostri*";[15] but in order to do that he had to blend the myth with certain occurrences involving not very important contemporaries on a particular though not particularly very important day, 16 June 1904.

Much more might be said about Joyce's success in his stated purpose of keeping the professors busy, but I can now proceed to explain why I have brought him in. There is need of only one more word of caution. It would be possible to diminish the whole subject by saying that Joyce, after all, was a very odd fellow. For example, he had a picture of the city of Cork framed in cork; and Yeats, a poet by no means hostile to occult correspondences, was shocked by this and pronounced it "mania."[16] Others might think it no more than a joke or whimsy, and reserve the word *mania* for the insertion of thousands of similar jokes into the language of *Finnegans Wake*. But it is well to remember that these jokes and puns are tokens of a far from absurd attitude to the world as language expresses it. It is presupposed that only by using the resources, even the most hidden resources, of language can we apprehend the world in its inexhaustible variety, its millions of senses and correspondences; and that no expenditure of wit and learning is too profligate if devoted to the discovery of its occult connections. Joyce was a superstitious man, but superstitions may only be the vulgar day-to-day dress of an altogether nobler confidence in the world and its language. In Joyce a nineteenth-century hermeticism is matched with a rabbinical passion for the world as coextensive with Torah, another work of infinite self-correspondence that has kept the professors busy for centuries.

We have seen by this example that a "low-mimetic" story can contain a metaphoric or mythic plot. In order to do so it constantly refers beyond itself to another text, a text believed to be encyclopedic, a verbal model of the world. That text chooses the color of Dignam's face, determines his address in Dublin and his drinking habits. It is responsible also for a great many other details; we are not always sure which. The crumbs on the seats of the carriage carrying the mourners—are they manifestations of myth or scandal? Once the general correspondence is established there is no obvious limit to particular correspondences—no guarantee that the author perceived every one, that the professors in their commentaries may not find more. If the truth of the world is to be got into a book, it will be a book shaped by and at least in part containing an earlier book that contains everything except a complement of commentary, a modern excess, to make it valid now. The new book will add to the old only by exploring the senses of the old as they appear in a world in which everything has changed except the deeper plot, the radical and never fully understood truth.

It will be apparent that I have now left *Ulysses* behind. If we think of the Gospels as having a place in a temporal plot, the first thing we notice is that they come in near the end of it. They remember the beginning, if only to rewrite it, as John did in his opening verse; but they remember it when the end which will finally give sense to the whole is imminent. That end is predictable only in types and figures, as in the synoptic apocalypse, or in the imagery of harvest and thrust-in sickle. But from their position, privileged though not absolutely so (for the end is not yet), they can claim a fuller view of the whole than was formerly available. The claim is implicit in their rhetoric. There is the device of "how much more" ("shall he not much more clothe you?") or the one that develops or controverts an existing adage ("you have heard it said . . . but I tell you") or the one that claims fulfillment of some hint or promise never before understood ("that what was spoken might be fulfilled"). These are not isolated rhetorical tricks; they reflect the design of the whole.

In each of these devices there is a clear dependence on something written earlier, and it is important for any understanding of this literary aspect of the Gospels to see that they have as it were a double view of their own plots. Behind all of them is a Bible, thought of as complete and authoritative, a world-book credited with the power to explain everything: a key to the creation. Such books are definitive except—and of course it is a large exception—for commentary, which will end only with the end. They have that property of eternity to which Augustine's psalm was moving; but in the world of time, where we read them, they call incessantly for supplement. And indeed there is a sense in which they are not complete without it. For the Jews it came to constitute an oral Torah, conceived, once it had passed through time, as coeval with the text itself.

Hence the double view: although the text is complete, it still calls for completion. The means by which this is done can be codified as a body of regulations or recommendations, like the rabbinical *middot,* which has items very like the rhetorical devices I mentioned earlier as occurring in the New Testament.

Comment on the mysteries of the old Bible assumes that it is inexhaustibly full of them; as when one remote verse requires to be read with another that resembles it, perhaps only in its use of a similar word or phrase. These mysteries, though eternally present, have their most urgent meanings exposed only at the end, or, since all comment then ceases, when the end is most imminent, whether at Qumram or with the first Christians. It is at such times that one most clearly sees the detailed ways in which the old plot shapes the new, which completes it although it is complete already.

More must always be said. This is a kind of excess. When an antitype completes what is in itself already a completed thing, a type, there must be excess. The antitype declares itself in a context of event or scandal; and to perceive that occurrence amid the events and scandals of the last days is to understand fulfillment, but it is also to demand excess. One thinks of Matthew 5:47, which has given the translators some difficulty: "What do ye more than others?" says the King James Bible; "what is extraordinary about that?" asks the New English Bible, very loosely; the Vulgate, more accurately, has *quid amplius facitis?;* and the Greek, literally translated, "What excess do ye?". It is an encouragement to interpretative excess; yet it conforms with the text of the world-book because, though valid forever, that text requires, at every moment of time but especially when (as it nearly always is) the end is nigh, our supplement to complete it.

Now if all that seemed a little cloudy, the extreme familiarity of the examples I shall now offer may make it seem too clear; but I mean them to be looked at in this rather more obscure context. They are taken mostly from the Birth narratives, partly because these are so familiar, partly because here, deprived of their Marcan guidelines, Matthew and Luke exercised what must surely be properly called their distinctive literary talents to such varying effect. No doubt they wrote under similar constraints and treated topics in some sense prescribed for both of them; but the differences, elided as they have been in the traditional Christmas stories, are great enough for us to think of the two as individual talents transforming a tradition.

Each (to use another Augustinian expression) needed figures of the truth, and each sought them in the Bible. A divine child is to be born, and there is an annunciation of a kind so familiar in the Old Testament that it has been labeled a "type-scene." Matthew selects the unique instance of annunciation to a husband, which is that of the angels to Abraham in Genesis 18. Robert Alter has shown how this situation is varied in subsequent annunciations—to Rebecca, to Rachel, to the wife of Manoah, mother of Samson, to Hanna, and to the Shunamite woman in 2 Kings 4.[17] Various as these are, they are all annunciations made to the woman concerned; and Luke followed them. We can make guesses about the different choices of Matthew and Luke, but it is in any case clear enough that their narratives are founded on the old type; how else could matters have fallen out?

Paul had treated the birth of Isaac from Sarah's barren womb as a type of the resurrection, and Matthew takes it with equal plausibility as a type also of the birth of Jesus. The annunciation to Abraham ("Behold, Sarah thy wife shall bear thee a son . . . and thou shalt call his name Isaac," Genesis 17:19) is associated, in the rabbinical manner, with the remote echo in Isaiah 7, where the Greek version says that a *parthenos* shall bear a son, "and thou shalt call his name Emmanuel." Michael Goulder, commenting on this juxtaposition, says there are few clearer illustrations "of the steps by which an evangelist has found history in scripture." But that is not all. "If Mary was virgin and yet the announcement was to be made to Joseph, then they were not yet married but must be engaged. If they were engaged and she pregnant, then the proper attitude" called for the dissolution of their bond. "Nevertheless mercy is still proper even in such cases . . . The angel calls Joseph the son of David, which . . . underlines the ironical contrast between Joseph's restraint with Mary and David's laxity with Bathsheba."[18]

Whether or not one agrees with every point of such exegesis, it is true enough that the narrative is here shaped in accordance with a reading of the old text; if it is an excessive reading, then excess is the rule in these matters as in Bloom's carriage ride.

Does the account of conception by the Holy Spirit echo Psalm 100:30? Does the ambiguous marital status of Mary echo the ambiguities, moral and racial, of the four women mentioned in Matthew's genealogy? The one thing certain is that in writing of this kind all the elements are, as Luke calls them, "signs"; all the words point, whether by direct intention or not, toward that world-book from which all figures of the truth derive. R. E. Brown reminds us that Luke's manger comes from Isaiah 1:3 (LXX), "The ox knows its owner, and the donkey knows the manger of its lord; but Israel has known not me." He adds that Luke may also be recalling a midrash on the curse of Adam. Here he is taking Luke at his word; there is no end to these possible relations, these signs, and their truth must be the truth of the new, excessive narrative. The swaddling clothes are a sign: to Lancelot Andrewes the sign of a suffering Messiah with "poor clouts for his array"; to Brown the sign of royal birth; and perhaps, in this generous plenitude of senses, both are right.[19]

Let me add one or two more instances of the shaping of the later narrative by the secrets of the old one. Did Joseph, in Matthew 2, take his family to Egypt so that Jesus, like the first Israel, could be called out of Egypt, as Hosea said (Hosea 11:1)? And why, later, did he settle in Nazareth? The answer is, "that it might be fulfilled which was spoken by the prophets, He shall be called a Nazarene *(Nazoraios)*" (Matthew 2:23). But perhaps this is an almost Joycean pun. For the word seems to be related to the Hebrew word for "branch" (of the house of David, the stem of Jesse); and also to Nazir, a holy one, separate to God like Samson in Judges 16:17; so perhaps residence at Nazareth has a multiple determination.[20] Bethlehem came in because of its association with David (and perhaps because Jews would not believe in a Messiah who came from Galilee). We know how boldly Luke solved the Bethlehem problem, by inventing a universal census; yet even that may derive from Psalm 87:6, which, in one version, reads "in the census of the peoples this one will be born there."[21] If that is right, a very obscure promise receives a very bold fulfillment, and all the world is taxed.

Dibelius, speaking of the Passion narratives, felt a need to distinguish between passages having historical reference and passages in which, as he put it, history was "begotten" by the Old Testament, such as the Judas story.[22] In some contexts of discussion this is clearly a relevant issue; but it need not be considered in a purely literary treatment like mine, for here the interest is only in the dialogue between two "plots." Dodd observed that, in order to give the story of Doubting Thomas its extremely important place in his narrative, John had to arrange for that disciple to be absent when Jesus appeared to the other disciples, though in "the common tradition" all eleven loyal disciples are present.[23] Such perceptions confirm the general proposition that what is sometimes called "kerygmatic history" may involve the kind of maneuver and the kind of choice we remarked in Joyce. But it inevitably leads us to further consideration of the nature of the choice. For example, Thomas's mention of the print of the nails in Jesus' hands (John 20:25) is the only mention of such nails, though they may be implied by Luke 24:39–40, where there is a possibility that some scribe has added to the original an echo of John.[24] The question is complicated, but it is at least possible that the nails are attributable to Psalm 22:16, "They pierced my hands and feet"[25]—another link between the old and the new plot, or (since they came to be one) between the end of the book and its middle and beginning.

Hebrews 12:2 calls Jesus *archēgos* and *teleiōtēs,* author and finisher, and we might borrow these terms for the Old Testament and the evangelists; in the end the two come together, bound in one volume, and the *sensus plenior* is revealed to understanders of the plot of the book, though the finishing goes on throughout, and continues in *our* interpretations.

"If only the church did not attach so much importance to the Old Testament," sighed Erasmus. "It is a thing of shadows."[26] And much later Gunkel spoke for many, perhaps most, when he noted with regret that the trouble with Marcion had forced the Church to make up its mind on the Old Testament so long ago that there now seemed little prospect of changing it. But he added that the old way of reading the Old Testament was important because evidently Jesus and the disciples thought it was, seeing a pattern of fulfillment, a huge repository of testimonies.[27] Indeed we are told by von Campenhausen that it was mostly because of the value of these testimonies that the Old Testament survived Marcion's assault.[28] But modern historical criticism discounts them, except in so far as they are a part of history; for it tends to fragment the book and interests itself in the events to which the words appear more or less obscurely to refer, and not in occult relations between the words.

Of late, however, we have seen a new "canonical" criticism speak, according to its lights, for the book and against mere history. And it seems open to secular critics, according to theirs, to read the Bible as a book, a book with a plot, made of two plots, a book like a world, in which there are promises and fulfillments, fulfillments in excess of all but the most minutely researched premises or promises. Its secret connections and relations, beloved of the rabbis and the evangelists, are still open to inquiry, which may be made by methods proposed or revived by modern secular literature and its interpreters.

For it is no longer a question of abandoning our own sense of history in order temporarily to share, say, Matthew's. What Martin Hengel calls the "flight from history"[29] has resulted not only in existentialist and structuralist exegesis, but in a hermeneutics that makes the appropriation of the past a complicated matter, a combination of historical situations. Literary criticism has tended toward what has been called, figuratively, spatial interpretation, which means only that books are considered not *sub specie temporis* but rather as what Augustine thought of as images of eternity. It looks for secrets, for what is not declared overtly, for the occult or secret plots in poems and narratives. Its interpretations complete what is already in principle complete by revealing those hidden plots, the mysteries and the ground of the mysteries.

If we now look once more at Joyce we see at once that he conceived his relation to Homer as that of finisher to author, *teleiōtēs* to *archēgos*. We saw also that his critics divide into those who think the Homeric relations important in themselves, and those who think them important only because Joyce did. He was writing a spiritual encyclopedia, a world map, and he used the old map as a guide. He was willing, as Matthew and Luke and John were willing, to arrange his narrative in obedience to that guide, to provide characters with significant names and send them to places which had real existence but also belonged—as lying-in hospital, library, brothel, and cemetery belong—to an allegorical geography. Homer, as spiritual encyclopedia, lacked nothing but Joyce's excess, his supplement, or *telos;* so Joyce gives us his day that is a last day, passed in a city which is a humdrum Jerusalem and dominated by his good man, his parodic Ulysses who is also his parodic Elijah. In reducing the creative word to the scandal, the interior mumblings and random conversations of his day, in spiritualizing the topography of his city, he treats Homer as a sacred book, and perhaps his true model is the New Testament in relation to the Old. Nor is all this mere scaffolding, as some say, and best ignored. He has made explicit our ways of reading and our passion for a kind of consonance. There is a reason for Paddy Dignam's red face, as there is for the names of Jesus. There is also a reason why, for all its enormous rhetorical repertoire, Joyce's book is for the most part in what is sometimes called the low-mimetic mode, the late descendant of that *sermo humilis,* the mode of realism, of event—of the "archive of excesses"—that according to Auerbach had its origin in the gospels.[30]

So *Ulysses,* thought by most to be the exemplary novel of our age, may offer a strong hint as to the right way, or at any rate one right way, of reading the Bible. It is not exactly a new way, having much in common with the methods of first-century exegesis. It is unlikely to be a permanent way, for the great early-twentieth-century myth of the book as world, which has taken so many different forms in modern creative and critical writing, may not survive for long into a future where information is processed in disparate bits. But for the time being—and that is the time with which interpretation properly concerns itself—we can once again see the Bible as a book rather than as a collection of edited and sometimes duplicated material. We can see it not as a bundle of documents to be sorted by the ingenuity and patience of scholars, but as a book with a plot, fecund in metaphoric relations, out of time, recurring amid the scandals and excesses of time and shaping them to itself; as Matthew saw his Bible, and Joyce his Homer. To say that it is complete, and yet in constant need of interpretative excess, is after all to say that its senses are inexhaustible. And perhaps we should in consequence register our difference from Erasmus and Gunkel; we owe Marcion thanks if indeed he was, however unwillingly, responsible for the preservation of the book as a whole, as "inspired unity"[31] concealing behind its stories an occult plot which is a master version of the plot of our world.

# Notes

*Prologue*

1. Frank Kermode, *The Art of Telling* (Cambridge, Mass., 1983). In Britain the book was titled *Essays on Fiction;* it was published by Routledge & Kegan Paul.
2. Frank Kermode, *The Genesis of Secrecy* (Cambridge, Mass., 1979).
3. Robert von Hallberg, ed., *Canons* (Chicago, 1984).
4. Barbara Herrnstein Smith, *Contingencies of Value: Alternative Perspectives for Critical Theory* (Cambridge, Mass., 1988).
5. Frank Kermode, *Forms of Attention* (Chicago, 1985).
6. Frank Kermode, *History and Value* (Oxford, 1988).
7. Robert Alter and Frank Kermode, eds., *The Literary Guide to the Bible* (Cambridge, Mass., 1987), pp. 600–610.
8. Paul de Man, *The Resistance to Theory* (Minneapolis, Minn., 1986), pp. 3–20; Jacques Derrida, *Mémoires* (New York, 1986), especially pp. 41–43.
9. The best way into that controversy is to read Stanley Fish, "Profession Despite Thyself: Fear and Self-loathing in Literary Studies," *Critical Inquiry,* 10 (1983), 349–364; and the collection *Against Theory,* ed. Walter Benn Michaels and Stephen Knapp (Chicago, 1985), based on another issue of the same journal.
10. Gerald Graff, *Professing Literature* (Chicago, 1987), pp. 68, 114, 161, 218.
11. Jonathan Culler, *Framing the Sign: Criticism and Its Institutions* (Norman, Okla., 1988).
12. J.-M. Goulemot, "Histoire littéraire et mémoire nationale," in *Between Memory and History,* ed. M. N. Bourguet, L. Valensi, and N. Wachtel (*History and Anthropology,* 2 [October 1986], 225–235).
13. Hillis Miller, the doyen of imperialist Theory, has an essay with the neat and aggressive title "The Function of Rhetorical Study at the Present Time." Like Culler, he is glad that works of literature now, after the theoretical takeover, "tend to be redefined as 'examples' demonstrating the productive effectiveness of this or that theory"; and he laments the fact that for

some of these theories, set forth in books composed in foreign languages (such as French and German), students are often forced to wait, translations being sometimes tardy. What he doesn't seem to think a cause for lamentation is the monoglot character of the students' education. It might have been thought that instead of hanging about awaiting the translators' pleasure they could learn the foreign language in which their favorite reading is to be found; but this might not leave time to keep up with the neocritical journals as Miller thinks they must. (See James Engell and David Perkins, eds., *Teaching Literature* [Cambridge, Mass., 1988], pp. 87–109.)

14. Alvin Kibel, "The Canonical Text," in *Reading in the 1980s,* ed. S. Graubard (New York, 1983), pp. 239–254.

15. I gratefully acknowledge that what I know about the Ratio Club derives from the conversation of Jonathan Miller.

16. René Wellek, *The Attack on Literature and other Essays* (Chapel Hill, N.C., 1982).

17. Frederick Crews, *Skeptical Engagements* (Oxford, 1986), p. 170.

18. Terry Eagleton, *Literary Theory: An Introduction* (Minneapolis, Minn., 1983), pp. 200ff.

19. Robert Scholes, "Deconstruction and Communication," *Critical Inquiry,* 14 (1988), 284–285.

20. See Richard Poirier, *The Renewal of Literature,* (New York, 1987).

21. "Parmi ces hommes sans grand appétit de Poésie, qui n'en connaissent pas le besoin et qui ne l'eussent pas inventée, le malheur veut que figurent bon nombre de ceux dont la charge ou la destinée est d'en juger, d'en discourir, d'en exciter et cultiver le goût; et, en somme, de dispenser ce qu'ils n'ont pas. Ils y mettent souvent toute leur intelligence et tout leur zèle: de quoi les conséquences sont à craindre." Quoted by Maria Corti, *An Introduction to Literary Semiotics,* trans. M. Bogat and A. Mandelbaum (Bloomington, Ind., 1978), epigraph.

22. Here is an instance, not to be attributed: "The allegory of 'The Dead' is therefore cautionary rather than expressive, less a dramatisation of Gabriel's fatuity than a structure of deferred action that serves as a pedagogical instance for the relief of the anxiety of belatedness that *Ulysses* will formalize. The future, the later, thus takes a logical if surprising advantage over a past that otherwise precedes it and so makes it anxious. The future, after all, is the ineluctable site of the past's enduring presence, its putative *histoire* always already a function of a *récit* belated to it phenomenologically but precedent to it discursively. Such an ap-parent evasion of the Oedipal paradox . . ." This, though full of fun, is not intended as parody, and its absurdity is not unique. One sees why the ancients find it easy to avoid reading the moderns.

23. Hayden White, "Historical Pluralism," *Critical Inquiry,* 12 (1986), 480–493.

24. Paul de Man, "Hypogram and Inscription," in *The Resistance to Theory,* p. 29. "Return to Philology" is in the same volume, pp. 21–26.

25. Paul de Man, "Autobiography as De-facement," in *The Rhetoric of Ro-*

*manticism* (New York, 1984), pp. 69–70. Derrida quotes this passage (*Mémoires,* pp. 22–23) and agrees that "this undecidability itself remains untenable," though without telling us how to get out of the door or off the wheel.

26. *Dissemination,* trans. Barbara Johnson (Chicago, 1981), p. 223. For a more subtle discussion of what is meant by this statement, see Rodolphe Gasché, *The Tain of the Mirror* (Cambridge, Mass., 1986), pp. 256ff.

27. Gasché, *The Tain of the Mirror,* p. 261.

28. Robert Scholes, *Textual Power* (New Haven, Conn., 1985), p. 24.

29. Scholes, "Deconstruction and Communication," p. 283.

30. David Brooks, "From Western Lit to Westerns as Lit," *Wall Street Journal,* February 2, 1988.

31. Vincent B. Leitch, *American Literary Criticism from the Thirties to the Eighties* (New York, 1988), p. xiv.

32. Ibid., pp. 223–224.

33. Lionel Trilling, *Beyond Culture* (London, 1966), pp. 4–6.

34. Ibid., pp. 10–11.

35. Lionel Trilling, "The Function of the Little Magazine," in *The Liberal Imagination* (New York, 1950; reprinted 1961), pp. 93–103.

36. William Empson, *Argufying,* ed. John Haffenden (London, 1987), p. 104.

## 1. *The Common Reader*

1. Helen Gardner, *In Defence of the Imagination* (New York, 1982), pp. 41–42, 47.

2. Erich Auerbach, *Literary Language and Its Public in Late Latin Antiquity and the Middle Ages* (London, 1965), p. 333.

3. *Boswell's Life of Johnson,* ed. G. B. Hill and L. F. Powell (Oxford, 1964), pp. iv, 218 (May 1, 1783).

4. Garnett's role is documented in George Jefferson's *Edward Garnett: A Life in Literature* (London, 1982).

5. Peter Uwe Hohendahl, *The Institution of Criticism* (Ithaca, N.Y., 1982).

6. Ibid., p. 133.

7. "The Work of Art in the Age of Mechanical Reproduction," in Walter Benjamin, *Illuminations,* ed. Hannah Arendt (New York, 1968), pp. 219–253.

8. Edmund Wilson, *Classics and Commercials* (London, 1950), pp. 204–208.

9. *The London Review of Books,* 4(15) (August 19–September 1, 1982), 18.

10. Philip Rieff, *Fellow Teachers* (London, 1975), p. 97.

11. Donald Davie, *These the Companions* (Cambridge, 1982), p. 78.

12. Rieff, *Fellow Teachers,* p. 175.

## 2. *Milton in Old Age*

1. The following paragraphs are based on the account of Godfrey Davis, "Milton in 1660," *Huntington Library Quarterly,* 18 (1954–55), 351–363.

### 3. *Wallace Stevens*

1. Wallace Stevens, *Opus Posthumous* (New York, 1957); hereafter cited as *OP* in the text.

2. *Letters of Wallace Stevens,* ed. Holly Stevens (New York, 1966); hereafter cited as *L* in the text.

3. Margaret Peterson, "*Harmonium* and William James," *Southern Review* (Summer 1971), 664ff.

4. Wallace Stevens, *The Necessary Angel* (New York, 1951); hereafter cited as *NA* in the text.

5. "Und keinen Waffen brauchts und keinen / Listen, so lange, bis Gottes Fehl hilft." Text and translation from Michael Hamburger's complete parallel text, *Friedrich Hölderlin: Poems and Fragments* (London, 1966), pp. 176–177 (translated from *Hölderlin: Sämtliche Werke* [Stuttgart, 1961]).

6. Friedrich Hölderlin, *Poems and Fragments,* trans. Michael Hamburger (bilingual edition; Cambridge, 1980), p. 250.

7. Ibid., pp. 600–601. The prose poem "In lieblicher Bläue," from which these lines derive, is not certainly Hölderlin's own, but Heidegger treats it without question as authentic.

8. Thomson, "The City of Dreadful Night"; Whitman, "A Clear Midnight." Both quoted in *NA,* p. 119.

9. Wallace Stevens, *Collected Poems* (New York, 1954); hereafter cited as *CP* in the text.

10. Jarrell, *The Third Book of Criticism* (New York, 1969), pp. 57–58.

11. Heidegger, *Poetry, Language, Thought,* trans. Albert Hofstadter (New York, 1971), p. x.

12. Heidegger, "The Origin of the Work of Art [Der Ursprung von Kunstwerkes]," in *Poetry, Language, Thought,* pp. 17–81.

13. "The Thinker as Poet," in *Poetry, Language, Thought,* p. 4.

14. Heidegger, "Hölderlin and the Essence of Poetry," trans. Douglas Scott, in Heidegger, *Existence and Being,* comp. Werner Brock (Chicago, 1949), p. 310.

15. Commentators on Stevens appear not to have interested themselves much in this affinity, always supposing that it exists. They have not, to my knowledge, spoken of Stevens in relation to late works of Heidegger (that is, from the 1936 Hölderlin essay on). But Richard Macksey freely alludes to *Sein und Zeit* (along with Husserl and Merleau-Ponty) to illuminate late Stevens. He observes, in part, that "Stevens grounds his poetics and defines his individuality in terms of a death which always *impends* even in 'the genius of summer'" (*CP,* p. 482). See his "The Climates of Wallace Stevens," in Roy Harvey Pearce and J. Hillis Miller, eds., *The Act of the Mind: Essays on the Poetry of Wallace Stevens* (Baltimore, 1965), p. 201. Heidegger argues that *my* death alone achieves and delimits wholeness of Being (cf. "Every man dies his own death" [*OP,* 165]); and the project of the late Stevens recalls Heidegger's *Sein*

*zum Tode* ("when *Dasein* reaches its wholeness in death, it simultaneously loses the Being of its 'there'"). Macksey cites as his epigraph Heidegger's favorite Hölderlin quotation ("dichterisch, wohnet der Mensch auf dieser Erde") but does not otherwise refer to the philosopher's later work. An essay by J. Hillis Miller in the same collection sounds as though Miller could have had these later essays in mind, but he does not allude to them explicitly.

16. In *Being and Time,* trans. John Macquarrie and Edward Robinson (New York, 1962), p. 80, Heidegger explains (though that is not the right word) that the word *innan (wohnen)* collects the senses of "to dwell" *(inn)* and "accustomed," "familiar with," and "look after something" *(an).* But there is no substitute for a reading of that passage and related passages.

17. Quoted by Heidegger in "Hölderlin and the Essence of Poetry," p. 296.

18. Heidegger, "Building Dwelling Thinking," in *Poetry, Language, Thought,* pp. 143–162.

19. Heidegger, "Remembrance of the Poet," trans. Douglas Scott, in *Existence and Being,* p. 281.

20. Heidegger, "Hölderlin and the Essence of Poetry," pp. 293ff.

21. Heidegger, "Remembrance of the Poet," p. 264.

22. Heidegger, "The Origin of the Work of Art," p. 41.

23. Ibid., p. 47.

24. Heidegger, "What Are Poets For?" in *Poetry, Language, Thought,* p. 97.

## 4. *T. S. Eliot*

1. *Autobiography of William Carlos Williams* (New York, 1967), pp. 146, 174–175.

2. Richard Poirier, *The Renewal of Literature* (New York, 1987), pp. 21–22.

3. Harold Bloom, *The Breaking of the Vessels* (Chicago, 1982), pp. 17–20.

4. *The Letters of T. S. Eliot,* vol. 1, ed. Valerie Eliot (Orlando, Fla., 1988), p. 57.

5. Ibid., p. 310.

6. Herbert Howarth, *Some Figures behind T. S. Eliot* (London, 1965), chap. 1. Dickens, in his *American Notes* (1842), described him as "a gentleman of great worth and excellence" (quoted by Valerie Eliot, *Letters,* p. 7).

7. T. S. Eliot, *To Criticize the Critic* (New York, 1965), p. 44.

8. "The Influence of Landscape upon the Poet," *Daedalus* (Spring 1960), 421–422. Cited by Robert Crawford, *The Savage and the City in the Works of T. S. Eliot* (New York, 1987), p. 6. Crawford adds considerably to our knowledge of the St. Louis days.

9. Howarth, *Some Figures behind T. S. Eliot,* p. 29.

10. *Times Literary Supplement,* January 13, 1961, quoted by George Watson, "The Triumph of T. S. Eliot," *Critical Quarterly* (1965), reprinted in *T. S. Eliot: The Waste Land* (Casebook), ed. C. B. Cox and A. Hinchliffe (London, 1968), pp. 47–50.

11. G. M. Young, *Daylight and Champaign* (1937), p. 202, quoted in Bevis Hillier, *Young Betjeman* (London, 1988), p. 333.

12. Bernard Bergonzi, *T. S. Eliot* (New York, 1972), pp. 117–118.

13. See Eugen Weber, *Action Française* (Stanford, Calif., 1962), p. 480.

14. Lyndall Gordon, *Eliot's New Life* (New York, 1988), p. 92.

15. "The Urban Apocalypse," in *Eliot in his Time,* ed. A. Walton Litz (Princeton, N.J., 1973), pp. 23–49.

16. Gareth Reeves, "*The Waste Land* and the *Aeneid,*" *Modern Language Review,* 82 (1987), 555–572. Reeves adds to the list of parallels proposed by Kenner.

17. For detail, see my book *The Classic* (Cambridge, Mass., 1983), chap. 1. Eliot, in 1923, called England "a Latin country"; in 1949, however, he wrote: "When we consider the western world, we must recognize that the main cultural tradition has been that corresponding to the Church of Rome. Only within the last four hundred years has any other manifested itself; and anyone with a sense of centre and periphery must admit that the western tradition has been Latin, and Latin means Rome . . . From this point of view, the separation of Northern Europe, and of England in particular, from communion with Rome represents a diversion from the main stream of culture." Nevertheless we remain (exiled) citizens of the Empire.

### 5. *William Empson*

1. William Empson, *Argufying* (London, 1987).

2. William Empson, *The Royal Beasts* (London, 1986).

3. An essay on "The Faces of the Buddha" appeared in *The Listener,* February 5, 1936, and is reprinted in *Argufying,* pp. 573–576.

4. William Empson, *Some Versions of Pastoral* (London, 1935); hereafter cited as *SVP* in the text.

5. *The Review,* 6–7 (1963), p. 4.

6. T. E. Hulme, *Further Speculations,* ed. Samuel Hynes (Minneapolis, Minn., 1955), pp. 108–109.

7. See the essay "Ballet of the Far East" published in *The Listener,* July 7, 1937, and reprinted in *Argufying,* pp. 577–582.

8. William Empson, "Rescuing Donne," in *Just So Much Honor* (Philadelphia, 1972), p. 95.

9. *New York Review of Books,* December 3, 1981, pp. 42–50.

10. Ibid., March 4, 1982, p. 43.

11. William Empson, *Milton's God* (London, 1961), pp. 45–46.

12. William Empson, *Essays on Shakespeare* (Cambridge, 1986).

13. Ibid., p. 10.

14. Ibid., p. 84.

15. Ibid., p. 107.

## 6. Freud and Interpretation

1. M. Foucault, *The Order of Things,* trans. A. Sheridan Smith (1966; London, 1970); Foucault, *The Archaeology of Knowledge,* trans. A. Sheridan Smith (1969; London, 1972).

2. P. Mahony, *Freud as a Writer* (New York, 1982), pp. 11–12.

3. P. Brooks, "Freud's Masterplot: Questions of Narrative," *Yale French Studies,* 55–56 (1977).

4. S. Freud, "Introductory Lectures on Psycho-analysis: III," in *The Complete Psychological Works: Standard Edition,* ed. James Strachey (London, 1966), vol. 16, pp. 389, 397.

5. S. Freud, "From the History of an Infantile Neurosis," in *Standard Edition,* vol. 17, pp. 50–51.

6. Ibid., p. 97.

7. S. Ferenczi, *Thalassa,* trans. H. A. Bunker (New York, 1968), p. 66.

8. *Letters of Sigmund Freud,* ed. E. L. Freud (London, 1961), p. 323.

9. F. J. Sulloway, *Freud: Biologist of the Mind* (London, 1979).

10. E. Jones, *Life and Work of Sigmund Freud* (London, 1957), vol. 3, p. 313.

11. S. Freud, "Moses and Monotheism," in *Standard Edition,* vol. 23, p. 130.

12. S. Freud, "Introductory Lectures on Psycho-analysis," pp. 370–371.

13. F. de Saussure, *Course in General Linguistics,* trans. W. Baskin (1915; London, 1974).

14. Ibid., p. 81.

15. E. Gombrich, *Aby Warburg: An Intellectual Life* (London, 1970), pp. 238ff.

16. J. R. Moore, *The Post-Darwinian Controversies* (Cambridge, 1979), pp. 148ff.

17. F. Nietzsche, *The Use and Abuse of History* (1874; Indianapolis, 1949), pp. 7, 28.

18. W. Dilthey, "The Types of World View and Their Development in Metaphysical Systems," in *Dilthey: Selected Writings,* ed. H. P. Rickman (Cambridge, 1976), p. 135.

19. C. Lévi-Strauss, *The Savage Mind* (1962; Chicago, 1966), p. 261.

20. S. Freud, "The Future of an Illusion," in *Standard Edition,* vol. 21, p. 29.

21. Ibid., p. 36.

22. S. Freud, "Civilisation and Its Discontents," in *Standard Edition,* vol. 21, p. 123.

23. S. Freud, "On the History of the Psycho-analytic Movement," in *Standard Edition,* vol. 14, pp. 17ff.

24. S. Freud, "On Narcissism: An Introduction," in *Standard Edition,* vol. 14, p. 77.

25. S. Freud, "Constructions in Analysis," in *Standard Edition,* vol. 23, p. 269.

26. J. Neu, "Genetic Explanation in *Totem and Taboo*," in *Freud: A Collection of Critical Essays,* ed. R. Wollheim (New York, 1974), pp. 366–393.
27. P. Ricoeur, *Freud and Philosophy* (New Haven, 1970).
28. Ibid., pp. 374–375.
29. J. Habermas, *Knowledge and Human Interests,* trans. J. J. Shapiro (1968; London, 1972), p. 189.
30. Ibid., p. 193.
31. M. A. Skura, *The Literary Use of the Psychoanalytic Process* (New Haven, 1981), pp. 22ff.
32. M. M. Schwartz, "Critic, Define Thyself," in *Psychoanalysis and the Question of the Text,* ed. G. Hartman (Baltimore, 1978).
33. Skura, *Literary Use,* p. 271.
34. R. Schafer, "Wild Analysis" (unpublished paper, 1983).
35. D. A. Spence, *Narrative Truth and Historical Truth* (New York, 1982).
36. Ibid., pp. 165–166.
37. J. Malcolm, review of *Narrative Truth and Historical Truth* by D. A. Spence, *New Yorker,* November 24, 1982.

## 7. *Divination*

1. *The Printing and Proof-reading of the Shakespeare First Folio,* 2 vols. (Oxford, 1963).
2. George Steiner, "The Uncommon Reader," *Bennington Review,* no. 3 (December 1978).
3. L. D. Reynolds and N. G. Wilson, *Scribes and Scholars,* 2nd ed. (Oxford, 1974), p. 212.
4. James Thorpe, *Principles of Textual Criticism* (Pasadena, Calif., 1972), pp. 30, 27.
5. *Dunciad* III.27–28; see Aubrey L. Williams, *Pope's Dunciad* (London, 1955), pp. 82–83.
6. In the Arden Shakespeare (6th ed., 1958).
7. Richard Levin, *New Readings versus Old Plays* (Chicago, 1979).
8. *The Classic* (New York, 1975), chap. 3.
9. Reynolds and Wilson, *Scribes and Scholars,* p. 211. Incidentally, a compositor setting Massinger's play *The Emperor of the East* changed the word *Courte* into *Constantinople;* a copy survives in which the author corrected it. (See John Crow, "Editing and Emending," in *The Practice of Modern Literary Scholarship,* ed. Sheldon P. Zitner (New York, n.d.), pp. 161–175.

## 8. *The Plain Sense of Things*

1. Wallace Stevens, *Collected Poems* (New York, 1957), p. 502; hereafter cited as *CP* in the text.
2. See F. O. Matthiessen, *The Achievement of T. S. Eliot,* 3rd ed. (New York, 1958), p. 90.

3. Northrop Frye, *Anatomy of Criticism: Four Essays* (Princeton, N.J., 1957), p. 76.

4. J. Barton, *Reading the Old Testament* (London, 1984), p. 85.

5. *De libero arbitrio,* quoted in *Cambridge History of the Bible,* vol. 3, *The West from the Reformation to the Present Day,* ed. S. C. Greenslade (Cambridge, 1969–1970), p. 28.

6. John Lyons, *Semantics,* vol. 1 (Cambridge, 1977), p. 237.

7. Bruno Bettelheim, *Freud and Man's Soul* (New York, 1983).

8. *Cambridge History of the Bible,* vol. 3, p. 11.

9. Gerald Hammond, *The Making of the English Bible* (Manchester, 1982), p. 10.

10. Beryl Smalley, *The Study of the Bible in the Middle Ages,* 2nd ed. (Oxford, 1952), p. 15; D. S. Wallace-Hadrill, *Christian Antioch: A Study of Early Christian Thought in the East* (Cambridge, 1982), chap. 2.

11. *City of God,* XVI, 2.

12. *Cambridge History of the Bible,* vol. 2, pp. 252ff.

13. Smalley, *Bible in the Middle Ages,* chap. 4.

14. Ibid., p. 151.

15. Ibid., p. 163.

16. Ibid., p. 362.

17. J. S. Preuss, *From Shadow to Promise: Old Testament Interpretation from Augustine to the Young Luther* (Cambridge, Mass., 1969), p. 53.

18. Ibid., p. 69.

19. Ibid., p. 81.

20. J. T. Burtchaell, *Catholic Theories of Inspiration since 1810* (London, 1969), p. 32.

21. Ibid., pp. 69–70.

22. Ibid., chap. 5.

23. *Papers of the Institute of Jewish Studies, London,* vol. 1, ed. J. G. Weiss (Jerusalem, 1964), pp. 141–185.

24. John Searle, "Literal Meaning," in *Expression and Meaning: Studies in the Theory of Speech Acts* (Cambridge, 1979).

## 9. *The Argument about Canons*

1. W. G. Kümmel, *The New Testament: The History of the Investigation of Its Problems* (London, 1973, from the German ed. of 1970), pp. 304–305.

2. Ibid., p. 373.

3. Hans-Georg Gadamer, *Truth and Method* (New York, 1975, from the German 2nd ed. of 1965; 1st ed., 1960), pp. 295–296.

4. Ibid., p. 301.

5. Ibid., pp. 307–309.

6. Gershom Scholem, *The Kabbalah and Its Symbolism* (New York, 1965, ed. of 1969, from the German ed. of 1960), p. 46.

7. Ibid., p. 21.

8. Ibid., p. 30.
9. Kümmel, *The New Testament*, p. 425.
10. D. C. Hoy, *The Critical Circle* (Berkeley, Calif., 1978), p. 139.

## *10. The Bible: Story and Plot*

1. See Paul Ricoeur, *Time and Narrative,* trans. Kathleen McLaughlin and David Pellauer (Chicago, 1984), pp. 5ff., for a valuable discussion of Augustine's passage in relation to plot.
2. Jurij M. Lotman, "The Origin of Plot in the Light of Typology," *Poetics Today,* I, 1–2 (1979), 161–184.
3. Henry James, *The Art of the Novel,* ed. R. P. Blackmur (New York, 1934), p. 313.
4. Frank Kermode, "Secrets and Narrative Sequence," in *Essays on Fiction 1971–1982* (1983), chap. 6.
5. E. M. Forster, *Aspects of the Novel* (1927; Orlando, Fla., 1956), chap. 8.
6. *The Letters of D. H. Lawrence,* ed. Harry T. Moore (London, 1962), p. 1076.
7. Eliot observed that "Bloom told one nothing." *The Diary of Virginia Woolf,* ed. Anne Olivier Bell (Orlando, Fla., 1978), II, 203 (February 26, 1922).
8. Frank Budgen, *James Joyce and the Making of "Ulysses"* (London, 1934; ed. of 1972), p. 18.
9. The most interesting of the changes to the received text proposed in a new edition occurs in a famous passage where Stephen Dedalus is confronted by the ghost of his mother. He asks her, "Tell me the word, mother, if you know now. The word known to all men." She does not tell him. But now, in a passage the printer inadvertently omitted from a different episode, the text reads "Love, yes. Word known to all men," and goes on to give a Thomist definition of love. Bloom speaks elsewhere for love against "force, hatred, history"; so it is fitting that the same word should be there, though unspoken, at the climax of this "spiritual encyclopedia." See Richard Ellmann's review of *Ulysses: A Critical and Synoptic Text,* ed. H. W. Gabler (1984), in *New York Review of Books,* October 25, 1984.
10. Stuart Gilbert, *James Joyce's "Ulysses": A Study* (1930; rev. ed., New York, 1952).
11. T. S. Eliot, "*Ulysses,* order and myth" (1923), in *Selected Prose of T. S. Eliot,* ed. F. Kermode (New York, 1975).
12. Ezra Pound, *"Ulysses"* (1922), in *Literary Essays of Ezra Pound,* ed. T. S. Eliot (New York, 1954), pp. 403ff.
13. Hugh Kenner, *"Ulysses"* (London, 1980), pp. 26–30.
14. Richard Ellmann, *The Consciousness of Joyce* (New York, 1977), p. 33.
15. *The Letters of James Joyce,* ed. S. Gilbert (New York, 1957), I, 146–147.
16. L. A. G. Strong, *The Sacred River* (New York, 1949), pp. 144–145.
17. Robert Alter, "How Convention Helps Us to Read: The Case of the Annunciation Type-Scene," *Prooftexts,* 2 (1983), 115–130.

18. M. D. Goulder, *Midrash and Lection in Matthew* (1974), pp. 234–235.
19. R. E. Brown, *The Birth of the Messiah* (New York, 1977), pp. 418–420.
20. Ibid., pp. 207ff.
21. Ibid., p. 417.
22. M. Dibelius, *From Tradition to Gospel* (1919), trans. B. L. Wolf (Greenwood, S.C., 1971), pp. 188ff.
23. C. H. Dodd, *Historical Tradition in the Fourth Gospel* (New York, 1963), pp. 145–146.
24. I. Howard Marshall, *The Gospel of Luke: A Commentary on the Greek Text* (Grand Rapids, Mich., 1978), p. 902.
25. R. E. Brown, *The Gospel according to John, XIII–XXI* (New York, 1970), p. 1022.
26. Erasmus, *Collected Works: Correspondence,* trans. R. A. B. Mynors and D. F. S. Thompson (Toronto, 1979), vol. 5, p. 347.
27. E. G. Kraeling, *The Old Testament since the Reformation* (New York, 1955, 1969), p. 140.
28. H. von Campenhausen, *The Formation of the Christian Bible,* trans. J. A. Baker (Minneapolis, Minn., 1972), p. 64.
29. M. Hengel, *Acts and the History of Earliest Christianity,* trans. J. Bowden (Minneapolis, Minn., 1979), p. viii.
30. E. Auerbach, *Mimesis* (1946), trans. W. Trask (Princeton, N.J., 1953), chap. 2; *Literary Language and Its Public in Late Latin Antiquity* (1958), trans. R. Manheim (1964), pp. 27–66.
31. Campenhausen, *Formation of the Christian Bible,* p. 101.

# *Index*

# Index